D0087697

Combating Human Trafficking

A Multidisciplinary Approach

Combating Human Trafficking

A Multidisciplinary Approach

Edited by
Michael J. Palmiotto

CRC Press
Taylor & Francis Group
Boca Raton London New York

CRC Press is an imprint of the
Taylor & Francis Group, an **informa** business

Contents

Preface

This book on human trafficking fills a void on a major social, criminal, and human rights issue affecting the world in the first decades of the twenty-first century. Unlike most books that deal with international human trafficking and women and child abuse, *Combating Human Trafficking: A Multidisciplinary Approach* provides a broader perspective than current books on the market dealing with the subject of human traffic.

Human trafficking must be considered the most heinous crime against humanity in a world considered to have the most technologically advanced civilizations. The offense of human trafficking must be considered the twenty-first century form of slavery. Slavery as a major form of violation against fellow human beings can be traced to ancient times. This inhumane form of slavery has continued through the centuries to this day. It is occurring in developed countries as well as undeveloped countries. Slavery is simply the buying and selling of human beings for an economic profit without any concern for the person being sold.

Trafficking of people today includes the recruitment, transportation, and holding of individuals by unlawful means, which may include physical violence and possible threat. The victims of trafficking have their freedom taken from them by the trafficker. The trafficker intends to hold the victim as a modern-day slave. In this regard modern trafficking is similar to traditional slavery. Both traditional slavery and human trafficking remove the freedom from their victims. The captive is completely at the controller's mercy.

Human trafficking is considered a serious problem not only in the world but for the United States as well. Because it is difficult to identify victims of human trafficking, the actual number of human trafficking victims is unknown. Victims of human trafficking will not come forward even when hospitalized. They are fearful of their offenders and often consider them to be their protectors from government. One of the major issues in human trafficking is the lack of understanding regarding the seriousness and size of problem. As long as public and governmental agencies remain unaware of the seriousness of the problem, the more difficult it will be to get human trafficking under control.

For the United States, human trafficking has become a national problem and police departments are assigning investigators to investigate this specific crime. For example, Wichita State University and the U.S. Attorney Office for the District of Kansas along with the Kansas Attorney General's Office are collaborating on training police officers. Federal agencies and state agencies with local police are creating task forces to combat the growth of human trafficking.

Contributors to this book include former and current law enforcement practitioners, community organizers, and academic professors from several universities. This book has taken a multidisciplinary approach to provide a better understanding of what human trafficking is from a variety of perspectives. A human trafficking book with specialists from different disciplines can shed light on the human trafficking problem rather than receiving the information from a specialist from one discipline. *Combating Human Trafficking: A Multidisciplinary Approach* has 16 chapters from either different disciplines or from different positions dealing specifically with human trafficking.

The introduction, "Human Trafficking—Modern Slavery," provides an overview of human trafficking as it exists in the world today and introduces the topic of human trafficking. Ancient slavery is reviewed as well as how human trafficking can be considered modern slavery. Modern slavery as human trafficking exists in the United States as sex slavery and forced labor.

Chapter 1, by Caleb L. Seibel, focuses on the precursors of human trafficking, specifically slavery as it has existed in the United States. This chapter emphasizes society's opinions and understanding on the institution of slavery and how society's perceptions of historical forms of exploiting guide the nation's current approach to human trafficking.

Laurence Armand French's chapter, "Borderland: The Challenge of Cross-Border Trafficking of People, Drugs, and Guns between Mexico and the United States," provides insight on how these three issues are interrelated. Chapter 2 reviews the historical, geopolitical, and cultural analysis of the "borderland" region between Mexico and the United States in relation to current border issues including illicit trafficking of people, drugs, and firearms (Operation Fast and Furious). The chapter includes the role of Mexico in trafficking through both its southern and northern borders and how Mexico gained prominence in the "War on Drugs" at the expense of the successes of United States interventions in Colombia. Particular focus is on the exploitation of people, notably women, attempting to get to the United States to work at the border factories in Mexico.

The third chapter, by Christopher J. Moloney, deals with human trafficking from a sociological perspective. This chapter, "Sociology of Human Trafficking," recognizes that human trafficking is a global problem that transcends national borders. Whereas the global scale of human trafficking ensures that it occurs in various forms, it is still possible to discern distinct racial, ethnic, gendered, class, and cultural elements and patterns of the problem. Utilizing a sociological perspective, this chapter describes and analyzes these patterned aspects of human trafficking. In the concluding section a political–economic framework is utilized to gain greater understanding of how structural forces contribute to the patterned race, ethnicity, class, culture, and gendered dynamics of the human trafficking problem.

In the fourth chapter, "Psychology of Human Trafficking," author Jodie G. Beeson begins with an introduction to theory and roles before moving on to psychological risk factors, trauma, and treatment of victims. Next, traffickers, recruiters, and facilitators are explored. The chapter concludes with a psychological profile of consumers (buyers, or johns) of trafficking and the grooming process: finding victims and creating dependence.

Chapter 5, "Human Trafficking and the Internet," reviews the role of the Internet in human trafficking. In this chapter, Szde Yu reviews the following issues pertaining to human trafficking and the Internet: Internet and crime, human trafficking victimology on the Internet, the Internet as a hunting ground, the Internet as the marketing place, investigations on the Internet, and preventing human trafficking on the Internet.

Ryan J. Alexander in Chapter 6 writes on child victim recruitment into sex trafficking. The author divides the chapter into three major categories. The first discusses who the vulnerable children are, offender characteristics, and contact between victims and offenders. The second category is manipulative tactics, which cover financial and victim naiveté. The third category is coercion, which discusses kidnapping, slave trade, and threats against victims and their families.

Brian F. Kingshott in Chapter 7, "Investigation of Human Trafficking," provides information needed for the investigation of human trafficking. In this chapter, issues relating to the investigations of human trafficking focus on the victims and perpetrators of human trafficking. What is the scope of the problem and where are the major centers of human trafficking found? Who are the victims and who are the perpetrators? How do they become victims? What are the challenges facing investigators? What interagency protocols exist?

Jeffrey W. Weible is a lieutenant with the Wichita Police Department and responsible for the Child Exploitation Unit. He has firsthand knowledge of human trafficking. In Chapter 8, "What Does Human Trafficking Look Like in the Midwest?" Weible discusses the complex issue of human trafficking, specifically in the Midwest. This chapter examines the topic of why victims are chosen and get into this life. Furthermore, the chapter addresses why it is difficult to identify victims and to criminally investigate human trafficking cases.

D. G. Oblinger, author of Chapter 9, "Sex Trafficking in Sexually Oriented Businesses," obtained great insight into sex trafficking while assigned as a detective doing undercover work. Sex trafficking often smuggles people in order to facilitate commercial prostitution. Escort services, hostess bars, and massage parlors are a few of the sexually oriented businesses that can be fronts for sex trafficking. Investigating these types of criminal enterprises requires attention to detail and persistence.

Chapter 10, "Street Gangs and Human Trafficking," was written by Joseph Stearns, a former gang intelligence officer of the Wichita Police Department. This chapter explores how human trafficking has become more prevalent with local street gangs. National and local trends with street gangs show an overall lack of organization from the top down. This lack of leadership has caused gang members to commit crimes on an individual level instead of typical group activities. Human trafficking is a perfect example. Stearns explains how gang dynamics, for example, recruiting, intimidation, and moneymaking, have transformed amid the rise of social media. These dynamics greatly parallel how these gang members are carrying out their human trafficking activities. Local perspective by Stearns is the main focus, but similar national trends are used for support.

The next chapter, "Forced Labor in the United States," discusses the forced labor aspect of human trafficking. The various definitions of forced labor are reviewed and the definition that best describes forced labor in the United States is discussed. A review of illegal immigrants as forced labor and the reason why they are not considered victims but rather law violators is examined. This chapter looks at labor trafficking organizations, offenders, and their victims.

"Federal Law Enforcement and Human Trafficking" was written by Jeff Bumgarner, a former federal agent. Chapter 12 explores the various federal agencies in the United States responsible for confronting human trafficking, including the Federal Bureau of Investigation and Immigration and Custom Enforcement. This chapter highlights the strategies and initiatives employed by federal agencies.

Chapter 13, "Law Enforcement Awareness and Training in Human Trafficking," was written by Vladimir A. Sergevnin, an authority on training. This chapter discusses that human trafficking involves both national and transnational crime and that it is the local law enforcement officer who is most likely to encounter such crimes related to human trafficking. Chapter 13 compares different training efforts to combat human trafficking and suggests how to create awareness about human trafficking and improve the response of police agencies to the problem. This chapter is an exploratory assessment of the nature and extent of the local law enforcement training response to trafficking in the United States.

"Not in Our City," by Stacie Donaldson, discusses the difficulties people have believing that human trafficking happens in their communities—the initial idea of "not in my city," that surely it couldn't happen *here*. Chapter 14 covers the case that brought trafficking to the city of Wichita's attention as well as Jennifer White's response—donations, meeting with community and law enforcement, and the creation of a nonprofit organization. This chapter includes interviews from law enforcement and other agencies, the pros and cons of involving the public in the fight, and how citizens can be effective. To fight human trafficking the city of Wichita has three major goals:

- A shift in the community's perception (the need to view those who have been sexually exploited as victims and survivors—not criminals)
- A need for partnership (allowing the professionals to determine needs and provide direct services, while community members support them by providing volunteer hours, donations, and other resources)
- A focus on encouraging the public to be involved in prevention efforts

Chapter 15 by Dorthy Stucky Halley, Sharon L. Sullivan, and Jennifer Rapp, "Providing Effective Services to Victims of Human Trafficking: Theoretical, Practical, and Ethical Considerations," reviews the theoretical perspectives being used in the development of policy and service for victims of human trafficking in some of the leading states in the nation, the strengths and weakness of different approaches, and the challenges in practical application. Ethical challenges and dilemmas related to service delivery are explored.

In Chapter 16, "Human Trafficking Laws and Legal Trends," Alison McKenney Brown contends that in the media there exists the perception that victims of human trafficking bear a responsibility for their victimization, which has hampered the criminal justice process to effectively address the prevention and end of these offenses. The laws in many states only recently began to allow the criminal justice process to effectively address the crimes while protecting victims. This chapter provides an overview of federal human trafficking laws and reviews the legal trends within states associated with human trafficking and preventing and prosecuting these crimes.

About the Editor

Michael J. Palmiotto, PhD, is professor of criminal justice and undergraduate coordinator of the Criminal Justice Department at Wichita State University, Wichita, Kansas. He was formerly a police officer in New York State, serving in White Plains and Scarsdale. He has experience in establishing and operating a police training facility in Western Pennsylvania. Dr. Palmiotto earned a master's degree from John Jay College (CUNY) and a doctorate from the University of Pittsburgh. He has been a faculty member of several universities, including Western Illinois University and Armstrong State University.

Dr. Palmiotto has published eleven books, thirteen book chapters, and numerous articles on criminal justice and law enforcement. He has published in the areas of criminal investigations, community policing, police misconduct, police globalization, and police training, among others. He is the recipient of two Fulbright awards.

Contributors

Ryan J. Alexander
Washburn University
Topeka, Kansas

Jodie G. Beeson
Wichita State University
Wichita, Kansas

Alison McKenney Brown
Wichita State University
Wichita, Kansas

Jeff Bumgarner
North Dakota University
Fargo, North Dakota

Stacie Donaldson
ICT SOS
Wichita, Kansas

Laurence Armand French
Justiceworks Institute
University of New Hampshire
Durham, New Hampshire

Dorthy Stucky Halley
Topeka, Kansas

Brian F. Kingshott
Grand Valley State University
Grand Rapids, Michigan

Christopher J. Moloney
Center for the Study of Crime and Justice
Colorado State University
Fort Collins, Colorado

D.G. Oblinger
Wichita Police Department
and
Wichita Area Technical College
Wichita, Kansas

Michael J. Palmiotto
Wichita State University
Wichita, Kansas

Jennifer Rapp
Lawrence, Kansas

Caleb L. Seibel
School of Community Affairs
Wichita State University
Wichita, Kansas

Vladimir A. Sergevnin
Western Illinois University
Macomb, Illinois

Joseph Stearns
Wichita Police Department
Wichita, Kansas

Sharon L. Sullivan
Stop Trafficking and Reject Slavery
and
Washburn University
Topeka, Kansas

Jeffrey W. Weible
Wichita Police Department
Wichita, Kansas

Szde Yu
School of Community Affairs
Wichita State University
Wichita, Kansas

Introduction: Human Trafficking— Modern Slavery[*]

MICHAEL J. PALMIOTTO

Major Issues

- For more than a century, governments have tried to end slavery and human trafficking.
- Trafficking is a large industry that preys on the vulnerabilities of individuals, both foreign and domestic.
- The process of human trafficking includes a complex network of individuals.

Slavery can be traced to ancient times. The Bible, Islam Koran, and Greek classics all have described slavery. The term *slavery* simply means that one person owns another human being like a piece of property. The human being is property in a way similar to how a lamp or cabinet is owned. In earlier times people became slaves by being captured in war and they and their off-spring continued the slave culture. During the Middle Ages slavery evolved into a commercial enterprise. Slaves were hunted, captured, and sold into slavery. Commercial slavery is a business that still occurs in some parts of the world. For centuries it has been an inhumane and abusive form of treatment of one human being by another.

Most educated people have some knowledge of how Africans were hunted down, captured, and transported to the Americas. Slavery in America was introduced in 1619 when a Dutch ship brought the first slaves to America. The slave trade increased because cheap labor was important to the economy of the southern region of America.

The commercial slave business was referred to as transatlantic—the transporting of Africans across the Atlantic Ocean to the Americas. In 1807, Great Britain outlawed the slave business throughout its empire. However, slavery was not abolished. England abolished slavery in 1833, the United States in 1865, and Brazil in 1888. In 1926 the League of Nations called for an end to slavery. The United Nations in 1948 adopted a proclamation prohibiting slavery (Cullen-DuPont, 2009, p. 7).

---

[*] This chapter originally appeared in *Law Enforcement Executive Forum,* June 2012.

For the most part the transatlantic slave trade ended in the nineteenth century. Slavery in its various forms continues to take place to this present day. Human trafficking seems to be our modern form of slavery. This form of slavery was recognized in the early twentieth century when various governments of the world developed international agreements against human trafficking. In 1904 there was an International Agreement for the Suppression of White Slave Traffic and a 1910 international convention to stop the white slave trade. There was a 1921 international convention to suppress trafficking of women and children, another convention in 1933 with the same purpose, and the United Nations had a convention on human trafficking in 1949 (Lee, 2011, p. 26–27).

The International Abolitionist Federation at Geneva in 1877 brought to the world's attention the sex trade of women. In 1899 the International Congress met to oppose the white slave trade. The first agreement to suppress the white slave trade was adopted at the 1904 International Congress (Holman, 2008, pp. 104–105).

In the early nineteenth century the U.S. Congress acknowledged that human trafficking existed when it passed the White-Slave Traffic Act, known as the Mann Act, in 1910. The Mann Act prohibited the transportation of women and girls between various states or territories for the purpose of prostitution or debauchery, or for any other immoral purpose. In support of international agreements the Mann Act made it a crime to transport foreign women for the purpose of prostitution and debauchery (The Mann Act, 2005).

The 1978 amendment to the Mann Act was designed to protect minors who were being transported across state lines for immoral purposes. The amendment held that transportation by automobile would be sufficient for prosecution. Transportation by common carrier was not required, as originally stated under the Mann Act. The 1985 amendment made it a crime to transport a minor to produce pornography even for noncommercial purposes. The amendment is gender neutral, applying to males as well as females (Langum, 1994, pp. 249–250).

The United Nations defines *human trafficking* as

the recruitment, transportation, transfer, harboring, or receipt of persons, by means of the threat or use of force or other forms of coercion, of abduction, of fraud, of deception, of the abuse of power or of a position of vulnerability or of the giving or receiving of payment or benefits to achieve the consent of a person having control over another person, for the purpose of exploitation of the prostitution of others or other forms of sexual exploitation, forced labor or services, slavery or practices similar to slavery, servitude or the removal of organs. (As quoted in Aronowitz, 2009, p. 1)

The global economy has human trafficking as a by-product of the twenty-first century. Human trafficking is surpassed by drugs and weapons trafficking as the most profitable criminal actions. The crime of human trafficking is a serious human rights violation. The United States government believes that there are between 600,000 and 800,000 people trafficked across international borders. Of course, it is difficult to be exact in the number of people trafficked. Human trafficking is growing and it may be possible that within a decade trafficking of humans will surpass drugs and weapons trafficking (Holman, 2008, p. 102).

In 2000 the Trafficking Victims Protection Act (TVPA) was passed by Congress. The TVPA defines human trafficking as

> (A) Sex trafficking in which a commercial sex act is induced by force, fraud, or coercion, or in which the person induced to perform such act has not attended 18 years of age; or (B) the recruitment, harboring transportation, provision, or obtaining of a person for labor or services, through the use of force, or coercion for the purpose of subjection to involuntary servitude, personage, debt bondage or slavery. (As quoted in Wilson and Dalton, 2008, p. 297)

The main point of the act indicates that force or fraud cannot be used to take advantage of a person either for forced labor or sexual exploitation. The TVPA legislation does not require that a person be transported across geographical locations for it to be a crime. Also, individuals do not necessarily have to be transported from another country for it to be human trafficking. However, under the TVPA law a minor does not have to be forced if a third person benefits from sexual exploitation.

The TVPA should be considered significant United States legislation since it held those countries accountable that did not take constructive action to combat human trafficking. This legislation increased law enforcement in the United States with pressure on foreign countries to enforce stricter laws against human trafficking. Countries that did not take constructive action against human trafficking would not receive humanitarian aid from the United States (Holman, 2008, p. 101).

How serious of a problem is human trafficking? It is a serious problem but how serious appears difficult to determine. The number of people who are actual victims of human trafficking is unknown. According to the International Human Rights Law Institute report on trafficking in Central America and the Caribbean:

> In view of the clandestine and criminal nature of the phenomenon, the inadequate monitoring by law enforcement agencies, and public confusion

about the nature of the problem, accurate quantitative data on the trafficking for sexual exploration was impossible to obtain. In fact, available
quantitative data was purely speculative. (As quoted in Aronowitz, 2009,
p. 15)

What are the reasons for human trafficking? The fall of the Soviet Union
in 1989 led to economic upheaval not only in Russia but in countries under its
control. China, Nigeria, and Thailand contribute to trafficking. It should be
recognized that victims of trafficking can come from any country. Probably,
poverty has been considered the greatest contributor to human trafficking.
Those in poverty are unable to financially meet the basic needs of shelter,
food, or medical care. Parents and children go to bed hungry and are poorly
clothed, causing some adults to get into bondage to financial lenders trading
their freedom for some basic need. The majority of people who are trafficked
are women and girls, which is primarily due to gender inequality. Women
sometimes fall for lies that they will have their basic needs met with potential
employment (Cullen-DuPont, 2009, pp. 23–24).

The demand for human trafficking has increased with globalization, the
breakup of the Soviet Union, economic poverty, and lack of border controls.
Human trafficking results in human suffering. The control or elimination of
human trafficking is difficult to implement in society since there are monetary advantages to illegal and legal organizations. The profit motive for
human trafficking either by sex exploration or forced labor benefits those
in control. Factories, construction companies, or farmers can benefit by
the forced labor of human trafficking. Sex slavery has increased in the past
decade because of human trafficking (Shelley, 2010, p. 29–30).

The demand for women in the sex market and people for cheap labor
contributes to the demand of human trafficking to stay in operation. Women
are vulnerable and are in big demand for both legitimate and illicit businesses. The commercial sex and entertainment business make big profits.
The demand for women also exists as domestic workers or as caretakers.
Women are valuable to the fast food industry and low-paying factory positions (Aronowitz, 2009, p. 25–26). The Presidents' Interagency Council on
Women formulated a definition on trafficking of women and children:

Trafficking is all acts involved in the recruitment, abduction, transport, harboring, transfer, sale, or receipt of persons; within national or across international borders; through force, coercion, fraud or deception; to place persons
in situations of slavery or slavery-like conditions, forced labor or services, such
as forced prostitution or sexual services, or domestic servitude, bonded sweat
shops labor or other debt bondage. (As quoted in O'Neill Richard, 1999, p. v)

Women are trafficked into the United States from Eastern Europe, Asia, and Latin America. The simplest way to be trafficked into the United States is to overstay their visa. Human traffickers use business and tourists to traffic women to the United States. The time frames of the visas vary depending upon the country of origin. The traffickers recycle passports to be used for new women being trafficked. The human traffickers also use finance and entertainers' visas to get women into the United States. The human traffickers train the women on how to apply for a visa. They obtain phony employment letters and records or bank statements to support documentation for the visa. The human traffickers gain control over the women by taking their passports and visas. Phony passports have also been used to bring women to the United States (O'Neill Richard, 1999, pp. 3–8).

Victims of human trafficking are usually identified in several ways. First, law enforcement identifies victims either because they are trained in human trafficking or through a criminal investigation. Second, victims could be identified by coworkers, customers, or neighbors. Third, human trafficking victims could be identified if they seek medical, social, or employment services (Logan, Walker, and Hunt, 2009, p. 19).

A major question that should be asked pertaining to human trafficking victims is, what keeps them trapped in this inhumane condition? There appears to be several reasons why people feel imprisoned when in human bondage. Fear seems to be a big factor, which can include physical abuse and sexual violence. In addition, fear can include a number of threats such as threats to harm family members, send the victim to jail, or have victims deported. A lack of knowledge is another reason why trafficking victims do not report their bondage. Victims lack knowledge of their rights and how to handle the situation they are in. If the trafficking victim does not speak the language, they are at a big disadvantage. Isolation can play a major part in human bondage. Victims held in isolation can be controlled by the trafficker. Victims have limited contact with outsiders because their outside contact is monitored. Finally, physical and psychological confinement keep the victim imprisoned in an unpleasant situation. Victims may be kept under physical control. Psychological control may include holding the victim's passport, visa, money, or other documents they possess (Logan et al., 2009, pp. 13–14).

The enforcement of criminal laws predominantly falls upon local policing agencies, which include cities, counties, and state investigative agencies. These local and state agencies reflect a diverse social–economic community. Who better to investigate human trafficking than local and state police agencies? Who knows their communities better than local police agencies? To support local law enforcement agencies, the federal government funded task forces to identify trafficking offenders and to prosecute human traffic violators. It appears that human traffickers are not being prosecuted in large numbers. A reason could be that police administrators do not consider it a major problem or perhaps not a serious problem to them. Bigger cities are more likely to consider human trafficking to be a major concern and, thus, they investigate human trafficking cases. Police agencies that have training programs and police personnel who specialize in human trafficking also have protocols to identify human trafficking cases (Farrell, 2009, pp. 246–251).

In March 2011, several strategies were suggested for law enforcement personnel to handle human sex trafficking. These suggestions were for patrol officers and investigators and included general indicators, physical indicators, financial/legal indicators, and brothel indicators. For example, patrol officers should document calls and complaints on police information reports, even if the details seem trivial.

Investigators should monitor websites that advertise dating and escort services. For the indicators, a general indicator could be a large number of people living in a small area; physical indicators could include injuries from beatings or cigarette burns; financial/legal indicators could be that someone else has an individual's travel documents; and brothel indicators could be men coming and going constantly (Walker-Rodriquez and Hill, 2011, pp. 5–6).

Human trafficking can take place in any country in the world. This inhumane offense can transport humans across national borders or across state borders. Since human trafficking in its entirety is too vast to review in this section, we will primarily discuss the human trafficking trade in the U.S. Midwest.

Human traffickers have been arrested in Kansas City, Missouri. There have also been international traffic labor cases. Victims would come to the United States based on the promise of a legitimate job only to be held in bondage. Women have been transported from China to Kansas City for the sex trade. Kansas City, like several cities, has received grants to fight human trafficking (Human Trafficking Project, 2009).

In the last several years, human traffickers have received more attention in Kansas. During 2011, domestic violence and sexual assault programs have reported working with 26 human trafficking victims. Eight victims were from the Wichita area. Wichita police statistics report human trafficking has more than tripled in the last four years. In 2011, the Wichita Police had 28 cases involving human trafficking. Kansas sits on a major human trafficking route favored by human traffickers of forced labor and the sex trade. The Kansas Attorney General wants to improve efforts to eliminate human trafficking ("Tougher Laws," 2012).

There exists little knowledge of human trafficking in the Midwest and little research in America's heartland. One study (Wilson and Dalton, 2008) looks at human trafficking in two urban communities: Columbus and Toledo, Ohio. Examined was the public's response to human trafficking and media reports. Toledo had 10 domestic cases that involved the commercial sex trafficking of juveniles from the Toledo area. There was also ongoing investigating of adults. During the period of this study, the police were investigating 60 possible human traffickers. Columbus has had five transnational cases; all involved forced labor either as domestic workers or hotel workers (p. 300).

A study by Williamson and Prior (2009) reviews the underground network of players involved in the domestic traffic of minors for the sex trade. There are several players identified in the social network: connectors, recruiters, groomers, traffickers, bottoms, watchers, and wife-in-laws. Connectors are neighborhood residents who hook the victim up with someone who knows how to make money in prostitution. Recruiters are closely linked to the traffickers, and their job is to find new prospects. Groomers prepare the victim for prostitution. Traffickers are pimps whose only goals are to control and exploit the victim. A bottom is a woman close to the pimp who is trusted by the pimp. Wife-in-laws are partnered with each other and belong to the same pimp (pp. 8–10).

When young people are rescued from traffickers, they are usually arrested and the victims are incarcerated in juvenile facilities. They don't receive treatment to overcome the trauma of their victimization (Williamson and Prior, 2009, p. 13).

Human trafficking is a crime that has been difficult to quantify. Estimates on the number of victims have been difficult to obtain accurately. There seems to be a great unknown about human trafficking. In 2010, there were 49,105 human trafficking victims worldwide who were identified. This was a 59 percent increase over 2009 (Office of Justice Programs, 2011, p. 1).

Action needs to be taken to combat human trafficking. Wilson and Dalton (2008) make several recommendations:

- Improve awareness and response through training, education, and outreach.
- Improve law enforcement capacity.
- Improve practitioner collaboration.
- Refine department policies.
- Use analysis to develop evidence-based programs and responses.
- Consider and assess legislative, legal, and regulatory changes. (pp. 309–311)

Summary

Human trafficking is a serious problem that is taking place in our country. We as Americans may find it hard to believe that something this inhumane can occur here. We like to think it takes place in developing countries in the world. In recent years, more attention is being paid to human trafficking, which seems to be divided into the sex trade and forced labor. Not only should the police be trained in spotting human trafficking, but the general public should be as well. Citizens who reside in neighborhoods are generally familiar with their neighbors and their comings and goings. Hopefully, in the coming decade, human trafficking can be eliminated.

Key Terms

Agreement for the Suppression of White Slave Traffic (1904)
commercial slavery
human trafficking
Presidents' Interagency Council on Women
Trafficking Victims Protection Act
White-Slave Traffic Act (aka Mann Act) (1910)

Review Questions

1. Explain why victims of human trafficking might not seek assistance.
2. Explain the several strategies suggested to aid law enforcement officers in handling human trafficking.
3. Discuss why Kansas might have seen more evidence of human trafficking in recent years.
4. Identify the underground network of players and their key roles in the Williamson and Prior (2009) study.

References

Aronowitz, A. (2009). *Human Trafficking, Human Misery*. Westport, CT: Praeger.

Cullen-DuPont, K. (2009). *Human Trafficking*. New York, NY: Infobase Publishing.

Farrell, A. (2009). State and local law enforcement responses to human trafficking: Explaining why so few trafficking cases are identified in the United States. *Sociology of Crime Law and Deviance*, 13, 243–259.

Holman, M. (2008). The modern-day slave trade: How the United States should alter the Victims of Trafficking and Violence Protection Act in order to combat international sex trafficking more effectively. *Texas International Law Journal*, 44(1/2), 99.

Human Trafficking Project. (2009). Human trafficking in the Midwest. Retrieved from http://www.traffickingproject.org/2009/05/human-trafficking-in-midwest.html.

Langum, D. J. (1994). *Crossing over the Line*. Chicago, IL: The University of Chicago Press.

Lee, M. (2011). *Trafficking and Global Crime Control*. Los Angeles, CA: Sage.

Logan, T. K., Walker, R., and Hunt, G. (2009, January). Understanding human trafficking in the United States. *Trauma, Violence, & Abuse,* 10(1), 3–30.

Office of Justice Programs. (2011). OJP Fact Sheet: Human trafficking. Retrieved June 7, 2012, from www.ojp.usdoj.gov/newsroom/factsheet/ojpfs_humantrafficking.html.

O'Neill, R. A. (1999). International trafficking in women to the United States: A contemporary manifestation of slavery and organized crime. Washington, DC: US Government Center for the Study of Intelligence.

Shelley, L. I. (2010). *Human Traffic: A Global Perspective.* New York: Cambridge University Press.

The Mann Act. (2005). www.pbs.org/unforgiveable/knockout/mannact_text.html.

Tougher laws sought on human trafficking. (2012, January 18). *Wichita Eagle,* pp. 1B, 6B.

Victims of Trafficking and Violence Protection Act of 2000 (TVPA), Public Law 106-386, Statutes at Large 114 (2000), 1464.

Walker-Rodriguez, A., and Hill, R. (2011, March). Human sex trafficking. *FBI Law Enforcement Bulletin.* Retrieved May 30, 2012, from www.fbi.gov/stats-services/publications/law-enforcement-bulletin/march_2011/human_sex_trafficking.

Williamson, C., and Prior, M. (2009). Domestic minor sex trafficking: A network of underground players in the Midwest. *Journal of Child & Adolescent Trauma,* 2, 1–16.

Wilson, J. M., and Dalton, E. (2008). Human trafficking in the Heartland: Awareness and response. *Journal of Contemporary Criminal Justice,* 24(3), 296–313.

Human Trafficking and the History of Slavery in America

1

CALEB L. SEIBEL

Contents

Introduction

The issue of human trafficking is a complex problem that involves numerous levels of exploitation defined by the various situations of the individual victims involved. The use of broad terminology like *human trafficking* and *modern slavery* often overshadows the most crucial elements that define who is considered a victim and how they are victimized. Due to the complexities in human trafficking, it is important to possess a historical perspective of the evolution of American slavery and how it relates to the human trafficking that takes place in the United States. Without understanding how human trafficking fits into the historical development of slavery it is likely that today's abolitionists will stumble into some of the same pitfalls abolitionists of the 19th century faced.

North American Slavery

Throughout the history of the world, slavery has been institutionalized in many forms by many people; however, slavery can refer to a near infinite number of specific forms of human bondage. Although early North America was dominated by only one form of slavery, at the same time in British India there were 14 different variations of legally recognized slavery. In the same period, Central Asian slaves were not recognized as fully persons or fully property, and in comparison to North American slaves could be viewed as privileged. As a result, discussing all forms of human bondage and exploitation under the wide umbrella of slavery deemphasizes the differences separating these various forms of exploitation and collectively contrasts them against the equally broad concept of freedom (Hopkins, 2008, pp. 631–634).

In the United States the word *slavery* is strongly associated with images of the cruel, racially defined bondage of the Atlantic slave trade utilized by plantation owners in North and Central America. The *Atlantic slave trade*, which spanned the 16th to 19th centuries, refers to the exchange of goods and slaves between Europe, Africa, and the Americas. The Atlantic slave trade forcibly removed an estimated 11.5 million people from Africa and was characterized by the brutal exploitation of Africans by Europeans and colonists (Fage, 1989, pp. 97–101).

More precisely the form of slavery practiced in colonial America and the early years of the United States is referred to as *chattel slavery*. Chattel is a term meaning personal property and is distinguished by its ability to be moved like livestock or tools, and is not permanently fixed to a location like land or buildings ("Chattel," n.d.). Chattel slavery is the most easily defined and recognized form of slavery because it clearly places slaves in the category of property with no claim to being a person. Because slaves were not recognized as persons by the government, they were not afforded any rights, as decided by the Supreme Court in the *Dredd Scott* case (Zuckert, 1992, p. 75). In addition to being denied rights, slaves prior to the Civil War were not punished through the criminal justice system but according to *slave codes* that allowed barbaric and public punishments, including a Louisiana slave code in 1724 that stated that a slave would be killed for striking his or her master (Bales and Trodd, 2009, p. 3). Whereas whites were punished for violating the laws of free men, slaves were punished for rejecting the rules of their captivity. Since imprisoning those already in captivity was recognized as redundant and deprived slave owners of labor, the dehumanizing slave codes were enforced to enable masters to maintain control of their slaves (Adamson, 1983, pp. 555–557).

Emancipation

As the Atlantic slave trade grew, in both numbers and brutality, so did its opposition, with tensions concerning slavery and its abolition in the United States culminating in the Civil War. Although the war began as a means to preserve the Union, it was the argument around slavery that had led Southern states to secede. Also as the Union came nearer to victory, Lincoln became bolder about the goals of the war and issued the *Emancipation Proclamation* in January of 1863, freeing slaves in the states that remained in rebellion. Although the executive order by Lincoln was the first major step toward abolishing chattel slavery in the United States, it allowed slavery to continue in the states that remained in the Union (Bales and Trodd, 2009, p. 13). Only after the conclusion of the Civil War was the North able to add the *Thirteenth Amendment* to the U.S. Constitution, formally abolishing slavery and involuntary servitude except as punishment for duly convicted crimes. The amendment also granted Congress the "power to enforce this article by appropriate legislation" (U.S. Constitution Amendment 13, Section 2). It is at this point, when chattel slavery is legally ended, that other forms of exploitation began to spring up in its place (Bales and Trodd, 2009, p. 13).

Although the Thirteenth Amendment was intended to completely free those who had previously been bound in chains physically and legally, it failed to produce any significant form of freedom for the newly emancipated blacks. Following the Civil War, the abolitionist-controlled Congress had begun to consider the need for an amendment to the Constitution to completely and permanently abolish slavery. The need for a constitutional amendment was based on two fears concerning the revival of slavery in the United States. First, there was concern whether a federal law prohibiting slavery could be enforced upon the states without being struck down by the Supreme Court for infringing upon states' constitutional rights. Second, it was recognized that although the current Congress was opposed to slavery it was possible for supporters of slavery to regain control of Congress in the future and repeal the law prohibiting slavery. As a result, abolitionists came to support amending the Constitution to ensure that slavery could not be easily reinstated if they lost their political power (tenBroek, 1951, pp. 179–201). As the abolitionists began making their case for adopting the 13th amendment, a new debate arose in Congress.

Despite the absence of Southern representatives in Congress immediately following the Civil War, there was still opposition to the Thirteenth Amendment. Arguments surrounding the amendment revolved not around the effect of the amendment on slavery and freed slaves but rather if such an amendment would be in contradiction with the spirit of the Constitution by regulating an area that had originally been left to the discretion of the states individually. Opponents also complained that the amendment would not only free blacks from slavery but raise them to an equal status before the law, and allow Congress to "invade any state to enforce the freedom of the African in war or peace," with freedom being recognized as more than "exemption from personal servitude." These debates illustrate that prior to implementation of the amendment, though not everyone favored it, all agreed that it would mean former slaves would not merely become a new form of subjects but instead would become full citizens (tenBroek, 1951, pp. 174–175). Although there was initial consensus as to what the amendment would mean, once implemented its opponents began interpreting it in a much narrower fashion.

After the ratification of the Thirteenth Amendment and formal emancipation, the debate over what constitutes slavery reached its peak. Northern Democrats, who argued they were never pro-slavery but rather noninterference, and Southern Democrats, who had fought to defend slavery, agreed that the Thirteenth Amendment had brought a complete and sudden end to slavery. This standpoint is illustrated by Representative Phelps' statement that only "purblind patriots … predict the revival of even affirm the actual present existence of slavery." In their view, the Thirteenth Amendment had clearly moved the United States into a new postslavery era and nothing else could or should be done regarding slavery. Democrats now argued that the Thirteenth Amendment had been fully implemented with the formal emancipation of slaves. Contrary to their earlier debates, Democrats began contending that the amendment could not be and was never intended to do more than end the ability to formally own another human. Although Democrats claimed the Thirteenth Amendment settled the issue of slavery, the more radical Republicans realized their work was incomplete as previous slave owners and their respective state governments developed new methods to perpetuate the exploitation of former slaves (Brandwein, 2000, pp. 324–331; tenBroek, 1951, p. 189).

Freedom for Freedmen

The addition of the Thirteenth Amendment in 1865 released more than 4 million slaves from bondage; despite the formal end of slavery these 4 million people could hardly be considered free. Once liberated, many former slaves, out of necessity, returned to the same work and similar conditions that they had prior to the Civil War. Lacking resources and land, ex-slaves became reliant on credit for tools and supplies. Many freed slaves also turned toward *sharecropping*, a system where the tenant works the land and pays the landowner with a share or portion of the crop produced, from white land owners. Although freed from bondage, former slaves that entered sharecropping agreements often had the size, type, and method of agricultural production dictated to them by landowners and merchants. These arrangements were rarely fair and frequently led the former slaves from being reliant on white merchants and landowners to being indebted to them, resulting in a cycle of continued exploitation. Exploitation of black labor was further exacerbated by new state laws passed in the wake of the Thirteenth Amendment with the specific intent to control the newly freed slaves (Brandwein, 2000, p. 324; Ruef and Fletcher, 2003, pp. 447–450).

Although the passing of the Thirteenth Amendment meant Southern states could no longer have formal slave laws, states were able to enact new laws such as the *black codes* that provided a means to continue the exploitation of black labor. With the constitutional prohibition of slavery, Southern states began to pass black codes to explicitly govern the behavior of all blacks in a nearly identical way that slave codes had previously controlled the same population. The new laws blurred the distinction between slave and free by perpetuating the slave status despite the legal change from chattel slavery to wage labor. The creation of black codes continued the distinction between black and white populations by "enacting harsh vagrancy laws, apprenticeship laws, and criminal penalties for breach of contract, and extreme punishments for blacks" (Brandwein, 2000, p. 324). Even though former slaves were no longer legally recognized as property and the use of physical coercion was reduced, the new situation closely mirrored the old with former slaves being tenants to landlords who were former slave owners (Fuef and Fletcher, 2003, p. 448).

As Republicans became aware of the enforcement of black codes and the continued exploitation of black labor by new methods like sharecropping, they began raising the argument that former slaves were still not free. Referring to the Southern black codes, Representative Ingersoll stated that the South "will seek to again enslave [the freedmen] not perhaps by a sale on the auction block as in the olden time, but by vagrant laws and other laws and regulations concerning the freedman," while Senator Henry Wilson stated, "In several of these States new laws are being framed containing provisions wholly inconsistent with the freedom of the freedmen." Republicans believed that in order for blacks to truly be free from slavery, they needed the civil rights associated with full citizenship such as the ability to own property, enter contracts, receive an education, to sue and be sued, to be subject to the same criminal laws. Without these basic rights Republicans argued that despite its intent the Thirteenth Amendment had left slaves half emancipated or free in body but not in spirit (Brandwein, 2000, p. 346).

Radical Republicans were clear from the beginning that the Thirteenth Amendment had the intention of providing complete freedom to the slaves. Freedom was not merely seen as being free from chattel slavery but also from the "lingering vestiges of the slave system; its chattelizing, degrading and bloody codes; its dark, malignant barbarizing spirit." Abolitionists' arguments had long opposed slavery not solely for treating humans as chattel but also for repressing what were seen as natural and God-given rights. These rights included the equal treatment under the law along with the ability to own property, obtain an education, and speak freely. It was understood that without these rights former slaves would never be free (tenBroek, 1951, p. 177). When the weaknesses of the Thirteenth Amendment were realized, the Republican-controlled congress developed the *Fourteenth Amendment* to reattempt to secure the rights of former slaves as full citizens of the United

States. The new amendment redefined citizens as all persons born or naturalized in the United States. The new definition of citizenship included former slaves and prohibited states from infringing upon the privileges and immunities of citizenship and required states to allow them due process and equal protection of the laws. Despite the adoption of the Fourteenth Amendment, the privileges of full citizenship were still withheld from African Americans for many more years due to intentionally restrictive interpretations of the amendment by the Supreme Court. Although its proper implementation underwent significant delays, the Fourteenth Amendment was eventually the basis by which African Americans began to experience more freedoms (Zuckert, 1992, pp. 77–92).

The historical progress of slavery and the legislation against it is relevant to today's abolitionists because past trials in implementing effective anti-slavery legislation can guide current efforts. Despite the addition of the Thirteenth Amendment, the replacement of slave codes with black codes ensured those who had been emancipated would remain disadvantaged and controlled. Even with the passing of the Fourteenth Amendment African Americans did not receive the freedoms due to them as citizens. It is these outcomes that today's abolitionists must be aware of; if history is ignored, current and future legislative efforts will not end the oppression of human trafficking but only change the way in which people are oppressed.

Human trafficking is not a new issue, but a topic of renewed interest. To ensure that new interest is effectively channeled into combating human trafficking, abolitionists must be aware of the progress that has been made in past decades along with the shortfalls of recent steps forward. In conjunction with this knowledge, abolitionists must also be conscious of how they frame the issue of human trafficking to be inclusive of the many shapes, sizes, styles, and depths of victimization. Without a conscious effort to address the numerous variables present in the complex equation that leads to being trafficked, the majority of legislative gains will be made hollow by those who benefit from the exploitation of other humans.

Human Trafficking: The New Slavery

When abolitionists from the 1800s were working toward ending chattel slavery they were very clear about their goals and who they saw as victims of the tragic institution. Although those who were enslaved and treated like animals were the most prominent victims, they also recognized that a broader population including free blacks were also being victimized by the institution (tenBroek, 1951, p. 179). Although abolitionists recognized the broader implications of slavery, their early legislative efforts failed to rectify the wider issue of oppression facing African Americans both free and enslaved. Shortly after the passing of the Thirteenth Amendment, abolitionist Frederick Douglass gave a speech concerning the need for continuing anti-slavery work. In his speech Douglass stated:

> Slavery has been fruitful in giving itself names. It has been called "the peculiar institution," "the social system," and the "impediment" … It has been called by a great many names, and it will call itself by yet another name; and you and I and all of us had better wait and see what new form this old monster will assume, in what new skin this old snake will come forth next. (Douglass, 2000, p. 579)

Following the Civil War, slavery reemerged under the black codes. Although the method and structure of oppression changed, little else changed for former slaves. Today slavery goes by a new name and uses new methods of oppression, but human trafficking is the same old monster.

To recognize the old snake in its new skin, abolitionists must continue to look beneath the surface and beyond the most obvious victims. Early abolitionists recognized slavery defined the lives of free blacks as well as the lives of those bound in chains, in the same way those wishing to combat modern slavery must be aware that being unbound and unbeaten does not preclude you from being enslaved. When considering victims of human trafficking it is easy to become focused on ideal victims and overlook those who do not fit the same image. Although human trafficking is the new form of slavery, calling it modern slavery can unintentionally create the impression that today's human trafficking looks like the chattel slavery of early American history. Despite the similarities of chattel slavery and human trafficking, they often utilize different methods of exploitation. When the ideal victim is consciously or unconsciously adopted as the definition of being victimized, it leaves those who are not ideal victims trapped in a cycle of exploitation because they are not labeled as victims by themselves or others.

According to criminologist Nils Christie, the five attributes of *ideal victimization* include a weak victim, the victim is doing something respectable, the victim was somewhere he or she can't be blamed for being, the offender is big and bad, and the victim does not know the offender (Hoyle, Bosworth, and Dempsey, 2011, p. 315). Although these attributes make compelling news stories, they are highly restrictive when it comes to identifying victims. Unfortunately the attributes of ideal victimization characterize many of the news stories about human trafficking. Too often those who write about human trafficking either for news media or nonprofit organizations focus on details that make victims seem ideal or attributes that are not ideal are left out. One such example is the story of a sex trafficking ring in Detroit. According to the article by *Detroit Free Press* the primary victim was a young girl who had been abducted while waiting for a bus and had been forced by a man and older woman to have sex with strangers (Bales, Fletcher, and Stover, 2004, p. 12). Although the story clearly depicts a victim of human trafficking, the young girl is no more a victim than a 30-year-old woman who is coerced into having sex with acquaintances of her boyfriend. Sadly, if attention continues to focus on ideal victims, then more victims will be overlooked and slavery will yet again shed its skin and take on a new form.

Summary

It is likely that anti-trafficking efforts will meet some of the same challenges anti-slavery efforts met in past decades, and if abolitionists want to continue making progress and not lose ground, then a conscious and concerted effort to champion the cause of more than the ideal victim must be made. To prevent the monster of slavery from shifting into another ugly form, legislation and the general public must recognize the broadest group of trafficking victims. Without proper legislation the public is largely unarmed in the conflict against trafficking and will struggle to adequately punish those involved in this exploitative enterprise. Yet, even if the best legislation is in place, without a properly informed and supportive populace the exploitation will continue in defiance of the law in the same way the Thirteenth and Fourteenth Amendments were disregarded by the Supreme Court and many of the states. Besides the importance of a supportive public and well-formed legislation, today's abolitionists can learn several things from past anti-slavery efforts.

From historical observation, today's abolitionists should recognize that even if a state regulates and controls an institution or industry, it does not become any less oppressive. Among the many views regarding the relation of prostitution and sex trafficking is the idea that legalizing prostitution will decrease the amount of trafficking (Marinova and James, 2012, p. 235). History shows that after the Thirteenth Amendment formally abolished slavery, many Southern states adopted black codes that not only continued the oppression of African Americans but made the states more involved in the process by leveraging the criminal justice system as a means of exploitation. Although state regulation of prostitution might improve the environment in which it takes place, it will not change prostitution's exploitative nature. Instead of curbing sexual exploitation, the state would gain a vested interest in the continuation of prostitution to maintain its source of revenue.

Modern abolitionists should also consider following the historical precedent of amending the Constitution to ensure the permanence of legislative progress. Although human trafficking is a popular subject today with broad public support, it is inevitable that public awareness will wane and even possible that popular opinion could change direction. With this in mind abolitionists should contemplate the possibility of making a constitutional amendment. The decision to push for constitutional amendments prohibiting slavery in the immediate aftermath of the Civil War was undoubtedly wise, because although the amendments faced numerous obstacles early on, the fact that they were amendments to constitutional law rather than statutory law allowed them to persist despite initial opposition.

Key Terms

Atlantic slave trade

black codes

chattel slavery

Emancipation Proclamation

Fourteenth Amendment

ideal victim

sharecropping

slave codes

Thirteenth Amendment

Review Questions

1. Describe how slavery evolved after the adoption of the Thirteenth Amendment.
2. What significance is there in seeing human trafficking as part of the evolution of slavery?
3. In what way could the association of human trafficking with chattel slavery have a negative impact?
4. What attribute is most likely to cause a victim to be ignored if they do not match the ideal victim?

References

Adamson, C. R. (1983). Punishment after slavery: Southern state penal systems, 1865–1890. *Social Problems, 30*(5), 555–569.

Bales, K., Fletcher, L., and Stover, E. (2004). Hidden slaves: Forced labor in the United States. Retrieved from http://escholarship.org/uc/item/4jn4j0qg.

Bales, K., and Trodd, Z. (2009). *Modern Slavery: The Secret World of 27 Million People.* Oxford: Oneworld.

Brandwein, P. (2000). Slavery as an interpretive issue in the Reconstruction Congresses. *Law & Society Review, 34*(2), 315–366.

Chattel. (n.d.). In *Wex*. Retrieved from http://www.law.cornell.edu/wex/chattel.

Douglass, F. (2000). *Frederick Douglass: Selected Speeches and Writings* (abridged). P. S. Foner and Y. Taylor (Eds.). Chicago: Chicago Review Press.

Fage, J. D. (1989). African societies and the Atlantic slave trade. *Past & Present, 125,* 97–115.

Hopkins, B. D. (2008). Race, sex and slavery: 'Forced labour' in Central Asia and Afghanistan in the early 19th century. *Modern Asian Studies, 42*(4), 629–671.

Hoyle, C., Bosworth, M., and Dempsey, M. (2011). Labelling the victims of sex trafficking: Exploring the borderland between rhetoric and reality. *Social & Legal Studies, 20*(3), 313–329.

Marinova, N. K., and James, P. (2012). The tragedy of human trafficking: Competing theories and European evidence. *Foreign Policy Analysis, 12,* 231–253.

Ruef, M., and Fletcher, B. (2003). Legacies of American slavery: Status attainment among southern blacks after emancipation. *Social Forces, 82*(2), 445–480.

tenBroek, J. (1951). Thirteenth Amendment to the Constitution of the United States: Consummation to abolition and key to the Fourteenth Amendment. *California Law Review, 39*(2), 171–203.

Zuckert, M. P. (1992). Completing the Constitution: The Fourteenth Amendment and constitutional rights. *Publius, 22*(2), 69–91.

Borderland
The Challenge of Cross-Border Trafficking of People, Drugs, and Guns between Mexico and the United States

2

LAURENCE ARMAND FRENCH

Contents

Major Issues

Illegal immigration has become a heated political flashpoint in the United States during the twenty-first century, making it one of the main domestic issues dividing politicians, law enforcement, the courts, and the public. The fear of "foreign-born" immigrants has long been a part of America's history placing "native-born" whites against "foreign-born" newcomers, especially those of color or of different religious affiliations. The political rhetoric, then as now, is that these immigrants, legal or illegal, will bring with them a host of social ills that will ultimately undermine the basic fabric of American society. From this general perspective, the general distrust intensifies where undocumented (illegal) immigrants are concerned. Here, a common causal but largely unfounded assumption is that illegal immigrants are potentially "criminal immigrants." This perception prevails among an adamant and vocal segment of U.S. society despite a lack of evidence to support this contention. Today, Hispanics, notably those of Mexican origin, are targeted as the largest group of criminal immigrants in need of policing.

Introduction

Although the bulk of Mexican immigrants in the United States, regardless of status (licit or illicit), are productive, compliant members of society, it is the criminal enterprise associated with border activity that has gained attention among law enforcement agencies in the United States, especially since the advent of the Department of Homeland Security following the terrorists attacks of September 11, 2001. Now the U.S.–Mexico border is seen not only as a funnel for Mexicans to enter the United States but for others who may be intent on harming America. For this reason alone, the U.S.–Mexico and U.S.–Canada borders require greater scrutiny and protection, resulting in corroborative efforts between these three NAFTA (North American Free Trade Agreement) partners. Mexico differs from Canada, which has historically had a virtually "open" border with the United States. Mexico, on the other hand, has maintained a frontier region known as the *Borderland,* which transcends portions of both countries' geographic borders. The nearly 2,000 mile shared border between Mexico and the United States was finally settled through conflict and threat of war in December 1853. Today the Borderland has 22 million inhabitants and its own frontier culture. Borderland extends from Brownsville–Matamoros to San Diego–Tijuana, with Juarez–El Paso as its de facto capital. Within 30 miles of the region's major cities lies a rural area basically unaffected by time, interior Mexico, or the United States. That changed with the advent of NAFTA in 1994 and the September 11, 2001, terrorist attacks on the United States. A brief review of the Borderland is needed to best understand the current issues regarding human trafficking along the Mexico–U.S. border.

Historical Antecedents

Border issues with Mexico extend back to Spanish Mexico when it welcomed Anglo emigrants to settle its northern territory (Texas). Here, substantial *Empresario land grants* were awarded to U.S. citizens willing to convert to Catholicism and become Spanish citizens. The first land grant was awarded to Moses Austin on January 17, 1821, initially allowing him to settle 300 families in what is now Texas. Eight months later, on September 21, 1821, Mexico gained independence from Spain, becoming the Republic of Mexico. The new Republic continued the Empresario system established under the Imperial Colonization Law. The root of rebellion that fueled the Texas Revolution among the U.S. emigrants was Mexico's new constitution, which outlawed slavery. By 1835, the antislavery issue became paramount leading to the secession of the Anglo-dominated northern territory, known as Texas, on December 10, 1835. Another issue of contention was the constitutional protection offered Indian tribes within Mexico. Instead, Section 10 of the Constitution of the Republic of Texas states: "All persons (Africans, the descendants of Africans, and Indians excepted) who were residing in Texas on the day of the Declaration of Independence, shall be considered citizens of the republic, and entitled to all the privileges of such." Moreover, only U.S. slaves were welcomed in the new Republic: "No free person of African descent, either in whole or in part, shall be permitted to reside permanently in the republic, without the consent of Congress; and the importation of admission of Africans or Negroes into this republic, excepting from the United States of America, is forever prohibited, and declared to be piracy (Section 9)." Eventually, even the Tejanos (Texans of Mexican descent) would be disenfranchised and discriminated against by their Anglo counterparts.

On February 19, 1845 Texas ended its existence as a Republic and was annexed to the United States as a slave state. And in January 1846, President James K. Polk sent General Zachary Taylor across the Nueces River for the purpose of establishing U.S. military posts along the Rio Grande setting the stage for America's Mexican War (known as the War of Northern Aggression in Mexican history). Taking advantage of a weaker neighbor, the United States used the Mexican War (1846–1848) to expand the United States to the Pacific Ocean, a raw example of blatant imperialism according to former U.S. Attorney General Robert Kennedy. The acquisition of this vast territory ignited the slave debate in the United States, paving the way for the more devastating conflict—the War Between the States (U.S. Civil War).

The war with Mexico of 1846–1848 led to the signing of the Guadalupe Hidalgo Treaty on February 2, 1848. The terms of the treaty formally ended Mexico's claim to Texas while expanding the United States to the Pacific Ocean with the acquisition of New Mexico and the Upper California territories. In all, Mexico was forced to cede 55 percent of its territory, what are now the states of Arizona, California, New Mexico, and parts of Colorado, Nevada, and Utah. The 1848 treaty established the Rio Grande (Big River) as the official southern border for the state of Texas.

The Gadsden Purchase, obtained under threat of American armed intervention during the administration of President Franklin Pierce, in 1853 further expanded the U.S. territory in the southwest by 45,000 square miles by moving the Mexico–U.S. border south of the Rio Grande expanding the borders of New Mexico, Arizona, and California. The main purpose of the Gadsden Purchase was to provide a southern East–West rail link across the continent. The purchase was named after James Gadsden, Pierce's U.S. minister (ambassador) to Mexico. Gadsden, from South Carolina, previously served as President Monroe's agent in charge of removing Florida's Seminole Indians onto reservations. Gadsden was also the president of the Consolidated South Carolina, Louisville, Charleston, and Cincinnati Railroads, which wanted to construct a rail line to the Pacific Ocean in an attempt to beat northern rail efforts to connect the east with California. Gadsden's engineering plans indicated that the most efficient route for this endeavor was one south of the Gila River that delineated the U.S.–Mexico border under the 1848 Treaty of Guadalupe Hidalgo. The purchase also gave the U.S. ownership of the rich copper mines in the region. This land grab added Yuma, California; Tucson, Nogales, Wilcox, and Douglas, Arizona; and Lordsburg, Deming, Columbus, Mesilla, and Santa Rita in New Mexico as well as other villages and tribal homelands to the United States. Regarding local tribes, some of the fiercest Indian warfare occurred in this newly acquired territory in violation of the 1848 treaty relevant to Mexico's confirmation of citizenship to Native Americans with its 1821 constitution as well as the abrogation of Article XI of the 1848 treaty that obligated the U.S. Army to protect Mexicans from cross-border raids by aggressive Apache, Comanche, and Kiowa tribes residing in what was now the United States. Instead, the United States raged a war of genocide on Indians in the Southwest, treating them as less-than-human pests that needed to be removed or exterminated.

The Borderland

The Borderland, that region that transcends the 1,933 mile U.S.–Mexico border for a radius from 30 to 50 miles on either side of the international border, flourished under the long reign of Porfirio Diaz, who dominated Mexican politics from 1877 to 1911 either during his six terms as president or de facto leader, an era known as the *Porfiriato*. Porfirio Diaz was a Mexican general who distinguished himself in the *Cinco de Mayo* (5th of May, 1862) battle against Napoleon III's troops in support of Emperor Maximilian von Hapsburg, the European leader installed to run Mexico. During this time Mexico's foreign debt was paid and the national treasury was operating in the black. Crime was down as well but at the expense of the curtailment of civil liberties and rights. The *Porfirian* society preferred the upper class *Criollos* (Mexican-born whites) at the expense of the peasants that consisted mainly of *Mestizos* (mixed Indian/white) and full-blooded Indians, who comprised the vast majority of Mexican society. Diaz's success was due mainly to his introduction of foreign, mainly U.S., business interests designed to exploit both the country's vast untapped natural resources as well as its cheap workforce. This led to the development of the Borderland region, which traces it birth to 1882 and the U.S.–Mexico treaty allowing reciprocal border crossings. This class differential, along with its racist characteristics, and foreign exploitation of labor and resources led to the second Mexican Revolution (1911–1917) with General Carranza and Obregon fighting the peasant forces led by Generals Villa and Zapata. The United States played a major role in the Mexican Revolution, with U.S. troops occupying Veracruz in 1914 and ending in 1917 with General John (Black Jack) Pershing's 11-month Punitive Expedition into Mexico in search for General Villa for his 1916 raid on a U.S. military base in Columbus, New Mexico. Villas eluded Pershing but the expedition provided the U.S. with its first experience with a mechanized military preparing America for its role in World War I.

Immigration and Migrant Issues

U.S. immigration laws corresponded with the massive immigration wave of some 25 million people entering the country between 1880 until the borders were closed in 1930 due to the Great Depression. It was during this time that the first exclusionary legislation was enacted: the Chinese Exclusion Act of 1882. The immigration situation for Mexicans during this era, up to the Second World War, was focused mainly in the Borderland. The manpower drain of both world wars led to the need for a readily available workforce, albeit illegal, to accommodate the agricultural demands of ranchers and farmers from Texas to California, and the Borderland region provided these cheap seasonal laborers. This was a fluid process with demand for Mexican workers diminished during the Great Depression with the internal migration of unemployed men, mainly "Okies," providing the agricultural manpower resources. The transborder movement during this era was not seen as being problematic, as is evidenced by the relatively small size of the U.S. Border Patrol. Since its creation in 1924, the U.S. Border Patrol has remained relatively small for decades. Following the Great Depression the need for transient Mexican "day laborers" (braceros) led to an international agreement with the establishment of the *Bracero Program* (Public Law 45). Terrorists and drug and human trafficking were not seen as serious problems; in 1993, the Border Patrol had only about 4,000 agents, a figure that swelled to more than 21,000 following the September 11, 2001 attacks.

The Bracero Program did not initially include entry into the United States along the entire border region. Texas, with the longest section of borderlands, did not originally participate mainly because Texas farmers and ranchers thought that they could continue to get illegal Mexican *wetbacks* (*mojados*) at a cheaper rate and without adhering to the humane conditions spelled out by Public Law 45. Nonetheless, the Bracero Program was unique in that it allowed Mexico to establish the minimum standards for its workers in the United States. During the period covering the initial Bracero Agreement, from 1942 until 1947, some 200,000 braceros came to the United States as agricultural workers under these international provisions. They worked in agriculture in 24 states with the vast majority employed in California. Texas received no braceros during this contract period, but did participate in subsequent extensions of this program, which continued until 1964.

Theories and Policies

Theories relevant to intergroup interactions are complex and varied. We have already looked at the historical complexities of U.S. expansionistic policies and actions, notably those directed toward Mexico. Race and religion certainly played a role in the historical discourse. Mexico has long been seen as a human resource for cheap labor, either in agriculture in the United States or in the international manufacturing companies located on the Mexican side of the Borderland. Nonetheless, regardless of the nature of historical events, once boundaries are set, formal interactions arise in the form of national and international policy. The main tools for maintaining the international flow of people and material are policies determining border security.

Immigration Policies

The U.S. Congress has original jurisdiction and complete authority over immigration issues. While the U.S. president can suggest changes in the immigration laws, his or her authority is limited solely to proposing polices. By the same token, the U.S. judiciary is limited to acting on the constitutionality of aliens' rights. States have limited legislative authority and can only participate in immigration matters as invited partners with federal authorities. The combined effect of the turbulent protests of the 1960s during the Civil Rights and Vietnam era and the ending of the Bracero Program opened the border to a flood of illegal immigration entering the United States from Mexico resulting in the Immigration and Reform Control Act (IRCA) of 1986 (Reagan administration). The IRCA both toughened legal sanctions for employers hiring illegal aliens and provided amnesty for those already in the United States. This act also restrained illegal aliens from participating in federal welfare programs while the Immigration Marriage Fraud Amendment attempted to curtail the practice of phony marriages for the purpose of obtaining U.S. citizenship.

The Immigration Act of 1990 revised the standards set forth in 1952, which abolished the exclusions against Asians and gave preference based upon education and skill levels, by equalizing the allocation of visas across nations, thereby opening up immigration worldwide. Six years later, as a reaction of the Oklahoma City bombing (a domestic bombing terrorist act), the Illegal Immigration Reform and Immigration Responsibility Act of 1996 (IIRIRA) instituted stricter immigration policies. The IIRIRA addressed five major areas: (1) improvements to border control, facilitation of legal entry, and interior enforcement; (2) enhanced enforcement and penalties against alien smuggling and document fraud; (3) inspection, apprehension, detention, adjudication, and removal of inadmissible and deportable aliens; (4) enforcement of restrictions against employment; and (5) restrictions on benefits to aliens.

On March 1, 2003, following the terrorist attacks of 9/11, the United States created the Department of Homeland Security with oversight over three agencies: (1) U.S. Customs and Border Enforcement (CBE), (2) U.S. Citizenship and Immigration Services (USCIS), and (3) U.S. Immigration and Customs Enforcement (ICE). Under this arrangement, U.S. Border Patrol falls under the CBE while ICE took over the function of deportation. The USCIS deals with asylum, naturalization, and permanent residence functions. Since the establishment of the Department of Homeland Security, over 95 percent of all people arrested entering the United States illegally enter from the Mexican border—the Borderland.

Even before the terrorist attacks of September 11, 2001, efforts were being made to shore up border security at the major entry points within the Borderland, thus forcing illegal aliens into the more treacherous desert regions know as *death corridors.* As a consequence of these actions, the U.S. government makes running the border gauntlet all the more deadly. The increased militarization of the Borderland was conceived in 1993 during the Clinton administration and went in effect in 1994, the same year NAFTA went into effect. This new strategy, known as the Southwest Border Strategy, was designed to shore up the most porous sections of the border, those adjacent to San Diego, California; Tucson, Arizona; and El Paso, Texas; and coincided with the economic crisis in Mexico over the devaluation of the peso. Operation Hold the Line was initiated at the Ciudad Juarez, Mexico–El Paso, Texas, entryway, while Operation Gatekeeper addressed the main California entry from Ciudad Tijuana, Mexico, into the Imperial Beach–San Diego region, and Operation Safeguard reinforced the Nogales, Mexico–Douglas, Arizona entryway to Tucson, Arizona. These border operations also resulted in an increase in border patrol officers along the U.S.–Mexico border as well as the introduction of military personnel. In 2006, President George W. Bush reintroduced a plan for using U.S. military personnel along the southern border by enticing governors of California, Arizona, New Mexico, and Texas to authorize the use of their National Guard for this duty. This was known as Operation Jump Start.

The increase in border patrol activity coupled with deployment of the National Guard as well as the creation of numerous roads and the environmental damage done by construction vehicles has soured some Borderland residents. Other landowners have welcomed the intrusion of military, paramilitary, and increased border patrol personnel. Some even allow the Minuteman Civil Defense Corps to construct fencing on their property and to patrol with guns and dogs. Some residents and entire communities on the U.S. side of the border are concerned about the increasingly widening swath that border security is mandating, with the power of federal eminent domain, to confiscate their lands and carve up their backyards. Moreover, it is questionable if these efforts are really curtailing the drug trade itself especially with more border tunnels being discovered. Unfortunately, the majority of the million plus apprehensions along the U.S.–Mexico border per year are not drug dealers or terrorists but merely Mexicans coming to the United States for jobs. With the worldwide financial crisis that began in 2008, both the number of illegal immigrants and the resources for extending the border fence seem to be temporarily halted. Even then hundreds of deaths occur annually on the U.S. side of the Borderland. On the Mexico side of the Borderland, the numbers are much higher with drug-related massacres and the unsolved murders of young women drawn to the maquiladoras.

Major Issues Discussed

Trafficking of People

Economics is the main force that drives the human trafficking through Mexico to the United States. NAFTA was a major factor for the internal migration of working class Mexicans from the interior to the Borderland. By the same token, poverty and discrimination against indigenous peoples in war-torn Central American countries was the main incentive for the migration of non-Mexican Hispanics who traversed Mexico's southern border with Guatemala in order to get to the Borderland and hopefully into the United States. Regarding the internal Mexican migration, not everyone had the intention of crossing into the United States. For the most part, many young females were enticed by their families to migrate to the Mexican side of the Borderland to work in the maquiladoras. The NAFTA-driven migrations led to an increase of both licit and illicit enterprises within the Borderland, resulting in the flooding of the slums within the cities and the emergence of unincorporated squatter settlements in the rural regions, known as *colonials.*

For the most part mere shantytowns, these communities posed challenges for both the Mexican federal and state governments regarding not only adequate housing, but schools, water and sanitation, roads, and safety. Granted, many of the maquiladoras provided dormitories especially for their predominately single female workers, but entire families migrated to the Borderland as well, being forced into the slums and colonials. Human trafficking also involved prostitution, which is not illegal in Mexico. With the advent of a flood of young, single, or unaccompanied females, the sex market in the Borderland was a draw for Mexican and American males, especially within the bar districts of the major Mexican Borderland cities as well as within the rural areas. An unfortunate consequence of the Borderland sex trade is that of child sex tourism where Mexico is one of the leading magnets for child sexual exploitation along with Thailand, Cambodia, Colombia, India, and Brazil. According to the U.S. Department of State, "Human Rights Report: Mexico," the most vulnerable groups to be exploited are women and children, indigenous persons, and undocumented migrants. The majority of non-Mexican trafficking victims entering the Borderland are from Central America, but this population also represents people from the Caribbean, South America, Asia, and Eastern European countries. Houston, Texas, is a major hub for human trafficking for all nationalities seeking entry into the United States. This includes those entering from Mexico. Houston's large geographic area; large Hispanic population; and land, air, and sea entry points, along with its job opportunities make it a convenient magnet for illegals and those willing to exploit people eager to enter the United States. While some of this population attempt to enter the United States on their own, many rely on traffickers to gain entry. *Coyote* is the term used to describe the traffickers taking illegal aliens through Mexico to the Borderland region, mustering on the Mexican side and then traversing the international border into the United States. Often they do this in concert with unsavory farmers, ranchers, and construction firms seeking cheap labor.

Drug and Weapons Trafficking

With the U.S.-sponsored war on drugs in Colombia and the conclusion of the civil wars in Central America, Mexico became the major transit route for drugs, both homegrown and in transit. Often it is difficult to separate drug trafficking from human trafficking since the major drug cartels run both types of rackets. Regardless, there has been a high toll on human lives during the 21st century. Both the drug trade and death count has risen rapidly since the demise of the Colombian Cali and Medellin cartels in the 1990s. Ironically, the Mexican drug cartels emerged in the 1980s as a subsidiary of the Medellin cartel run by Pablo Escobar. The "Godfather" of the Mexican drug trade was Miguel Angel Felix Gallardo, a former member of the

Mexican Judicial Federal Police. Felix Gallardo held a monopoly on the drug trade with his Guadalajara cartel with considerable support from corrupt police, judges, and politicians and with minor interference from the United States. Things changed with the torture and murder of Drug Enforcement Administration (DEA) Agent Enrique Camarena. The United States imposed its influence into the Mexican drug trade forcing the Guadalajara Cartel to go underground and to encourage splinter cartels throughout Mexico. Felix Gallardo divided the drug trade so that now there was the Tijuana route run by the Arellano Felix brothers; the Ciudad Juarez route under the Carrillo Fuentes family; the Sonora Cartel run by Miguel Caro Quintero; and the Matamoros/Tamaulipas Gulf Cartel run by Juan Garcia Abrego. It was during this time that the Sinaloa Cartel took over the Pacific Coast operations using innovative techniques such as ships and submarines to distribute their drugs. In the first decade of the 21st century, Mexico was plagued with seven major drug/smuggling cartels, often competing with each other resulting in a blood bath among both cartel members and innocent civilians. The competing combatants are the Tijuana Cartel, the Beltran Leyva Cartel, the Sinaloa Cartel, the Juarez Cartel, the La Familia Michocana, the Gulf Cartel, and the Los Zetas.

The availability of military and military-like assault weapons (e.g., AK-47, M16, M4, AR15, riot 12-gauge shotguns, large capacity pistols) has contributed to the deadly cartel wars. Although some items are smuggled from Mexico's southern borders, most come from the United States. For the most part, gun trafficking originates with gun shops in borderland states, notably Arizona. In order to trace the origin of these weapons entering Mexico from the United States, in 2006 the Arizona Field Office of the U.S. Bureau of Alcohol, Tobacco, Firearms and Explosives (ATF) initiated what it hoped to be a sting operation: Project Gunrunning. For 5 years (2006–2011) the ATF purposely allowed licensed firearm dealers, mainly in Tucson and Phoenix, to sell assault-type weapons to illegal straw buyers in order to trace the guns to Mexican drug cartels. This was known as *gun walking* and the largest of these projects was known as Operation Fast and Furious. Of the 2,000 guns involved in Operation Fast and Furious only 710 were recovered as of February 2012. Those guns that were tracked were involved in crimes on both sides of the Mexico–U.S. border, including the killing of U.S. Border Patrol Agent Brian Terry on December 14, 2010. An investigation by the Mexican Attorney General found that some 150 civilian casualties were linked to the gunrunning operations. The exposure of the gunrunning programs did little to improve Mexicans' perception of the United States, especially in light of the over 60,000 drug-related deaths, including hundreds of young females along the Borderland. Although these controversial programs began under President George W. Bush, President Obama effectively sealed the details of

Project Gunrunning by invoking executive privilege leading to a Contempt of Congress directed to Attorney General Eric Holder on June 28, 2012.

Solutions

Short of a total fence along the U.S.–Mexico border along with a 24/7 military and police presence, human trafficking will continue as long as there is a demand for people to work in jobs that are considered undesirable by U.S. residents. Indeed, an influx of young workers is desired in societies that have a substantial aging population, like the United States and many European societies. Toward this end, countries like England have enticed outsiders to migrate as long as they know the language, are adequately educated, or have sufficient financial resources to bring with them. Even then, illegal immigrants will find a way into societies that they perceive as being more desirable than their own country. In the United States, President Obama bypassed the congressional gridlock by instituting the Development, Relief, and Education for Alien Minors Act (DREAM Act) protecting children of illegal immigrants from deportation and allowing them to pursue the same future offered children of legitimate citizens. This opened educational opportunities for this population with many states following suit by allowing this group in-state tuition at state colleges and universities. As of February 2014, 14 states have passed legislation allowing high school students of illegal immigrants to pursue higher education at the same savings of legal state residents. Seven other states have legislation pending. Three of the four Borderland states—Texas, New Mexico, and California—were quick to provide these services to their substantial Hispanic population, despite outcries from vocal conservative groups opposed to any concessions to illegal immigrants.

Another federal initiative is for the deportation, as against incarceration, of illegal immigrants arrested, convicted, and sentenced for nonviolent offenses. Here the U.S. Department of Homeland Security (DHS) can remove illegal immigrants arrested for nonviolent crimes as long as it feels that this is in the best interest of the country. This provision became available at the federal level in 2012 and those already serving sentences for convictions prior to enactment of this law can petition the U.S. Department of Justice for their participation, once the law was approved by the U.S. Attorney General. Since passage, the DHS has encouraged individual states to participate in the program (ICE Rapid REPAT). This would require legislation to alter existing laws, many which require that the offender complete at least half of their sentence before qualifying for early deportation. However, a December 2013 survey of Hispanic and Asian Americans by the Pew Research Center found that the vast majority of (89 percent) favor legislation creating pathways for citizenship for unauthorized immigrants as against current deportation policies. This is important given that Hispanics account for about three-quarters of the nearly 12 million immigrants in the country illegally.

Nonetheless, continued cooperation between U.S. and Mexican law enforcement and the military (seen as less corruptible than either local, state, or federal law enforcement agencies) resulted in the arrest of Mexico's top drug lord, Joaquin "El Chapo" Guzman, on February 22, 2014. El Chapo headed the deadly Sinaloa Cartel responsible for tens of thousands of deaths and was on the U.S. DEA's most wanted list as well as held the title of "Public Enemy, No. 1" in Chicago, a title last bestowed on Al Capone. He ran the largest and most notorious drug cartel in Mexico with a drug empire that extended throughout the United States and Canada to Europe and even Australia. His capture by Mexican Marines was assisted by U.S. intelligence. That is the good news. The not so good news is that Mexican President Enrique Pena Nieto insists on having El Chapo tried in Mexico and sentenced to its notoriously corrupt penal system where he escaped from prison 13 years ago. Moreover, drug leaders incarcerated in Mexico allegedly continue running their operations from within prison walls.

Ostensibly, any viable solution to drug and human trafficking through the Borderland into the United States is contingent upon two major factors, both determined by the world market economy. Illegal trafficking from Mexico depends on the Mexican economy. Post-NAFTA indicates a swelling of the emergent middle-class as well as better employment opportunities for the working class in such areas as the auto industry. Continued growth and economic improvements depend on the curtailment of corruption within Mexico, notably within public agencies including the courts and police. President Pena Nieto's proposed reforms, including allowing foreign investment in Mexico's oil sector and eliminating single-term requirements for political office, can backfire given these abuses in the past. Optimism for change is mixed given that many of these past abuses occurred during the long reign of the Institutional Revolutionary Party (PRI) to which President Pena Nieto belongs. The drug trade, on the other hand, is contingent on the U.S. and Canadian market demands. A partial solution is the movement to decriminalize marijuana, and, in a number of states, to legalize its production for medical or personal use. This, in itself, should serve to put a dent in the illicit market demand.

Another critical solution involves efforts at better control over Mexico's southern borders with Guatemala and Belize. Drugs, guns, money, and human cargo from outside Mexico cross these borders into Mexico with much of this contraband targeted for the Borderland. Any viable solution for Mexico's southern borders needs to take into account the plight of the Mayan Indians that transcend both regions of these borders. Indeed, Mexico's southern borders represent a historic Mayan borderland itself. The North American partners—Canada, Mexico, and the United States—need to work with the Mayan Indians to meet their demands for the preservation of their traditional customs and practices, which are often at odds with the capitalist interests of non-Indians within these regions.

Summary

Human trafficking is a worldwide phenomenon driven by a number of factors including cheap labor and the sex market. People are often enticed to migrate to another country, either legally or illegally, only to find themselves held in servitude or as a sex slave. Here, the exploitation of children and youth, regardless of gender, is the worst case situation. Currently there are a number of international efforts to curb these practices, especially those involved in child pornography. Moreover, more countries are considering legalizing adult prostitution in order to better protect both the practitioner and the client from disease and violence. Drug trafficking and other transborder movement of illicit contraband, such as motor vehicles, can only be addressed by better international and interagency cooperation. But in the final analysis, efforts need to be made to diminish the market for these items as well. The Mexico–USA example speaks to the limitation of increased policing and militarization of borders as well as the increased criminalization of the recipient of these services (notably drug laws), whether it be a cheap labor resource or the drug market.

Key Words

Border Patrol
Bracero Program
coyotes
drug cartels
Homeland Security
Operation Gunrunning
North American Free Trade Agreement (NAFTA)
maquiladoras
militarized border
sex trade
terrorist attacks (9/11)
World Trade Organization (WTO)

Review Questions

1. What role did the early history of U.S. expansionism play in the overall geopolitics of Borderland issues today?
2. To what extent does race/ethnic national orientation seem to influence public opinion and public policy regarding border security along America's borders: U.S.–Mexico versus U.S.–Canada?
3. To what extent does the world economy and the agreements such as NAFTA and the WTO influence border politics?

Bibliography

"ATF Fact Sheet: Project Gunrunning," http://www.atf.gov/publications/factsheet/factsheet-project-gunrunning.html.

Akins, S. "State and Local Enforcement of Immigration Law." *Criminology & Public Policy*, vol. 12, no. 2 (May 2013): 227–236.

Bracero Agreement. Public Law 45. August 2, 1942–December 31, 1947.

Bureau of Democracy, Human Rights, and Labor. U.S. Department of State. 2009.

Central Intelligence Agency (CIA). "Belize," *The World Factbook*, http://www.cia.gov/library/publications/the-world-factbook/geos/bh.html.

Crowley, M. "The committee to save Mexico," *Time*, vol. 183, no. 7 (2014): 34–39.

Early Release Programs for Nonviolent Offenders Pursuant to 8 U.S.C.: 1231 (a) (4) (B). 2012.

"Fast and Furious: The anatomy of a failed operation," http://oversight.house.gov/wp-content/uploads/2012/07/7-31-12-FF-Part1-FINAL-REPORT.pdf. United States Congress.

French, L. A. *Running the Border Gauntlet: The Mexican Migrant Controversy*. Santa Barbara, CA: Praeger Press, 2010.

French, L. A., and M. Manzanarez. *NAFTA & Neocolonialism: Comparative Criminal, Human, & Social Justice*. Lanham, MD: University Press of America. 2004.

Graham, M. "Human trafficking begins to eclipse during drug trade in Mexico," *Spero News*, http://www.speroforum.com/site/print.asp?id=41874. October 17, 2010.

Grillo, I. *El Narco: The Bloody Rise of Mexican Drug Cartels* (2nd ed.). New York, NY: Bloomsbury Publishing, 2012.

"Human Rights Report: Mexico," http://www.state.gov/g/drl/rls/hrrpt/2008.

Immigration and Custom Enforcement. Fact Sheet: Delegation of Immigration Authority Section 287(g) Immigration and Nationalization Act. U.S. Department of Homeland Security. 2012a.

Immigration and Custom Enforcement. "Activated jurisdictions." U.S. Department of Homeland Security. 2012b.

Immigration and Custom Enforcement. "Fact sheet: Criminal alien program." U.S. Department of Homeland Security. 2012c.

Longmire, S. "The irony of Mexico's problem along its southern border," *Mexidatainfo*. December 7, 2009. http://www.mexidata.info/id2481.html.

Lopez, M. H., P. Taylor, C. Funk, and A. Gonzalez-Barrera. "On immigration policy, deportation relief seen as more important than citizenship: A survey of Hispanic and Asian Americans." Pew Research: Hispanic Trends Project, December 19, 2013. http://www.pewhispanic.org/2013/12/19/on-immigration-policy.

Mexican Law Agreement of 1951; 1961; 1963 (Public Law 78).

Rosenblum, M. R., and K. Brick. *US Immigration Policy and Mexican/Central American Migration Flows: Then and Now*. Washington, DC: Migration Policy Institute, 2011.

Shepard-Durini, S. "Mexico's other border: Issues affecting Mexico's dividing line with Guatemala," Council on Hemispheric Affairs. September 12, 2008. http://www.coha.org/mexico's-other-border-issues-affecting-mexico's-dividing-line-with-guatemala/.

Wallner, P. A. *Franklin Pierce: Martyr for the Union*. Concord, NH: Plaidswede Publishing, 2007.

Sociology of Human Trafficking

3

CHRISTOPHER J. MOLONEY

Contents

Major Issues

- What is a sociological perspective?
- Culture and human trafficking
- Race, ethnicity, and human trafficking
- Gender and human trafficking
- Exploring sociological explanations of human trafficking

Introduction

The topic of this chapter, like the others in this volume, is human trafficking. What differs substantially here is the perspective through which that issue is understood. Utilizing a critical sociological perspective, we examine the human trafficking problem along the dimensions of culture, race, ethnicity, and gender. Ultimately, these social factors interact with each other and larger societal issues like poverty to produce and sustain human trafficking around the globe. This chapter concludes with a brief look at how different types of sociological explanations can generate important knowledge about how and why human trafficking occurs and persists.

What Is a Sociological Perspective?

The sociological imagination enables us to grasp history and biography and the relations between the two within society. This is its task and its promise.

—**C. Wright Mills**

In a classic sociological work of the same name, C. Wright Mills discussed his concept of the *sociological imagination,* which conveyed a unique method of examining social life by taking into account not only individual characteristics, or personal "biography," but also historical and structural events and processes (Mills, 1959). Today, Mills' concept of the sociological imagination is analogous to what sociologist Randall Collins (1998) referred to as the *sociological eye.* Collins argued that what characterizes sociology, and sociologists, is a unique, critical way of seeing the social world so that we avoid taking things for granted. Utilizing our sociological eye reveals hidden and taken-for-granted meanings, patterns, trends, causes, and consequences that might otherwise go overlooked. These meanings and patterns are everywhere around us leading Collins (1998:2) to conclude: "There is a sociology for everything."

The dual concepts of the sociological imagination and sociological eye speak to what is more generally referred to as a *sociological perspective.* A sociological perspective sees the "general in the particular" (Berger, 1963) and among other things, emphasizes how our *social location,* our specific place and category within society (i.e. male, female, young, old, American, etc.), shapes our individual life experiences in a variety of ways (Macionis, 1999).

A sociological perspective obligates us to explore a global social problem like human trafficking as if it were a diamond with multiple facets. Each time we pick up and analyze the human trafficking issue, we should flip it over, turn it around, and rotate it to reveal and inspect a new facet. This emphasis upon appreciating and analyzing the multiple, interrelated facets of social problems that define sociology and the sociological perspective.

Thus, one crucial difference between a sociological analysis of human trafficking and a psychological one is that a sociological approach moves beyond the individual, without discounting the importance of individual decisions, beliefs, and attitudes. Those factors are situated within broader, macrostructural ones. Ultimately, a sociologist views human actions as shaped and constrained by larger forces. Important structuring aspects of human social life—including culture, race and ethnicity, and gender—are crucial factors shaping our individual existence and experience, our social worlds, and problems like human trafficking. Developing stronger understandings of how those factors intersect with the human trafficking dilemma benefits the development of policies and other responses for controlling and responding to the problem.

Culture and Human Trafficking

Culture teaches us how to be human. It encompasses commonly shared and transmitted patterns of human activity represented in things like norms, behaviors, beliefs, practices, and language (Chambliss and Eglitis, 2013). Our individual socialization experiences—whether from family, peers, school, or work—are shaped by the culture surrounding us.

Culture and cultural differences are observable, though we often take for granted that our particular culture, which we absorb and help re-create on a daily basis, is typical of other cultures around the world. *Cultural relativism*, however, encourages us to appraise other cultures by their standards and not our own. Practicing cultural relativism reveals many examples of difference that we otherwise might take for granted as being the "normal" way of life. For example, within certain cultures spitting in public is frowned upon, while in others it is perfectly acceptable; the same is true for burping and a host of other behaviors. Gestures like the thumbs up sign can also convey drastically different meanings depending on the culture one is in.

Not surprising, the concept of culture is a key component in many sociological analyses. Indeed, most introductory sociology textbooks devote their entire second chapter to a discussion of culture. The reason culture is so important is because it is omnipresent and, therefore, a significant variable in explaining sociological phenomena of all kinds. Culture is intimately connected to the socialization process, and to important spheres of social life like politics and economics. Culture exerts such strong influences within human societies that it is difficult to understand most issues without accounting for its impact. In short, a sociological understanding of human trafficking would be insufficient without attending to the powerful influence of culture, or the cultural contexts within which human trafficking occurs.

Several important facts guide our understanding of how culture and human trafficking intersect. First, human trafficking is a global social problem existing in both postindustrial, advanced capitalist countries like the United States, in still-developing countries like Cambodia, and in hybrid communist countries like China all with distinct cultures. Second, while human trafficking is a global problem, it is not an equally distributed one. Certain places and cultures are more likely to be involved in all phases of the human trafficking problem (International Organization for Migration, 2012). Typically, the trend is for trafficking victims to originate in poorer nations and be trafficked into wealthier ones, though this is not a rule (Burke, 2013; United Nations Department of Public Information, 2001).

Thus, the ubiquitous quality of human trafficking and its unequal dispersion means there are aspects of culture—in the form of variations and influences—that contribute to, and sustain, the trafficking problem where it occurs. Therefore, a sociologist would ask what cultural factors influence human trafficking and what other variables intersect with those cultural factors making human trafficking more likely? Cultural factors impacting human trafficking might include dominant religious beliefs, the degree to which a society is patriarchal or adheres to an idea of individualism or communalism, attitudes toward sex, and ideas about family composition and gender roles. Those cultural factors might intersect with other factors like race, ethnicity, and gender, as well as larger issues like poverty, political, economic, and social turmoil or conflict. Analyzing the role of culture and its interaction with other variables helps explain how human trafficking occurs and why it is responded to in particular ways in specific places.

Current research conducted in places around the world indicates that cultural factors influence all aspects of the human trafficking problem. For example, Tiefenbrun and Edwards (2008) conducted an analysis that explored the impact of China's one-child policy on the trafficking of women. The author's argue that China's one-child policy ultimately reflected a deep-seated cultural affinity for, and valuing of, male children and heirs over female children. Once China legislatively institutionalized its one-child family planning policy—ostensibly to reduce the negative effects of overpopulation—this created an environment that encouraged families to have male children, leading female children to be considered disposable. Female children in China—often given up or placed in overcrowded group homes—thus became easy victims for traffickers to prey upon, especially those involved in sex trafficking.

Hume, Cohen, and Sorvino (2013) recently described the plight of a variety of Cambodian and Vietnamese girls who were sold into sex trafficking rings by their own parents for less than $500. Significant differences between Asian and Western cultures exist in relation to family dynamics and expectations placed upon female children, which certainly contribute to the discoveries made by the authors. However, Hume, Cohen, and Sorvino's research highlights the fact that cultural factors often intersect with other political and, especially, economic variables. The pressures of poverty—many Cambodian workers earn less than $3 per day—when combined with existing cultural dynamics (e.g., ideas about familial obligation) raise the chance of some people becoming trafficking victims. At the same time, cultural pressures and other factors may make selling one's daughter into sex work seem like the only option available to secure a better future for the entire family unit.

In a related report, Yun, Saborey, and Lippes (2013) indicate that cultural barriers in Cambodia and other nations may thwart the prosecution of human traffickers. For example, in Cambodia it is considered culturally taboo to "speak out against perpetrators" of crimes, especially the most prevalent forms of modern slavery: labor and sex trafficking. Additionally, there is a cultural tendency among Cambodians to resolve conflicts outside of the formal legal system. Given these cultural barriers, it is likely that many human trafficking incidents in Cambodia go unreported because victims fear retaliation or do not believe the legal system can resolve the situation.

United Nations (UN) officials have noted that cultural barriers in many other human-trafficking hotspots—often developing nations in Asia and Africa—detrimentally impact the ability of law enforcement agencies to combat human trafficking when it occurs or is discovered:

> A diplomat close to the UNODC [United Nations Office on Drugs and Crime] said its campaign was running up against cultural traditions in … developing nations that tolerated human trafficking … outlawed by U.N. conventions. "In cases of human trafficking, until now it often hasn't been tracked. It's only now that police in some countries are coming to realize that it's a crime … Normally, they would arrest a load of women and treat them like prostitutes and completely miss the point that they are actually victims of horrendous (trafficking to clients abroad)." (Heinrich, 2007)

The UN diplomat quoted obviously expresses a concern that in many places where trafficking occurs, cultural attitudes and beliefs inhibit people from revealing the extent, or even the existence, of the problem. Underfunded and inadequately trained law enforcement agencies, or a culture of corruption among law enforcement and government agents may make recognizing human trafficking when it occurs even more difficult. Add issues like poverty, food shortages, disease, and conflict to those potential cultural and institutional barriers and it becomes easier to see, sociologically, how police officers might assume that a truckload of young women are prostitutes, rather than trafficking victims, especially if prostitution is one of the only viable means for women to financially support themselves. Likewise, if sex tourism and prostitution are tacitly condoned by the state government, as is the case in Thailand, then deciphering unwilling sex-trade participants who were trafficked into the industry from those who entered voluntarily becomes an even more complicated issue.

Clearly, cultural factors contribute to the human trafficking problem. At the same time, the examples in this section demonstrate that cultural factors often intersect with other political, economic, and social issues to exacerbate the problem. A sociological perspective helps expose those interconnections as well as the cultural barriers inhibiting our ability to effectively respond to and control the trafficking problem.

Perhaps, then, it would be appropriate for the UN, international non-governmental organizations (INGOs), nongovernmental organizations (NGOs), and governmental and law enforcement agencies to adopt some of the principles of the *problem-oriented policing* (POP) approach. From the POP perspective, it is crucial to identify the underlying problems causing, or sustaining, crime events, rather than responding simply to the symptoms of those problems. Cultural attitudes, norms, beliefs, and barriers could all be seen as underlying contributing factors that must be strategized and addressed in order for progress to be made in combating human trafficking around the world. The fact that culture is not static, but, in fact, can and does change, gives hope to any efforts to address human trafficking at the cultural level.

Race, Ethnicity, and Human Trafficking

From a sociological perspective, *race*—often equated with skin color and other primary physical characteristics—is considered a *social construct*: something that has meaning because society instills it with meaning (Flores, 2012). In considering race to be socially constructed, sociologists highlight how many societies, especially the United States, imbue race, which is ostensibly a biological term, with an extraordinary amount of symbolic, social meaning. The symbolic significance of race exceeds any actual differences that exist among people of different racial groups. However, racial differences are often utilized "to justify existing social inequalities" and stratify the allocation of rewards and privileges within society (Kendall, 2014, p. 8).

By contrast, *ethnicity* refers primarily to cultural differences distinguishing one group of people from another. Ethnicity is a much more sociological agreeable concept than race. A person's distinct ethnicity may be reflected in things like their religious affiliation, language or dialect, country/region of origin, tribal affiliation, cultural heritage, or other unique practices (Kendall, 2014). Different ethnic groups may possess physical, or racial, characteristics that distinguish them from other groups. But, this is not always the case. For example, the assorted ethnic groups of Central and Southern Europe (e.g., Serbs, Croats, Albanians, Roma) do not appear that dissimilar outwardly but are significantly different on many other counts. Likewise, people may be ethnically united by a shared religion but look quite physically disparate.

For many years the United States Census Bureau collected demographic information that reflected primarily racial differences by asking people to identify as white, black, or other. Obviously, such a system would fail to capture the diversity of the U.S. population, which is comprised of many different racial and ethnic groups. Now, the U.S. Census provides a variety of both racial and ethnic categories (e.g., white, black, Hispanic, white [Latino or Hispanic origin], Pacific Islander, etc.) so people can choose to self-identify along whatever racial or ethnic lines they prefer.

Thus, sociologically speaking, both race and ethnicity are incredibly important concepts that are often studied jointly. Sociologists want to know how life differs as a result of a person's racial or ethnic category. Since so much sociological research is also concerned with understanding social problems and other societal issues, it makes sense to look for patterns underlying those problems. Often, those patterns have strong linkages to race and ethnicity. As we will see, the human trafficking problem is not evenly distributed among all racial or ethnic groups.

One way to consider the distinct racial and ethnic dimensions of the human trafficking problem is to look at country-level race, ethnicity, and human trafficking data. The International Office for Migration (IOM) provides direct assistance to trafficking victims and collects case data on those trafficking incidents. In 2011, the IOM collected case data on a total of 5,498 human trafficking incidents for which it provided assistance. That case data shows the following: (1) In Europe, Ukraine and Belarus accounted for nearly 60 percent of the region's 1,606 cases—the majority populations in both nations identify ethnically as either Ukrainian, Belorussian, or Russian and racially as "white"; (2) In the Middle East, 73 percent of human trafficking incidents took place in Yemen, or involved Yemeni nationals of various Arabic ethnicities; (3) Finally, for all of Central and South America, the small island nation of Haiti produced two-thirds of all IOM-assisted human trafficking cases (656 out of 984 total). The racial composition of Haiti is 95 percent black. Thus, around the world some places—regardless of their population size or political and economic power—are more likely to struggle with human trafficking. As a direct result, certain racial and ethnic groups are going to be disproportionately represented as both human trafficking victims and suspects.

This idea is illustrated within the context of human trafficking in the United States. The U.S. Department of Justice (DOJ) reports that for human trafficking cases in the United States occurring between 2008 and 2010, clear racial and ethnic distinctions can be observed (Banks and Kyckelhahn,

2011). For example, victims of sex trafficking incidents were predominantly black (40 percent) or non-Latino white (26 percent), while labor trafficking victims were more likely to be either Hispanic (63 percent) or Asian (17 percent). Most labor trafficking victims known to the DOJ during this period were also undocumented immigrants (67 percent), many hailing from Mexico and countries in Asia and Central and South America (Banks and Kyckelhahn, 2011).

Additionally, data from the DOJ show that the racial and ethnic dimensions of the trafficking problem persist in regard to the suspects involved in human trafficking cases. In the United States 62 percent of sex trafficking suspects are identified as "black," and 48 percent of labor trafficking suspects are identified as Hispanic (Banks and Kyckelhahn, 2011). Bureau of Justice Statistics data for 2007–2008 show that more than 70 percent of both suspects and victims of trafficking cases in the United States were members of racial or ethnic minorities (Kyckelhahn, Beck, and Cohen, 2009).

A clear implication drawn from the patterns presented in these data that may be useful to law enforcement agencies is that human trafficking, as with other serious crimes within the U.S. context, is often committed by suspects who share common racial/ethnic attributes with the majority of their victims.

Research by the Polaris Project (2014)—an organization devoted to ending modern slavery worldwide—points out that most human trafficking victims come from already vulnerable populations, including migrants, at-risk youth, the poor and lower classes, and members of oppressed or marginalized groups (see also Cottingham et al., 2013, p. 9). Empirical evidence from the United States demonstrates that individuals within these high-risk populations are also more likely to be members of racial or ethnic minorities. For example, the 2011 poverty rates for black and Hispanic Americans were nearly 3 times the rates for non-Hispanic whites, despite the fact that non-Hispanic whites comprise far more than half of the total U.S. population (National Poverty Center, 2014; U.S. Census Bureau, 2013). In other words, racial and ethnic minority groups are likely to be overrepresented not only as victims of poverty but also in terms of incarceration rates, and as suspects and victims of human trafficking.

Members of minority populations and marginalized groups are more susceptible to various forms of victimization during periods of *social conflict*, including revolution and civil war. Many social conflicts polarize populations along religious, racial, and ethnic lines, disproportionately harming certain racial or ethnic groups more than others and raising their risk of victimization.

Consider for a moment the following list of nations compiled by the IOM with the largest number of human trafficking incidents:

Top 5
  Ukraine
  Haiti
  Yemen
  Laos
  Uzbekistan
Next 5
  Cambodia
  Kyrgyzstan
  Afghanistan
  Belarus
  Ethiopia

You will notice that some nations previously mentioned—Ukraine, Haiti, Yemen, and Belarus—are on this list. Exploring the recent histories of a few of these nations and others highlights the connections between social conflicts and the proliferation of various forms of human trafficking, often with adverse results for already marginalized groups.

Ukraine experienced a series of revolutions (i.e., the "Orange" revolution) in the early 2000s and is now sliding toward civil war (Spiegel Online International, 2014). Keep in mind that both Ukraine and Belarus accounted for more than 60% of human trafficking cases in Europe. Haiti suffered a catastrophic earthquake in 2010 that killed over 220,000 people, left 1.5 million homeless, and destroyed numerous infrastructures and government buildings (OxFam International 2014). Prior to the earthquake in 2010, Haiti was considered a volatile nation prone to political and civil instability. It also had the lowest ranking of any nation in the U.N. Human Development Index (Disasters Emergency Committee, 2014). Of course, more human trafficking cases occur in Haiti than in any other nation in Central or South America. Yemen, which we already know produces a disproportionate share of human trafficking cases in the Middle East, experienced a civil war in 1994 and has since become a hub for terrorist organizations, like Al-Qaeda, as well as the site of many terrorist attacks. Finally, Afghanistan's history is rife with turmoil, war, and internal conflict, spearheaded in recent years by the U.S.-led invasion in 2001 that ousted the Taliban—a "government" that imposed severe restrictions on the freedoms of women.

Although the aforementioned data illustrate the point that human trafficking is more prevalent in some places and impacts certain populations and social groups more than others, it also presents hope for positive interventions. For example, directing resources toward resolving conflicts that place certain groups at higher risk of being trafficked is one obvious mechanism of intervention that may reduce the problem of human trafficking worldwide. In places like the United States, where domestic trafficking is an issue intimately linked with poverty and minority status, developing policies to increase the flow of resources to poor or minority communities and strengthen support networks in those communities may help reduce the trafficking problem.

Gender and Human Trafficking

The United Nations Department of Public Information released a policy brief following a 2001 conference in Durban, South Africa. In that brief, the interconnections between race, ethnicity, gender, and human trafficking were highlighted. The authors of the brief noted the following: (1) most human trafficking victims are women and (2) there is an undeniable "interaction of gender and racial discrimination" within the broader trafficking problem.

Examples of this *interaction effect* can be drawn from countries like Thailand and China, and show that the vulnerability of women to trafficking may increase because of their race or ethnicity. That is, racist, sexist, or other prejudicial beliefs may be held by trafficking suspects, their clients, or may be part of the broader culture of a place, and these attitudes and beliefs can result in certain groups of women becoming the primary targets of human traffickers. Police officers and other law enforcement agents are not above harboring racist, sexist, or other prejudicial beliefs, which could reduce the efficacy of law enforcement to combat the trafficking problem in some locales.

Indeed, a crucial concern for law enforcement agencies, domestic and international governing bodies, and various inter- and nongovernmental groups is the fact that women are disproportionately represented as victims in the global human trafficking problem. According to the IOM, over 60% of all trafficking victims are female, with the disproportionate victimization of women holding true across all regions and nations of the world.

The International Labour Organization and U.N. Office on Drugs and Crime report that most persons trafficked for both labor and sexual services are women (UNODC, 2010). An additional interaction effect between gender and age can also be perceived here, since many female children are trafficked into sexually exploitative industries or into domestic service. More generally, the U.S. State Department has cited the rise in "feminized economic sectors" such as "commercial sex and ... domestic service" as significant contributing factors to the worldwide problem of trafficking in women. A report by the U.S. State Department's Office to Monitor and Combat Trafficking in Persons (2009) describes the process that leads women in many places to become the victims of human trafficking:

Both the supply and demand sides of the trade in human beings are fed by "gendered" vulnerabilities to trafficking. These vulnerabilities are the result of political, economic, and development processes that may leave some women socially and economically dependent on men. If that support from men becomes limited or withdrawn, women become dangerously susceptible to abuse. They often have no individual protection or recognition under the law, inadequate access to healthcare and education, poor employment prospects, little opportunity to own property, or high levels of social isolation. All this makes some women easy targets for harassment, violence, and human trafficking.

Certainly, cultural factors impact the process of exploiting women and contribute to their prevalence as victims in the human trafficking trade. Some cultures may utilize antiquated and discriminatory, or patriarchal, laws that decrease women's independence while increasing their vulnerabilities to various hardships, turning them into easier targets for traffickers.

One glaring example illustrative of the preceding point is the treatment of women in Afghanistan under the Taliban government, which removed women and girls from schools, limited their ability to move freely, and condoned various abuses against them (U.S. Department of State, 2001). Social conflicts, for example, civil war and revolution, further contribute to these existing issues in places around the world. Even natural disasters may disproportionately raise the stakes, and hardships, for mothers and their children, increasing their chances of becoming trafficked.

Within the U.S. context, the United Nations Department of Public Information (2011) estimates that upward of 45,000 women and children—many of whom are also female—are trafficked into the United States each year. Moreover, 94 percent of all sex trafficking victims in the United States are also female (Banks and Kyckelhahn, 2011). These figures stand in stark contrast to the fact that more than 80 percent of trafficking suspects arrested in the United States are men (Banks and Kycklehahn, 2011). Clearly, the gendered dimensions of the human trafficking problem signal that there remain numerous obstacles to the equal treatment and consideration of women across the globe.

The recent prosecution of 25 suspected sex traffickers based in Georgia reveals the dire circumstances faced by trafficked women, highlights the gender divide between victims and suspects, and showcases some of the obstacles hindering the abolition of trafficking. According to various reports, women from Mexico were trafficked into the United States between 2008 and 2013, sold to various pimps and prostitution rings in Georgia and North Carolina, and forced to engage in sex 20 to 30 times per day for as little as $25 per client (Bynum, 2014). The defense attorney for one pimp and ringleader who was sentenced to life in federal prison argued that his client should be shown leniency because "many of the decisions made were influenced by ... poverty and the need to survive" (Bynum, 2014). That suspect, however, did have the financial wherewithal to send $1,500 per month back to his family living in Mexico, while the women who earned that money received only a small fraction (Bynum, 2014). The presiding judge in the case also engaged in a bizarre form of victim blaming, stating publicly, "I wonder if they [the trafficked women] really were vulnerable victims" simply because some of the women had cellphones and access to cars (Bynum, 2014). Evidence presented at trial, however, showed that the women were regularly beaten, threatened, and told harm would befall their families if they did not perform or attempted to flee (Bynum, 2014). Although it is certainly promising that prosecutions and convictions resulted in this sex trafficking case, it is obvious that many of the cultural and attitudinal obstacles noted in the previous sections of this chapter remain relevant within the U.S. context.

What do the data on the gendered nature of the human trafficking problem indicate for how we respond to the problem? First, it is clear that bolstering the rights, independence, and financial well being of women on a global scale is crucial. Success in those endeavors hinges in part on resolving existing social conflicts and large-scale economic issues, neither of which will be easy. Perhaps the longer road to remedying the gender discrepancies in human trafficking—and ultimately end trafficking altogether—is to effect change within the cultures of places where women are the primary victims of both trafficking incidents and other forms of struggle and deprivation. This applies to the United States as much as anywhere; clearly if a federal district court judge is capable of questioning the "vulnerability" of trafficked women, there is much work remaining. However, changing cultural attitudes and beliefs is neither easy nor always politically feasible. Cultural relativism preaches that there is no one universal cultural standard that all others should be held up to. Thus, ultimately, cultural change must originate and be driven from within a particular society rather than arising from external pressures. Nonprofit, human rights, and other organizations that work to empower women, improve living conditions, and contest ignorance and intolerance around the world will likely be crucial to this process of positive cultural change.

Exploring Sociological Explanations of Human Trafficking

The preceding sections have demonstrated that factors such as culture, race/ethnicity, and gender are linked to another, the human trafficking problem, and larger societal issues like poverty and conflict. Descriptively, the existing data on culture, race/ethnicity, and gender indicate that human trafficking is a more serious problem in some places than others, and is more likely to affect certain populations and groups (e.g., minorities, the poor, and women) than others.

However, sociologists are hesitant to simply describe the parameters of a problem. The goal is always to pair descriptions with potential explanations. Thus, in this final section, we explore some potential micro- and macrolevel sociological explanations of the human trafficking problem. Although not exhaustive, this section does offer additional insights that policy practitioners, law enforcement agents, and students can utilize to better understand the intricacies of the human trafficking problem and develop appropriate responses to it.

Microlevel Explanations

In general, microlevel explanations are concerned with individual-level interactions. Key foci and questions of microlevel explanations include (1) investigating how social situations are defined; (2) understanding the meanings of social interactions and how those meanings are created; and (3) determining how individual's make choices. Within explanations specifically focused upon crime, individual-level theories often focus on how criminal offenders decide to commit crimes or become engaged in different forms of deviance.

Sykes and Matza's (1957) theory of delinquency provides one interesting tool to aid our understanding of the human trafficking problem at the individual, decision-making level. Within their theory, Sykes and Matza discuss various "techniques of neutralization"—otherwise known as justifications— that could potentially enable, or sustain, an individual's involvement in deviance or criminality. These justifications include (1) denying injury/harm, (2) denying the victim, (3) denying responsibility, (4) appealing to higher loyalties, and (5) condemning the condemners.

Evidence shows that several of Sykes and Matza's techniques of neutralization are prevalently employed by suspects arrested in human trafficking cases. For example, the denial of injury/harm, denial of victim, and denial of responsibility techniques are all commonly employed by suspected traffickers who imply that the "victims" they exploited, whether for sex or labor, were willing participants who chose to become trafficked. Denying the existence of a victim, and thereby harm or responsibility, was demonstrated in the example from the gender section of this chapter. In fact, in that example the suspect, his defense attorney, and the presiding judge utilized those justifications or elements of them. Rationalizing and justifying that women and members of other racial and ethnic groups are deserving of being trafficked, or are not worthy of worrying about, or perhaps are not really victims at all, are discernible elements in many human trafficking narratives. Finally, justifying human trafficking by appealing to higher loyalties appears operative on the part of suspects within certain cultural contexts, especially when paired with other issues like poverty. Selling one's own daughter into the sex industry may be rationalized as the lesser of two evils, and ultimately less harmful than the extreme alternatives: starvation and death. People may justify their role in trafficking as serving some higher familial, community, or religious purpose.

Regardless of which justification is used, Sykes and Matza's theory is useful because it raises our sensitivity to those sorts of denials that otherwise might slip by us unnoticed. Raising our collective cognizance of when and how justifications are applied to lessen the sting of human trafficking is important for increasing our ability to negate those justifications when and where they occur.

Rational choice theory provides another avenue for understanding the human trafficking dilemma. The fundamental assumption of rational choice theory is that human beings make choices after they assess the costs and benefits of those choices (Cornish and Clark, 1987). This rational decision-making process carries over to decisions about whether to engage in crime or deviance as well. People, the theory argues, make rational choices about committing crimes by weighing the costs and benefits of their potential actions in relation to their ability to successfully carry out the crime, along with other "relevant information" (Cornish and Clark, 2014, p. 1). Applied to human trafficking, rational choice theory is potentially useful as a way to understand the decision-making processes of trafficking suspects. For example, one suspect may become involved in human trafficking because the benefits (e.g., money) outweigh the potential costs (e.g., arrest and prosecution). Rational choice theory has clear policy implications as well, most of which center on the concept of deterrence. That is, according to rational choice theory, thwarting crimes like human trafficking requires that the costs (i.e., punishments and penalties) of criminality be so high that they always outweigh the benefits. With human trafficking, this may be problematic since the costs of not engaging in trafficking may be more severe (i.e., starvation, poverty, death) than any penal costs of getting caught.

Ultimately, relying solely on microlevel explanations to understand human trafficking is unsatisfactory because those explanations divorce individuals—and their decisions—from the larger social contexts and forces surrounding them. The notion that people both shape their social contexts and are also shaped by them reflects a fundamental sociological concern with agency (i.e., free will) versus structure. Most sociologists adhere to a position known as *soft determinism*, where they accept that people are free to make choices, but acknowledge that ultimately those choices are influenced by a person's social location and other structural factors. Thus, from a sociological perspective microlevel explanations, while potentially helpful on a small scale, should always be paired and balanced by macrolevel explanations that explore how larger forces influence the choices and decisions people make.

Macrolevel Explanations

Macrolevel explanations are concerned with examining the impact that larger social structures, institutions, and phenomena have on societies and human behavior. There are a variety of explanatory paradigms and theories that operate at the structural level. Two dominant examples include *structural-functionalism*, which typically views society as a social system comprised of interdependent parts that function to maintain the health and stability of the whole, and the *conflict perspective*, which views society as a space of conflict among groups competing for scarce resources, including economic and other forms of power.

Both a functionalist and conflict approach to understanding human trafficking could begin from the same starting point: *globalization*. Globalization entails the increasingly fluid flows of people, products, services, and information between nations around the globe. The modern world is characterized by globalization, which has influenced the basic structure of all societies. Thus, many modern-day political, economic, and social issues intersect with the concept in some form. Indeed, human trafficking—modern-day slavery—can be seen as a product of an increasingly globalized world.

From a functionalist perspective, the fact that so many people are trafficked around the world for various purposes—agricultural labor, industrial labor, domestic labor, construction, sex—could be seen as a necessary, functionally important byproduct of globalization. In other words, functionally speaking, human trafficking may produce numerous positive, stabilizing benefits for the global social system, and its numerous societal subsystems. Thus, rather than view human trafficking as a social problem reflecting various conflicts and inequalities, a functionalist perspective might see it as a systems-level response to bring balance to and maintain the health of the global system. The fact that human trafficking occurs so frequently and universally would be cited as evidence of the system attempting to fix—or stabilize—itself, for example, by moving workers quickly and cheaply to places where labor is needed to sustain the healthy functioning of the global capitalist marketplace.

A functionalist view of the human trafficking problem, of course, must be interrogated critically since it implies that human trafficking is both a necessary and unavoidable consequence of contemporary human existence. This stability-enhancing functionalist view also rationalizes the actions of trafficking suspects by essentially stating that they are performing a vital service for society and the world. Moreover, functionalism glosses too quickly over other issues that might play a significant role in perpetuating and sustaining the human trafficking problem, like poverty. Obviously, a functionalist perspective is unsatisfactory for a variety of reasons, all of which push us further toward a macrolevel understanding of human trafficking rooted in a conflict orientation.

A conflict perspective argues that globalization and global capitalism produce positive and negative consequences for societies around the world. However, a conflict orientation also believes that most benefits of globalization accrue in already well-to-do places (e.g., the United States), while the negative consequences fall disproportionately, if not completely, upon the shoulders of the world's less wealthy, less powerful and more marginalized peoples and places.

A conflict perspective would point out that living conditions worsen and poverty increases in many places despite the positive aspects of globalization, creating a vacuum effect that draws individuals into desperate situations. Actual survival may depend on making choices that are largely conditioned and influenced by social structural forces and the individual's place (social location) within their society. Human trafficking may become a real—and sometimes the sole—possibility for improving one's life. Suspects may engage in human trafficking and the exploitation of their fellow men and women in order to improve their life, while the vulnerability of trafficking victims increases because they, too, are subjected to harsh realities that leave them few options for a better life and which also place them into vulnerable positions where they can easily become victims. Thus, from a conflict perspective human trafficking represents a unique form of conflict and exploitation that ultimately reflects underlying imbalances and conflicts in the "global political economy" of our modern world.

Clearly, from a conflict view, individuals have a much greater degree of freedom to make choices, but those choices are ultimately structured and conditioned by larger forces outside their direct control. Importantly, a conflict approach to understanding human trafficking does not preach stability or functional necessity and, therefore, opens many avenues for possible strategies at the structural (macro) and individual (micro) levels to mitigate or prevent human trafficking in the future.

Summary

Human trafficking is a complicated global problem intertwined with various political, economic, social, and cultural factors. Culture, race, ethnicity, and gender all intersect and interact with one another, other variables, and the human trafficking issue in ways that are sometimes clear and sometimes hidden. Disproportionately, human trafficking victims and suspects are drawn from marginalized racial and ethnic groups, including the poor. Women are vastly overrepresented as victims in both labor and sex trafficking cases. And, a variety of cultural factors both contribute to the problem of human trafficking and stand as barriers in the way of our attempts to respond to it.

A sociological perspective attending to the ways these important factors relate to one another and broader issues like globalization increases our collective knowledge of how and why human trafficking arises and persists. Additionally, by drawing attention to the multiple social facets and patterns of the human trafficking problem, a sociological perspective reveals important avenues that policy makers and law enforcement agencies might utilize in developing policies and other responses to mitigate, control, and, hopefully, prevent trafficking from occurring in the future.

Key Terms

conflict perspective
counterculture
culture
cultural relativism
ethnicity
globalization
interaction effect
problem-oriented policing (POP)
race

social conflicts
social construct
social location
sociological eye
sociological imagination
sociological perspective
soft determinism
structural functionalism
subculture

Review Questions

1. What is a sociological perspective and how does it provide unique insight into social problems like human trafficking?
2. How do cultural factors intersect with human trafficking? Provide several examples of how culture contributes to human trafficking as a primary cause of the problem and barrier to its prevention.
3. How do race, ethnicity, and gender relate to human trafficking and other issues like social conflict? Sociologically speaking, where are most trafficking victims and suspects drawn from in societies around the globe?
4. Describe the differences between micro- and macrolevel sociological explanations of human trafficking? How do explanations at both scales differ but also complement each other?

References

Banks, D., and Kyckelhahn, T. (2011). *Characteristics of Suspected Human Trafficking Incidents: 2008–2010.* U.S. Department of Justice, Bureau of Justice Statistics. Washington, D.C.: Office of Justice Programs.

Berger, P. (1963). *Invitation to Sociology: A Humanistic Perspective.* New York: Doubleday.

Bynum, R. (2014). "Mexican Gets Life Sentence in U.S. Sex Trafficking Case; Women Were Brought in from Abroad." *The Associated Press*, February 19.

Chambliss, W. J., and Egilitis, D. S. (2013). *Discover Sociology.* Thousand Oaks, CA: Sage.

Collins, R. (1998). "The Sociological Eye and Its Blinders." *Contemporary Sociology*, 27(1), 2–7.

Cornish, D. B., and Clarke, R. V. (1987). "Understanding Crime Displacement: An Application of Rational Choice Theory." *Criminology*, 25(4), 933–948.

Cornish, D. B., and Clarke, R. V. (2014). *The Reasoning Criminal: Rational Choice Perspectives on Offending.* New Brunswick, NJ: Transaction Publishers.

Cottingham, M., Nowak, T., Snyder, K., and Swauger, M. (2013). "Sociological Perspective: Underlying Causes." In M. C. Burke, *Human Trafficking: Interdisciplinary Perspectives* (pp. 51–72). New York, NY: Routledge.

Disasters Emergency Committee. (2014). "Haiti Earthquake Facts and Figures." Retrieved January 28, 2014, from http://www.dec.org.uk/haiti-earthquake-facts-and-figures.

Flores, L. (2012). "What Is a Social Construction?" Retrieved January 28, 2014, from Oakes College, University of California Santa Cruz, http://oakes.ucsc.edu/academics/Core%20Course/oakes-core-awards-2012/laura-flores.html.

Hume, T., Cohen, L., and Sovino, M. (2013). "The Women Who Sold Their Daughters into Sex Slavery." November 2, Retrieved 2013, from CNN.com, http://www.cnn.com/interactive/2013/12/world/cambodia-child-sex-trade/index.html?hpt=hp_t1.

International Organization for Migration. (2012). *IOM 2011 Case Data on Human Trafficking: Global Figures & Trends.* Washington: Humantrafficking.org.

Kendall, D. (2014). *Sociology in Our Times: The Essentials.* Belmont, CA: Wadsworth Cenage.

Kyckelhahn, T., Beck, A. J., and Cohen, T. H. (2009). *Characteristics of Suspected Human Trafficking Incidents: 2007–08.* U.S. Bureau of Justice Statistics, United States Department of Justice. Washington, D.C.: Office of Justice Programs.

Macionis, J. J. (1999). *Sociology.* Upper Saddle River, NJ: Prentice Hall.

Mills, C. W. (1959). *The Sociological Imagination.* London, UK: Oxford University Press.

National Poverty Center. (2014). "Poverty in the United States." Retrieved January 28, 2014, from National Poverty Center, http://www.npc.umich.edu/poverty/.

Office to Monitor and Combat Trafficking in Persons. (2009). "Gender Imbalance in Human Trafficking." U.S. State Department, June 15.

OxFam International. (2014). "Haiti Earthquake: 4 Years Later." Retrieved January 28, 2014, from OxFam International, http://www.oxfam.org/en/haitiquake.

Polaris Project. (2014). "The Victims." Retrieved January 28, 2014, from Polaris Project: For a World without Slavery, http://www.polarisproject.org/human-trafficking/overview/the-victims.

Spiegel Online International. (2014). "'Prepared to Die': The Right Wing's Role in Ukrainian Protests." Retrieved January 28, 2014, from Spiegel Online International, http://www.spiegel.de/international/europe/ukraine-sliding-towards-civil-war-in-wake-of-tough-new-laws-a-945742.html.

Sykes, G. M., and Matza, D. (1957). "Techniques of Neutralization: A Theory of Delinquency." *American Sociological Review*, 22(2), 664–670.

Tiefenbrun, S., and Edwards, C. (2008). "Gendercide and the Cultural Context of Sex Trafficking in China." Retrieved January 14, 2014, from Selected Works of Susan W. Tiefenbrun, http://works.bepress.com/susan_tiefenbrun/2.

United Nations Department of Public Information. (2001). *The Race Dimensions of Trafficking in Persons—Especially Women and Children*. World Conference against Racism, Racial Discrimination, Xenophobia and Related Intolerance.

United Nations Office on Drugs and Crime. (2010). "Factsheet on Human Trafficking." Retrieved January 30, 2014, from http://www.unodc.org/documents/human-trafficking/UNVTF_fs_HT_EN.pdf.

U.S. Census Bureau. (2013). "USA People Quick Facts." Retrieved January 28, 2014, from State & County Quick Facts, http://quickfacts.census.gov/qfd/states/00000.html.

U.S. Department of State. (2001). "The Taliban's War against Women." Retrieved January 30, 2014, from Bureau of Democracy, Human Rights and Labor, http://www.state.gov/j/drl/rls/6185.htm.

Yun, S., Saborey, O., and Lipes, J. (2013). "Cambodia Says Cultural Barriers Impeding Human Trafficking Fight." Radio Free Asia.

Psychology of Human Trafficking

4

JODIE G. BEESON

Contents

Major Issues

- Risk factors for human trafficking victimization
- How perpetrators recruit and manipulate victims (grooming/ seasoning)
- Personality characteristics of traffickers
- Impact of trafficking on mental health
- Treatment and rehabilitation of victims

Introduction

Human trafficking is often referred to as a form of "modern-day slavery" (Hoyle, Bosworth, and Dempsey 2011). Although this conceptualization of domestic human sex trafficking captures the involuntary nature of human trafficking, it fails to describe the coercive psychological processes used by traffickers to recruit and control human sex trafficking victims. In order to understand how this is possible in a world of Internet, cell phones, and 911, it is important to understand the psychological dynamics of human trafficking.

The psychology of human trafficking focuses on the roles of persons involved in trafficking, the risk factors for trafficking victimization, the characteristics of traffickers, the grooming or seasoning process, the psychological impact to trafficking victims, and the treatment of victims of trafficking.

Roles

It is easy to conjure up a picture of human trafficking that matches stereotypes of pimps and prostitutes. The pimp is an assertive male who dominates a helpless young female and forces her to have sex for money. However, this picture fails to capture the reality and complexity of domestic human sex trafficking. These stereotypes set up a dichotomous view of human trafficking roles. This dichotomous conceptualization results in an oversimplification of the definition of a human trafficking victim, which hampers efforts to provide appropriate and effective human services to victims of human sex trafficking (Buckland 2008).

Human trafficking organizations are typically hierarchical organizations. Although the complexity of the organizational structure varies, generally the organization consists of individuals who fill seven basic roles in the organization. One individual may fulfill one or more of the roles in the organization depending on the size of the organization (Parker and Skrmetti 2013; Reid 2012; Williamson and Prior 2009).

1. Trafficker—At the top of the organization is the trafficker or "pimp." The trafficker has a monetary interest in the recruitment and exploitation of victims of human trafficking.
2. Recruiter—The recruiter is responsible for identifying potential victims. Recruiters are often tasked with the job of identifying runaways, throwaways, or youth without adequate adult guardianship and enticing them to meet the trafficker. Often, a trafficking victim who has been with the organization for a longer period fills this role.
3. Connector—The connector is often a person in a community who, in exchange for money, drugs, or other favors, identifies potential victims and arranges a connection between potential victims and recruiters or traffickers.
4. Groomers—The groomer initiates the victim into the world of prostitution and or pornography. He or she employs psychological

methods to limit the victim's contact with those outside of the organization and to desensitize the victim to the negative aspects of the organization. This person is in charge of the "grooming or seasoning" process. In many cases, the recruiter assumes this role.

5. Watcher—The watcher is charged with transporting victims and ensuring that they do not have the opportunity to connect with persons outside of the organization or to escape.

6. Bottom (bottom bitch)—The bottom is a human trafficking victim who has the closest connection to the trafficker. The bottom is charged with managing other victims in the organization. Often the bottom assumes a caretaking role with other victims but must remain loyal to the trafficker. The victim's status as a bottom is a reward for loyalty within the organization, and this status is often used as an incentive to remain loyal to the trafficker and the organization.

7. Wife-in-law—Wife-in-laws are trafficking victims who live together and work together in the organization. These are often strategic matches in the organization to ensure loyalty of newer victims by pairing them with more seasoned victims.

Psychological Risk for Human Trafficking Victimization

There is no single portrait for a victim of human sex trafficking. Victims can be either female or male. Although most of the literature and research tends to focus on female victims, 20 percent of those arrested as "vendors of sexual services" in the United States are male (Dennis 2008). Trafficking victims come from various national, racial, and ethnic backgrounds (Banks and Kyckelhahn 2011). Age is a significant factor in domestic sex trafficking victims. The majority of victims are minors and 79 percent of adult victims had been sexually exploited prior to turning 18. Many victims are first recruited when they are 12 to 14 years old. Additional risk factors for domestic human trafficking include the following (Hardy, Compton, and McPhatter 2013; Wilson and Widom 2010):

- Runaway/thrown-away episode
- Previous sexual/physical abuse and early sexual initiation
- Parents/caretakers addicted to drugs/alcohol
- Neglect by parents/caretakers
- Youth drug use
- Juvenile crime
- School problems
- Childhood trauma

One common denominator in many of these risk factors is that the victim lacks protection from a capable guardian. A capable guardian is a person who has the personal capacity and the appropriate relationship to a youth to protect them from harm. A capable guardian would monitor a youth's interactions, either in person or through electronic means such as cell phones or the Internet, to ensure that they are not interacting with persons who pose a threat to the personal safety or emotional well-being. Victims often lack a family structure that would prevent a trafficker from gaining unobstructed access to a victim. This unobstructed access allows the trafficker to establish a connection with the victim and a trust relationship with the victim. The process of developing a trust bond with a victim and increasing their acceptance of circumstances and abuse is called "grooming" or "seasoning."

Grooming/Seasoning

The grooming process is a manipulative psychological process designed to capitalize on a potential victim's vulnerabilities to manipulate them into participating in the activities of the organization, whether it be prostitution or pornography. This process is an abusive cognitive conditioning process or "brainwashing" technique that can be compared to the techniques employed by those who sexually abuse children for personal gratification rather than monetary reasons. The process can also be compared to the dynamics of domestic violence relationships.

The trafficker uses both positive and negative reinforcement to condition a victim into "willingly" participating in prostitution or pornography.

Many traffickers assume the role of a "boyfriend" in the beginning of the relationship. Others may assume a feigned caregiver role. This is known as the "love" approach to recruiting victims. He or she may capitalize on the victim's emotional or physical needs by providing attention and support for a victim. Often, this "love" is provided in a way that excludes other relationships the victim may have. The trafficker is jealous and possessive. This technique is often used on victims who have no prior history of physical abuse. This type of grooming is designed to isolate a victim, create a sense of loyalty and trust, and to create a relationship based on domination and dependency. This relationship is marked by a continual process to maintain power and control over a victim (Annitto 2011; Birckhead 2011; Dutton and Painter 1993; Kennedy and Klein 2007; Kotrla 2010).

Another approach to grooming a potential victim is the "debt" approach. The trafficker provides protection, food, clothing, money, drugs, or other things that meet the victim's needs. Often these gifts are given under the guise that they are free and there are no expectations for reciprocation. Once the victim accepts these gifts, the trafficker introduces the expectation of repayment. Another person in the organization such as a "main girl" or a "bottom" often carries out this process. The victim may be told that they are in danger if they do not repay the debt in some manner. This approach is closely tied to the use of the "drug" technique. A victim is offered drugs free of charge until he or she is addicted to the drug. Once the trafficker recognizes that he or she is addicted, the victim is told he or she needs to pay for the drug by engaging in acts of prostitution or pornography (Kennedy and Klein 2007; Leidholdt 2013).

While the formerly listed approaches rely on enticements and fraudulent offers, the "gorilla" (or guerrilla) approach is based solely on physical abuse and fear. The gorilla trafficker uses beatings, rape, threats of abuse, threat to family or loved ones, kidnapping, and other brutal means to gain domination of the victim. This technique may be used on a victim following the use of one of the other techniques or in some cases the gorilla trafficker begins with this approach. Many traffickers consider the aforementioned approaches to be more sophisticated and do not solely rely on this method. Used alone, this approach does not engender loyalty, so the trafficker must rely on close supervision and continual threats to maintain this relationship (Dalla, Xia, and Kennedy 2003; Kennedy and Klein 2007; Leidholdt 2013).

Characteristics of a Trafficker

While the majority of research has been focused on victim characteristics, there has been research on the demographic characteristics of traffickers. A Bureau of Justice special report on human trafficking (Banks and Kyckelhahn 2011) describes the demographic traits of traffickers as well as victims. The majority of human trafficking incidents in the report are sex trafficking incidents. In the sex traffic cases, 81 percent of the traffickers were male. Considering the structure of trafficking organizations, it is likely that at least some of the female traffickers were functioning as a recruiter or a bottom in the organization at the time of the incident. The majority of traffickers were between 18 and 34 years old. Of the cases where the race of the suspect could be identified, 62 percent were black and 48 percent were Hispanic. An overwhelming majority (86 percent) of sex traffickers were U.S. citizens.

There has been very little research regarding the personality characteristics of traffickers. The research on the psychological processes of traffickers is limited. The majority of research is based on qualitative interviews with trafficking victims. However a Canadian study suggests that the Hare Psychopathology Checklist (PCL-R), along with variables such as educational attainment, psychiatric history, history of substance abuse, and history of violence may be valuable in understanding the psychological traits of a trafficker (Spidel and Greaves 2007). The PCL-R consists of the following traits (Hare and Neumann 2005):

- Glib and superficial charm
- Grandiose (exaggeratedly high) estimation of self
- Need for stimulation
- Pathological lying
- Cunning and manipulativeness
- Lack of remorse or guilt
- Shallow affect (superficial emotional responsiveness)
- Callousness and lack of empathy
- Parasitic lifestyle
- Poor behavioral controls
- Sexual promiscuity
- Early behavior problems
- Lack of realistic long-term goals
- Impulsivity
- Irresponsibility
- Failure to accept responsibility for own actions
- Many short-term marital relationships
- Juvenile delinquency
- Revocation of conditional release
- Criminal versatility

The sample of sex traffickers had significantly higher overall scores for psychopathy than a comparison sample of incarcerated individuals. Specifically, they scored higher in areas of superficial emotional responses, lack of empathy, cunning and manipulativeness, and failure to accept responsibility for own actions. This means that traffickers have the ability to feign emotional responses when recruiting potential victims and they do not feel a sense of remorse for harm done. They tend to prefer crimes where they are in control of the victim(s). They are also less likely to feel responsible for the harm they cause. In addition to higher levels of psychopathological traits, 95.5 percent of the sex traffickers had a history of both alcohol and drug abuse and 90.9 percent had a history of trafficking prior to the current conviction (Spidel and Greaves 2007).

Psychological Impact for Survivors

Survivors of sex trafficking are left with numerous mental health issues as a result of multiple exposures to traumatic events, social isolation, and degradation experienced during the time they were trafficked. Even when victims are not exposed to physical violence, the lack of predictability and lack of control victims experience are contributing factors for mental disorders. Substance abuse and health-related disorders are also contributing factors to the prevalence of mental disorders in trafficking victims (Adams 2012; Hossain et al. 2010; Zimmerman, Hossain, and Watts 2011).

Victims often enter the world at a young age and many had been emotionally, sexually, or physically abused prior to being trafficked. Many victims of trafficking were at high risk for mental disorders prior to exposure to human trafficking, adding to the complexity of diagnosis, treatment, and recovery posttrafficking (Abas et al. 2013; Banovic and Bjelajac 2012; Bjelajac, Spalevic, and Banovic 2013; Hossain et al. 2010). Survivors of human trafficking have been denied the opportunity to experience the social and emotional connections and experiences that contribute to healthy maturation. They have often lived in very isolated environments. Although their peers who have not been trafficked have had the opportunity to mature and explore life's possibilities, the victims have lived in a world focused on survival without the benefit of healthy support systems. They have lost a sense of "home" and the security and stability associated with it. As a result, survivors of trafficking lack the social and emotional skills to function in a world outside of trafficking and they lack social support systems to help them adapt to the mainstream world. Two of the most common psychological disorders associated with victims of trafficking are anxiety disorders and major depressive disorder (Bennett-Murphy 2012).

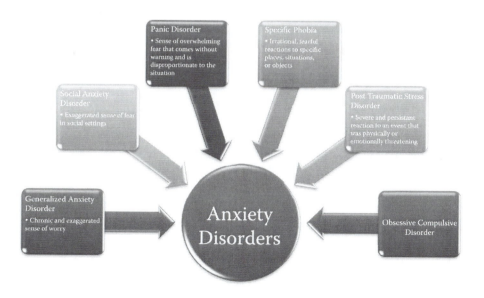

Anxiety Disorders and Posttraumatic Stress Disorder (PTSD)

Anxiety is a normal reaction to environmental or internal stressors. A person experiencing anxiety may feel a wide range of emotional or physical reactions. Under normal conditions, these are reactions that allow one to respond to danger and react accordingly. When an individual's anxiety response becomes chronic, out of proportion to the situation, and disrupts functionality it may be classified as an anxiety disorder. Anxiety disorders are a classification of psychological disorders that present in a variety of forms (see Anxiety Disorder Chart, below) (Kazdin 2000; National Institute of Mental Health 2009).

Trafficking victims live in environments that are unstable and full of environmental stressors. They face the additional stress of a lack of control of their environments and the inability to predict or prepare for stressful events. While being trafficked victims typically experience numerous traumatic events. They are often physically, sexually, and emotionally abused, witness horrific events, and live in a state of persistent anticipation of negative events. Upon leaving a trafficking environment, survivors face additional stress factors related to adjusting to life in an environment that they have not been prepared to live in. As a result, survivors are exposed to multiple factors that increase the likelihood of experiencing an anxiety disorder.

Posttraumatic stress disorder (PTSD) is an anxiety disorder that is the result of exposure to a severe or chronic fear-inducing situation. Studies indicate, that depending on the individual circumstances, around 40 percent of trafficking victims suffer from PTSD.

Symptoms of PTSD include the following:

- Recurrent and intrusive recollections of traumatic event
- Dreams of traumatic event
- Severe distress when confronted with stimuli associated with traumatic event
- Physiological reaction to stimuli associated with traumatic event
- Avoidance of thoughts, feelings, or conversation related to the event
- Detachment/estrangement
- Difficulties with sleeping
- Difficulty concentrating
- Irritability
- Outbursts of anger
- Hypervigilance

The symptoms of PTSD often interfere with a trafficking survivor's ability to cope with and adapt to a new living situation after leaving a trafficking situation. This has implications for the rescue and recovery for trafficking victims (Abas et al. 2013; Adams 2012; American Psychiatric Association 2013a; National Institute of Mental Health 2009).

Depression

Survivors of trafficking often experience depression. Although all victims of trafficking may be at higher risk for depression, those who are sexually abused are at significantly higher risk for mental health disorders. Studies indicate that between 59.4 and 100 percent of victims of trafficking suffer from a major depressive disorder (Oram et al. 2012).

Depression ranges from minor depression to major depressive disorder. The criteria for a major depressive disorder include the following (American Psychiatric Association 2013b):

- Depressed mood or a loss of interest or pleasure in daily activities for more than two weeks
- Mood represents a change from the person's baseline
- Impaired function: social, occupational, educational
- Specific symptoms, at least 5 of these 10, present nearly every day:

    1. Depressed mood
    2. Irritable most of the day, nearly every day, as indicated by either subjective report (e.g., feels sad or empty) or observation made by others (e.g., appears tearful)
    3. Decreased interest or pleasure in most activities, most of each day
    4. Significant weight change (5 percent) or change in appetite
    5. Change in sleep: Insomnia or hypersomnia
    6. Change in activity: Psychomotor agitation or retardation
    7. Fatigue or loss of energy
    8. Guilt/worthlessness: Feelings of worthlessness or excessive or inappropriate guilt
    9. Concentration: Diminished ability to think or concentrate, or more indecisiveness
    10. Suicidality: Thoughts of death or suicide, or has suicide plan

Feelings of entrapment, social isolation, humiliation, persistent environmental stressors, and exposure to trauma are key contributing factors to a major depressive disorder in victims of human trafficking. Victims experience a sense of hopelessness and a lack of social support. Trafficking victims lack the ability to control their environments and to engage in activities that promote self-esteem and a sense of self-actualization, which contributes to the prevalence of depression among victims of trafficking (Hossain et al. 2010; Ryan and Deci 2000; Zimmerman, Hossain, and Watts 2011).

Treatment for Victims of Trafficking

A variety of evidence-based treatments for individuals suffering from anxiety disorders including PTSD, major depressive disorder, substance abuse, and other mental health issues experienced by trafficking victims are used to treat victims of trafficking. However, in almost all cases, victims of trafficking have faced multiple traumatic events. Exposure to multiple traumatic events is referred to as "complex trauma." Research indicates that trauma-focused therapies are most effective with individuals who have experienced multiple traumatic events (Cohen et al. 2012).

Trauma-focused cognitive behavioral therapy (TF-CBT) is a cognitive-based treatment that places a high value on the therapeutic relationship. Although research regarding TF-CBT for use with trafficking victims is promising, the majority of research has been with other populations.

The therapy process is designed to include the caregiver in the process whenever possible (Child Welfare Information Gateway 2007; Cohen et al. 2012; O'Callaghan et al. 2013). TF-CBT is delivered in three basic phases.

Phase 1: Coping Skills

A victim of trafficking often lacks basic coping skills outside the trafficking environment. Personal safety is one of the essential skills that is particularly relevant to trafficking victims. Victims of trafficking have often experienced environments where they had no control over their own personal safety. They may engage in self-harming behaviors or risk-taking behaviors. The therapist works with the victim to develop the victim's skills in recognizing unsafe environments and behaviors. In addition to safety skills, a therapist works with the trafficking victim to develop other cognitive skills, such as relaxation, self-awareness, and coping skills.

Phase 2: Trauma Narration and Processing

The goal of the trauma narration and processing phase of treatment is to guide the trafficking victim through a process of identifying trauma types (rather than specific traumas) and to understand the anxiety and other emotions related to the experiences. Part of this process is recognizing maladaptive responses to the anxiety caused by the traumatic events and developing healthier strategies for coping.

Phase 3: Consolidation and Closure

The final phase is consolidation and closure. The therapist helps the trafficking victim incorporate the skills he or she has learned and to create a sense of closure regarding the traumatic events. If there is an available caregiver or person who is capable of providing ongoing emotional support to the trafficking victim, this person should be involved.

Summary

Understanding the psychology related to human trafficking is an important part of addressing the issue and developing both therapeutic and policy responses to the issue. It is important to understand the issues from various viewpoints. There are many stereotypes of both victims and traffickers. In order to develop effective prevention strategies, it is important to understand both the risk factors of potential trafficking victims and the characteristics of perpetrators of trafficking. In order to address the issues trafficking victims face, it is important to understand both the psychological impacts and the treatment necessary to restore the mental health of the trafficking victims. With these understandings, it is possible to develop comprehensive approaches to dealing with the issues of trafficking.

Key Terms

anxiety disorder
capable guardian
debt approach
gorilla approach
grooming/seasoning
love approach
major depressive disorder
psychopathy
PTSD
trauma-focused cognitive behavioral therapy

Review Questions

1. What are the major risk factors for becoming a victim of domestic human sex trafficking?
2. What are the major characteristics of a trafficker?
3. What are the six categories of anxiety disorders?

4. What are the symptoms of PTSD?
5. What is trauma-focused cognitive behavioral therapy and why is it appropriate for victims of trafficking?
6. What are the three phases of trauma-focused cognitive behavioral therapy?

References

Abas, Melanie, Nicolae V. Ostrovschi, Martin Prince, Viorel I. Gorceag, Carolina Trigub, and Siân Oram. 2013. "Risk Factors for Mental Disorders in Women Survivors of Human Trafficking: A Historical Cohort Study." *BMC Psychiatry* 13 (January): 204. doi:10.1186/1471-244X-13-204. http://www.pubmedcentral. nih.gov/articlerender.fcgi?artid=3737054&tool=pmcentrez&rendertype =abstract.

Adams, Christine B. L. 2012. "Beyond Attachment: Psychotherapy with a Sexually Abused Teenager." *American Journal of Psychotherapy* 66(4) (January): 313–330. http://www.ncbi.nlm.nih.gov/pubmed/23393991.

American Psychiatric Association. 2013a. *Diagnostic and Statistical Manual of Mental Disorders.* 5th ed. Arlington, VA: American Psychiatric Publishing.

American Psychiatric Association. 2013b. *Diagnostic and Statistical Manual of Mental Disorders.* Edited by American Psychiatric Association. 5th ed. Arlington, VA: American Psychiatric Publishing.

Annitto, Megan. 2011. "Consent, Coercion, and Compassion: Emerging Legal Responses to the Commercial Sexual Exploitation of Minors." *Yale Law & Policy Review.* http://search.ebscohost.com/login.aspx?direct=true&profile =ehost&scope=site&authtype=crawler&jrnl=07408048&AN=77407392&h =416VDwN12zuLBiyHC8qkyWfYgLzFHOX22nO%2Brv3UAQZYgSy3zbs COm9gfj3Jp5BvdA0Unbo93PDSNYp149q8Zg%3D%3D&crl=c.

Banks, Duren, and Tracey Kyckelhahn. 2011. *Characteristics of Suspected Human Trafficking Incidents, 2008–2010.* Bureau of Justice Statistics. http://policepro-stitutionandpolitics.com/pdfs_all/GOVERNMENT REPORTS US Justice Dept stats SEE ALSO TRAFFICKING ALL/Bureau of Justice Statistics/bureau of jus-tice stats 2008_2010.pdf.

Banovic, Bozidar, and Zeljko Bjelajac. 2012. "Traumatic Experiences, Psychophysical Consequences and Needs of Human Trafficking Victims." *Vojnosanitetski Pregled* 69(1): 94–97. doi:10.2298/VSP1201094B. http://www.doiserbia.nb.rs/ Article.aspx?ID=0042-84501201094B.

Bennett-Murphy, Laura M. 2012. "Haunted: Treatment of a Child Survivor of Human Trafficking." *Journal of Infant, Child, and Adolescent Psychotherapy* 11(2) (April): 133–148. doi:10.1080/152891 68.2012.673413. http://www.tandfonline.com/ doi/abs/10.1080/15289168.2012.673413.

Birckhead, T. R. 2011. "The 'Youngest Profession': Consent, Autonomy, and Prostituted Children." *Washington University Law Review* 88: 1055–1116. http:// works.bepress.com/tamar_birckhead/12/.

Bjelajac, Zeljko, Zaklina Spalevic, and Bozidar Banovic. 2013. "Psychophysical Status of Human Trafficking Victims." *HealthMed* 7(4). http://search.ebscohost.com/login.aspx?direct=true&profile=ehost&scope=site&authtype=crawler&jrnl=18402291&AN=87508738&h=KjvMKagAiUIoyIi1DswGa1sF3DTtBlqQAMoVNGo0Wkz1Nt52WODTaJzVP3djjM5LIY3SIhDW8qSlwk154S6soA==&crl=c.

Child Welfare Information Gateway, Children's Bureau/ACYF. 2007. *Trauma-Focused Cognitive Behavioral Therapy for Children Affected by Sexual Abuse or Trauma.* https://www.ncjrs.gov/App/Publications/abstract.aspx?ID=262302.

Cohen, Judith A., Anthony P. Mannarino, Matthew Kliethermes, and Laura A. Murray. 2012. "Trauma-Focused CBT for Youth with Complex Trauma." *Child Abuse & Neglect* 36(6) (June): 528–541. doi:10.1016/j.chiabu.2012.03.007. http://www.pubmedcentral.nih.gov/articlerender.fcgi?artid=3721141&tool=pmcentrez&rendertype=abstract.

Dalla, Rochelle L., Yan Xia, and Heather Kennedy. 2003. "'You Just Give Them What They Want and Pray They Don't Kill You': Street-Level Sex Workers' Reports of Victimization, Personal Resources, and Coping Strategies." *Violence Against Women* 9(11) (November 1): 1367–1394. doi:10.1177/1077801203255679. http://vaw.sagepub.com/cgi/doi/10.1177/1077801203255679.

Dennis, Jeffery P. 2008. "Women Are Victims, Men Make Choices: The Invisibility of Men and Boys in the Global Sex Trade." *Gender Issues* 25 (1) (May 20): 11–25. doi:10.1007/s12147-008-9051-y. http://link.springer.com/10.1007/s12147-008-9051-y.

Dutton, D. G., and S. Painter. 1993. "Emotional Attachments in Abusive Relationships: A Test of Traumatic Bonding Theory." *Violence and Victims* 8(2) (January): 105–120. http://www.ncbi.nlm.nih.gov/pubmed/8193053.

Hardy, V. L., K. D. Compton, and V. S. McPhatter. 2013. "Domestic Minor Sex Trafficking: Practice Implications for Mental Health Professionals." *Affilia* 28 (1) (February 7): 8–18. doi:10.1177/0886109912475172. http://aff.sagepub.com/cgi/doi/10.1177/0886109912475172.

Hare, Robert D., and Craig S. Neumann. 2005. "Structural Models of Psychopathy." *Current Psychiatry Reports* 7 (1) (March): 57–64. http://www.ncbi.nlm.nih.gov/pubmed/15717988.

Hossain, Mazeda, Cathy Zimmerman, Melanie Abas, Miriam Light, and Charlotte Watts. 2010. "The Relationship of Trauma to Mental Disorders among Trafficked and Sexually Exploited Girls and Women." *American Journal of Public Health* 100(12) (December): 2442–2449. doi:10.2105/AJPH.2009.173229. http://www.pubmedcentral.nih.gov/articlerender.fcgi?artid=2978168&tool=pmcentrez&rendertype=abstract.

Hoyle, C., M. Bosworth, and M. Dempsey. 2011. "Labeling the Victims of Sex Trafficking: Exploring the Borderland between Rhetoric and Reality." *Social & Legal Studies* 20 (3) (September 19): 313–329. doi:10.1177/0964663911405394. http://sls.sagepub.com/cgi/doi/10.1177/0964663911405394.

Kazdin, Alan E. 2000. *Encyclopedia of Psychology: Volume 8.* Edited by Alan E. Kazdin. Oxford; New York: Oxford University Press.

Kennedy, M. A., and C. Klein. 2007. "Routes of Recruitment: Pimps' Techniques and Other Circumstances that Lead to Street Prostitution." *Journal of Aggression, Maltreatment and Trauma* 15(2). doi:10.1300/J146vl5n02. http://www.tandfonline.com/doi/abs/10.1300/J146v15n02_01.

Kotrla, Kimberly. 2010. "Domestic Minor Sex Trafficking in the United States." *Social Work* 55(2) (April): 181–187. http://www.ncbi.nlm.nih.gov/pubmed/20408359.

Leidholdt, D. A. 2013. "Human Trafficking and Domestic Violence: A Primer for Judges." *Judges' Journal* 52(1): 1–8.

National Institute of Mental Health. 2009. *Anxiety Disorders.* Bethesda, MD: U.S. Dept. of Health and Human Services. doi:10.1037/e440272008-002.

O'Callaghan, Paul, John McMullen, Ciarán Shannon, Harry Rafferty, and Alastair Black. 2013. "A Randomized Controlled Trial of Trauma-Focused Cognitive Behavioral Therapy for Sexually Exploited, War-Affected Congolese Girls." *Journal of the American Academy of Child and Adolescent Psychiatry* 52(4) (April): 359–369. doi:10.1016/j.jaac.2013.01.013. http://www.ncbi.nlm.nih.gov/pubmed/23582867.

Oram, Siân, Heidi Stöckl, Joanna Busza, Louise M. Howard, and Cathy Zimmerman. 2012. "Prevalence and Risk of Violence and the Physical, Mental, and Sexual Health Problems Associated with Human Trafficking: Systematic Review." *PLoS Medicine* 9(5) (January): e1001224. doi:10.1371/journal.pmed.1001224. http://www.pubmedcentral.nih.gov/articlerender.fcgi?artid=3362635&tool =pmcentrez&rendertype=abstract.

Parker, Stephen C., and Jonathan T. Skrmetti. 2013. "Pimps Down: A Prosecutorial Perspective on Domestic Sex Trafficking." *U. Mem. L. Rev.* 1013–1046. https:// litigation-essentials.lexisnexis.com/webcd/app?action=DocumentDisplay&cra wlid=1&doctype=cite&docid=43+U.+Mem.+L.+Rev.+1013&srctype=smi&src id=3B15&key=7dafbab64cebae56770532e2e9915749.

Reid, Joan A. 2012. "Rapid Assessment Exploring Impediments to Successful Prosecutions of Sex Traffickers of U.S. Minors." *Journal of Police and Criminal Psychology* 28 (1) (June 23): 75–89. doi:10.1007/s11896-012-9106-6. http://link. springer.com/10.1007/s11896-012-9106-6.

Ryan, Richard M., and Edward L. Deci. 2000. "Self-Determination Theory and the Facilitation of Intrinsic Motivation, Social Development, and Well-Being." *American Psychologist* 55(1): 68–78. doi:10.1037/0 003-066X.55.1.68. http:// www.ncbi.nlm.nih.gov/pubmed/11392867.

Spidel, A., and C. Greaves. 2007. "The Psychopath as Pimp." *Canadian Journal of Police and Security Services* 4(4): 193–199. http://searchfortruth.info/sites/ default/files/_psychopath-as-pimp.pdf.

Williamson, Celia, and Michael Prior. 2009. "Domestic Minor Sex Trafficking: A Network of Underground Players in the Midwest." *Journal of Child & Adolescent Trauma* 2 (1) (February 3): 46–61. doi:10.1080/19361520802702191. http:// www.tandfonline.com/doi/abs/10.1080/19361520802702191.

Wilson, Helen W, and Cathy Spatz Widom. 2010. "The Role of Youth Problem Behaviors in the Path from Child Abuse and Neglect to Prostitution: A Prospective Examination." *Journal of Research on Adolescence: The Official Journal of the Society for Research on Adolescence* 20 (1) (January): 210–236. doi:10.1111/j.1532-7795.2009.00624.x. http://www.pubmedcentral.nih.gov/ articlerender.fcgi?artid=2825751&tool=pmcentrez&rendertype=abstract.

Zimmerman, Cathy, Mazeda Hossain, and Charlotte Watts. 2011. "Human Trafficking and Health: A Conceptual Model to Inform Policy, Intervention and Research." *Social Science & Medicine (1982)* 73(2) (July): 327–335. doi:10.1016/j. socscimed.2011.05.028. http://www.ncbi.nlm.nih.gov/pubmed/21723653.

Human Trafficking and the Internet

5

SZDE YU

Contents

Major Issues

- Internet and crime
- Human trafficking: Victimology on the Internet
- Human trafficking: Internet as the hunting ground
- Human trafficking: Internet as the marketing place
- Human trafficking: Investigating on the Internet
- Human trafficking: Crime prevention and the Internet

Internet and Crime

The Internet is a large network of smaller networks. It was first created in the 1980s so that various computer networks could communicate with one another through a standardized protocol suite, TCP/IP. Simply put, different computer networks were connected together to form a larger network, which allowed for electronic messaging, such as e-mail and electronic bulletin boards. Later the introduction of World Wide Web significantly enriched the Internet and the improvement on connection speed expanded the utility of the Internet to a scope limited only by imagination. By the year of 2012, the Internet had reached 2,405,000,000 users, a 566% worldwide growth from the year of 2000 (Miniwatts Marketing Group 2013). Since the Internet's original purpose was convenience, safety and regulation were not on top of the developers' list, not until recent years. As a side effect of the exponential growth of the Internet, criminal-minded people started to seek opportunities in cyberspace. The Internet not only offers easy and cheap access to a large group of potential victims but also provides a pseudo-anonymous environment for criminals to conceal or misrepresent their identities. It is pseudo-anonymous because technically a user's Internet activity is not entirely untraceable to the extent of being absolutely anonymous. Nonetheless, the sheer volume of Internet activities oftentimes renders undesirability for such tracing, and thus creates a sense of secrecy similar to anonymity, aka pseudo-anonymity. It is this sense of secrecy that not only attracts cybercriminals who commit crimes that could not be otherwise committed outside the cyberworld (e.g., hacking or digital piracy) but also tempts conventional criminals to exploit the Internet as a new playground (e.g., child pornography or cyberbullying). Very quickly, criminal activities on the Internet started to catch attention and call for concern because of its rampancy and the lack of effective curb. This type of crime is generally referred to as cybercrime.

Cybercrime, Internet crime, computer crime, electronic crime, and digital crime are often used interchangeably when referring to crimes that involve the Internet, computer systems, or other computer technologies. Technically, a crime involving a computer does not necessarily have to involve the Internet. For instance, storing child pornography on a computer can be accomplished without Internet connectivity. However, since Internet connectivity has become so prevalent and easily available nowadays, it is not terribly wrong to simply assume the Internet and a computer would come together for the sake of argument. It is important to be mindful that a computer may no longer take form of a desktop or a laptop as we used to conceptualize. A tablet and a mobile phone should be regarded as a computer as well. In fact, any electronic device that has the capacity to connect to the Internet or to transmit and receive digital data should be categorized as a computer in the discussion of cybercrime. For instance, some advanced printers can directly transmit digital files through the Internet to a website or a fax machine without the need to be connected to an additional device; therefore this printer itself should be seen as a computer in the context of cybercrime. Devices of this sort all can be used as a tool or be targeted as a victim in a cybercrime.

As mentioned, a cybercrime can be a novel crime that is only feasible on a computer or the Internet, but it can also be a crime that has existed for centuries in a new form with the help of modern technology. One example of the latter is fencing (i.e., selling stolen property). Traditionally, thieves and burglars would sell stolen goods to a middle man, a fence, and the fence then sells the goods to potential buyers for a higher price. Fencing provides a buffer for thieves to quickly get rid of incriminating evidence and avoid the trouble of finding buyers. On the other hand, the fence can claim no knowledge about the source of their products because the fence normally did not directly participate in the stealing. Many transactions were conducted in a seemingly legitimate setting such as a pawn shop as a front to disguise criminality. Sometimes, the fence or thieves would carry the stolen goods in a van and approach potential buyers in a parking lot. Either way, fencing traditionally requires contact in person and hence increases the chance of being recognized or falling into a police's trap. In modern times although much fencing is still done in the traditional way, e-fencing has become more popular as selling stolen property on the Internet makes it easier to sell the goods across borders and hence reduces the chance of being detected by law enforcement. The Internet gives the old crime of fencing a new avenue that is more convenient and safer, because local police generally does not have jurisdiction over interstate or Internet commerce. Recognizing this problem, in 2008 an E-fencing Enforcement Act was introduced in the U.S. Congress, but it was never enacted ("Bill Summary & Status: H.R. 6713"). Although understandably it is complicated to enact a new law, this is a salient example showing how legislation is consistently behind the new development of modern crime.

Another example of how the Internet assists in a century-old crime is human trafficking, including trafficking of humans (mostly women and children) for prostitution and trafficking of men (and women alike) for labor (Feingold 2005). According to the UN Protocol to Prevent, Suppress, and Punish Trafficking in Persons, signed in 2000, trafficking in persons also includes any forms of sexual exploitation, slavery, and the removal of organs (Gozdziak and Collett 2005). Surely, without the Internet, human trafficking can still be accomplished and certainly we cannot transfer a person via the Internet like an e-mail. It is fair to say the Internet is not a necessary component in human trafficking. However, the Internet may still play an important role in the modern form of human trafficking. In this chapter, the relation between the Internet and human trafficking is discussed. The role played by the Internet in human trafficking can be threefold. First, the victim may unknowingly fall into a snare by voluntarily engaging in Internet activity. Second, the perpetrator may utilize it as a tool to facilitate their criminal activity. Third, law enforcement may use the Internet to aid their investigation in human trafficking cases.

Human Trafficking: Victimology on the Internet

Victimology is an area of study that concentrates on the victim of crime. It studies the victim's suffering in the crime as well as the victim's behavior, characteristics, or lifestyle that might have directly or indirectly led to victimization (Fattah 1991; Karmen 2010; Yu 2013). Victimology can be useful for various purposes. It could help understand how to better assist the victim and the victim's family in the aftermath of crime. It could help crime investigators profile the offender, as it is believed that the victim's suffering reflects some crucial aspects of the offender, such as personality, mental state, and skills (Yu 2013). The subtle connotation of victimology sometimes sounds like blaming the victim for the crime as it suggests that something about the victim increases the chance of victimization. If that "something" had been identified and removed, perhaps crime would not have happened.

Conceivably, the risk factors that contribute to victimization would vary depending on the type of offense. For instance, promiscuous sexual activity and alcohol use are found to increase the likelihood of becoming a rape victim (Koss and Dinero 1989; Testa and Livingston 2009), while personality traits such as social anxiety and depression are usually found to have significant effects on increasing victimization of bullying (Marini and Dane 2005; Veenstra et al. 2005). However different these risk factors are, victimization probability for all crimes always requires one essential: opportunity. If you constantly give people opportunities to victimize you, you face a higher chance of victimization, especially when you lack sufficient ability to defend or protect yourself. For instance, if you walk home alone late at night, you present opportunities for victimization. If this is your daily routine, chances are sooner or later a criminal-minded person may take advantage of that opportunity. Sometimes, the victim creates opportunities by making bad decisions, but sometimes there is not much the victim can do to entirely remove such opportunities. Even if the victim has been extra cautious, some offenders would aggressively seek or manufacture opportunities. Consequently, it is safe to assume there are always opportunities for crime and hence victimization, although some victims indeed make it too easy to become a target. Likewise, the opportunities for victimization in human trafficking always exist.

A victim can be involved in human trafficking in many ways. Most commonly a trade can be made to purchase a person like a commodity or a victim could be abducted by force. Modern forms of human trafficking typically involve the use of fraud to lure victims, such as the promise of a better life in a foreign country or the prospect of becoming famous. This method is preferable rather than using brute force because when the victims come voluntarily, they are easier to manipulate and less likely to cause trouble. Moreover, when the victims fall for the false promises, oftentimes they would have to pay to be on board. It is almost as if the commodity is paying the merchant to be sold, which guarantees a profitable business for the merchant. By the time victims finally realize the promises are false, usually it is too late.

More and more victims are ensnared by human traffickers via the Internet. The people who are more likely to be victimized online typically are those who like to look for opportunities on the Internet. They look for opportunities to make money, to be famous, to gain a sense of accomplishment, to make friends, to have fun, or to realize their dreams. They tend to be more active online, as opposed to just passively receiving information. They are more likely to visit a variety of websites that allow for human interactions, such as social-networking, forums, chat rooms, fan clubs, and so on. Their looking for opportunities ironically makes them an opportunity for victimization, as these places also attract most predators who try to exploit unsuspecting Internet users. By frequently visiting these places on the Internet, the opportunity for victimization thus increases. Because these people are eager for something, they are most likely to be deceived by the ruse planted by human traffickers due to clouded judgment. Typically teenagers are the most vulnerable population but everyone has a chance. More important, the websites we visit and the information we leave on the Internet can reveal substantial information about who we are and what we want, which may translate into vulnerability. Unknowingly, for most Internet users the digital footprints they leave behind on the Internet can constitute a solid cyberprofile on themselves that reveals personal or even private information, and such information in the eyes of a predator can be more than useful. It might be used to gain more personal information. It might be used to establish false rapport or bonding. It might also lead to physical stalking. These can all be part of the human trafficker's methods to manipulate potential victims through intimidation, seduction, or other social engineering guiles. As discussed, sometimes victims unknowingly create too many opportunities for their own victimization. The use of the Internet can surely add to that. It is important to note, however, this is not to say using the Internet will always lead to victimization. Most Internet users are scrupulous enough. Although we may not be able to resist computer viruses or junk e-mails all the time, becoming a victim in human trafficking is more complicated than being bombarded by junk e-mails, for human trafficking cannot be accomplished by the Internet alone. Conversely, this also does not mean if you do not use the Internet you will never be targeted. Human trafficking does not require the Internet. The Internet simply paves a new avenue for victimization.

In sum, the people who are most likely to become a victim via the Internet are those who are most active in seeking life-changing opportunities on the Internet. Being active often entails revealing too much personal information. Such information once revealed on the Internet usually would stay there forever for criminals to collect and use for fabricating an opportunity you have been looking for. Even though most people would say they know they should not trust everything they see on the Internet, the reality is we are still prone to believe something we have been looking for. Because criminals cannot physically abduct a person on the Internet, this sense of safety would actually prompt potential victims to interact with those who they would otherwise find suspicious.

Human Trafficking: Internet as the Hunting Ground

Knowing that there are potential victims on the Internet eager to have a new life, modern criminals are actively seeking targets on the Internet. The Internet provides great assistance for human traffickers. As mentioned, the Internet allows for outreach to a wider audience. In the old days, criminals engaging in sex trafficking mostly would need to find gullible young girls in the neighborhood, while nowadays they can reach out to almost anyone via the Internet. It is not unheard of that a young girl dreaming about being a supermodel would be attracted by a false advertisement online and travel hundreds of miles to a big city to be "interviewed" and pay for expensive photo sets for "marketing." Via the Internet, after choosing the right venue to place bait (i.e., false advertisement) human traffickers can practically wait for preys to come to them as opposed to physically hunting them down. The Internet certainly widens the net for human traffickers.

With the Internet, criminals do not usually need to worry about finding suitable targets. Rather, how to intrigue and convince the target is the primary concern. Creating plausible websites and photos to seem legitimate has become one popular tactic for cybercriminals and human traffickers alike. In 2001, a number of young girls in China ran away from home and traveled 600 miles to Hong Kong because they believed a model agency based in Hong Kong can help them become a supermodel or a movie star. They were convinced the agency was legitimate because it had a well-designed website. On the website, there were testimonials claiming how helpful this model agency has been in creating future stars. There were also many photos showing models taking pictures with some famous movie stars and directors. For those girls, that was all the convincing they needed to believe this was a real opportunity. Unfortunately, this was a scam. The purpose was to attract young girls to come and pay for arrangements to receive professional training in America. Of course, there was no professional training waiting for them in America. The arrangements were made to sell these girls to a Chinese mafia in America that is known for sex slave operations.

Some methods are more refined than merely posting an advertisement. In the stage of luring, many human traffickers prefer a personal touch because there are too many false advertisements on the Internet nowadays and most Internet users are accustomed to being skeptical. To enhance conviction, they would target a particular person. With the help of social-networking sites, it is really not too troubling to identify someone who reveals enough personal information to stand out as a suitable target. For the purpose of sex trafficking, traffickers may target someone who is good-looking enough and seems gullible. As mentioned, the desire a person possesses makes him or her gullible, and more people are exhibiting those desires openly on the Internet without scruples. Perceived by human traffickers, a personal message would be sent to the target presenting false hopes in accordance with the desire. This method is more time consuming, but it is usually more effective and convincing. Even for the most gullible people, some convincing is needed. Besides, the message does not need to be really personalized as long as it looks personal to the victim. Once one target takes the bait, snowballing can be expected. One person would pass on the "good news" to friends and friends could spread the word to their friends. It usually works better for a prey to lead other preys to the trap.

In addition to using the Internet to target or attract potential victims, human traffickers utilize the Internet to facilitate communication and coordinate their operations. Tracking locations, sending messages, finding maps, and having a long-distance conference are just a few utilities the Internet can offer in human trafficking operations. The advancement in cell phone technologies makes these utilities even more convenient and mobile. Another usage of the Internet is to create a false sense of presence. When a victim has been taken away, it would be undesirable for the human traffickers if someone immediately notices the disappearance of the victim. The Internet allows criminals to create an illusion that seems the victim is not missing. A tweet or a status update on Facebook can easily accomplish this. The victims can be actually miles away, but an online presence may lead family and friends to think they are still around.

Although human trafficking is not technically a cybercrime, it does not stop human traffickers from benefiting from the convenience of the Internet in their criminal activity. In a world where people grow suspicion on other people but develop trust in technology, using the Internet to lure victims may be more efficient than face-to-face interaction. The Internet expands the comfort zone for criminals and offers easy disguise behind computers. Further, perhaps the best part about hunting on the Internet is the fact that even when they fail to lure the victim, criminals are facing a very small likelihood of being identified and caught. Most people simply do not bother to contact law enforcement for an unsuccessful online scam. Even if they do, it is highly unlikely any investigative action would be taken for practical or jurisdictional reasons.

Human Trafficking: Internet as the Marketing Place

In recent years, Internet marketing has been blooming. The Internet offers a much more colorful interface to interact with customers compared to traditional marketing strategies, such as phone marketing (Mohammed et al. 2007). Besides, a website can operate 24/7, which accommodates clients' various schedules. Depending on the methods, Internet marketing can be very economical. Many businesses, legal or illegal, have resorted to e-mail spam as a marketing strategy (Yu 2011). It costs very little to send bulk e-mails and the advertisements can potentially reach millions of people worldwide. With little chance of legal consequences in spite of the increasing legislations, the only major cost is to acquire a long list of e-mail addresses. Especially for illegal operations, Internet marketing provides convenience, cost efficiency, and anonymity. Many of such underground operations are held on the "Deep Web." Sites on the Deep Web are the websites (e.g., Silk Road) that exist on the Internet, but major search engines (e.g., Google) cannot index them. In other words, they are only accessible through special software, such as Tor (www.torproject.org/).

Human traffickers traditionally do not rely on Internet marketing to advertise their merchandise. Mostly they rely on building connections with local people who possess knowledge about potential clientele. However, the old-fashioned way could be restricted in scope and risky as law enforcement infiltrates the social network built by human traffickers. The incorporation of the Internet as the marketing place has its potential and this potential has been gradually recognized. By far, Internet marketing is more often used in sex trafficking. The Internet allows for a virtual showroom where clients can have a preview of the merchandise through arrays of photos or videos. An online profile can be created for each victim for sale. The client can make a choice while enjoying privacy for no one needs to know who is sitting in front of the computer. Further contact will only take place when the client is really interested and perhaps has paid the deposit. A web-based payment reduces the chance of double-crossing for the merchants. The increasing popularity of virtual currency (e.g., Bitcoin) is making online transactions easier and more secretive, which is certainly beneficial to black market businesses. A web-based marketing site can also control membership so as to exclude untrustworthy people from gaining access. In fact, some services in this business do not require physical contact. Some clients are simply paying for watching live shows through the Internet, like watching pay-per-view movies.

Even when human traffickers do not want to run a website, the Internet may still be of help. As mentioned, e-mail can be utilized as a marketing tool. Some human traffickers use email spam to explore potential clientele (Yu 2011). They do not usually directly advertise their sex slaves, however. Instead, human traffickers could pretend to be selling other products that are more conventionally found in spam e-mails, such as pornography or drugs, and thus lure people to contact them. After the potential client responds to the advertisement, human traffickers then introduce the real service they are providing. The assumption is those people who are responding to advertisements found in spam e-mails are already criminal-minded to some extent. Therefore, even if they are not interested in sex slaves, the chance of them actively drawing attention from law enforcement is slim. Human traffickers in general are most vulnerable in the scenario where their potential clients become whistle blowers, and the Internet offers a buffer zone for them to disguise themselves even when this scenario does happen.

Human Trafficking: Investigating on the Internet

When the Internet is involved in criminal activity, the two biggest hurdles in criminal investigation are, first, traceability and, second, quantity. Traceability means the ability for law enforcement to trace online activity back to the Internet user who participated in such activity. Quantity refers to the sheer volume of online activity. To date, there is no feasible method to monitor millions of Internet users and actually look into every activity they have participated in. No agency has the resources to accomplish this, not even the National Security Agency. Most cybercriminals hence count on these two hurdles and believe they will not be caught.

Although the Internet benefits human traffickers and cybercriminals alike, this is not to say it cannot be of help to law enforcement. Surely, it is by no means impossible for Internet activity to be traced, although at times it can be elusive. In terms of human trafficking, more often than not human traffickers cannot hide behind the Internet forever. A transaction usually needs to take place and requires offline contact. As stressed before, we cannot transmit a human being through the Internet. Therefore, from an investigative standpoint the Internet serves as an intelligence source that can lead to offline operations. Investigators should actively search for and solicit certain advertisements online that implicate human trafficking. For instance, some seemingly legal adult websites may contain secret portals that lead to a more ulterior site where human traffickers advertise sex slaves. This information usually is only shared among "insiders" or members. Some human traffickers use classified ads, such as Craigslist, to post advertisements. Another commonly used technique is to hide such information in an otherwise innocuous online message. For example, human traffickers could go on Yelp.com and respond to an innocent question about cats and leave contact information at the end of the posting as part of the "signature" that only experienced clients would recognize. Using coded messages for communication is very prevalent in cybercrime. It screens out outsiders (i.e., people who are not yet to be trusted with the code) and it renders deniability when the messages are discovered by law enforcement.

There are many ways human traffickers could use the Internet to communicate with clients, but these online operations are usually short lived as the website would be constantly changing places or the e-mail address would be frequently discarded. In today's Internet environment, it is fairly easy to create websites and untraceable e-mail accounts. Investigators need to constantly update their information and once information is acquired investigators need to act fast. Nonetheless, the information on human trafficking acquired from the Internet should offer a valuable profile about the human trafficker. Cyberprofiling is a technique using the known facts about the criminal's online activity to deduce the unknown characteristics of the criminal (Yu 2013). By applying cyberprofiling, investigators could start to understand what type of human trafficking they are dealing with, such as sex trafficking, organ black market, or slavery. Judging by the characteristics of the "products," geographical origin and affiliation may be determined. For example, if most sex slaves being sold are of the same ethnicity, it usually implies the involvement of certain ethnic criminal groups. Moreover, if human traffickers adopt some sort of online financial mechanism to receive payment, as most experienced investigators would know following the money is one promising way to trace criminals when their crime is financially motivated. More important, cyberprofiling allows investigators to determine the criminal's capability. Criminals are rarely specialists. Human traffickers could very well engage in other types of criminal activity or legal businesses. Knowing the full scope of investigation can avoid fatal mistakes, such as trusting the wrong informant or underestimating the criminal's legal clout.

Human Trafficking: Crime Prevention and the Internet

The Internet apparently can be utilized by human traffickers to facilitate their businesses. Nonetheless, as previously discussed, it can become an investigative tool as well. Furthermore, the Internet as an important information source nowadays can readily serve as the primary media that help disseminate educational messages to the most vulnerable populations (i.e., teenagers and young adults) as far as human trafficking is concerned. Some organizations, such as ECPAT-USA, have been actively providing resources to the people who want to help stop human trafficking. In the effort to prevent human trafficking, it is imperative to remember human trafficking is often a cross-border crime and therefore using the Internet to combat human trafficking becomes even more sensible considering its boundless outreach. Websites like humantrafficking.org garner ample information in relation to international human trafficking. Through these resources on the Internet, any concerned parties can educate themselves and become a helping hand in the endeavor.

However, the use of the Internet in current anti-trafficking coalitions is largely limited, as most of them only offer very generic information on human trafficking. In the future the utility of the Internet may be maximized by creating a web-based intelligence exchange hub that allows concerned citizens to share their observations and victims to anonymously share their experiences pertaining to specific criminal activity. Many, if not most, attempts to solicit victims on the Internet actually end in failure. Instead of being treated as trivial online scams, these unsuccessful attempts could provide useful intelligence about human traffickers. An online consolidation of these pieces of information can create valuable mapping of trafficking operations and also warn others of the schemes employed by criminals. Such effort is difficult for just one agency or interest group to accomplish. With the Internet it is also more convenient to consolidate intelligence coming from different regions or nations to ferret out human traffickers' network and movement. As mentioned, human trafficking is oftentimes transnational. A victim missing in Russia could appear in the United States a few weeks later. Hence, international collaboration is needed for rescue and prevention. It is easier to overcome language barriers and time differences on the Internet. Crime prevention is supposed to be a proactive strategy rather than reactively waiting for a crime to happen first. Therefore, it cannot rely solely on law enforcement agencies. Given a proper platform and official support, many Internet activists may gladly contribute to combating human trafficking.

Summary

In this chapter, we went through a few fundamental relations between human trafficking and the Internet. It is important to emphasize again that human trafficking traditionally is not a cybercrime and therefore the Internet is not a necessary component. Nonetheless, considering today's technology and its accessibility to the Internet, the likelihood of the Internet being part of the criminal operation is distinct. The Internet can be used as a hunting ground when targeting vulnerable populations, and it can be used to promote commodities, that is, the victims. In contrast, law enforcement can utilize the Internet to facilitate investigations and educate potential victims to be alerted. Crime prevention requires collective efforts, and for a transnational crime like human trafficking the Internet is an ideal tool to help consolidate resources and intelligence.

Key Terms

computer
crime prevention
cybercrime
cyberprofiling
Internet

marketing
pseudo-anonymity
quantity
traceability
victimology

Review Questions

1. What is the Internet? How is it related to crime?
2. Who are mostly likely to become victims on the Internet?
3. How might the Internet be used to facilitate human trafficking?
4. Discuss how law enforcement can find the Internet helpful in its investigations.
5. How does the Internet help stop human trafficking?

References

"Bill Summary & Status: H.R. 6713." The Library of Congress. Last modified January 4, 2013. http://thomas.loc.gov/cgi-bin/bdquery/z?d110:h.r.06713.

Fattah, Ezzat A. *Understanding Criminal Victimization: An Introduction to Theoretical Victimology*. Scarborough, ON, Canada: Prentice-Hall Canada, 1991.

Feingold, David A. "Human Trafficking." *Foreign Policy* 150 (2005): 26–30.

Gozdziak, Elzbieta M., and Collett, Elizabeth A. "Research on Human Trafficking in North America: A Review of Literature." In *Data and Research on Human Trafficking*, 99–128. Switzerland: International Organization for Migration, 2005.

Karmen, Andrew. *Crime Victims: An Introduction to Victimology*. Belmont, CA: Cengage Learning, 2010.

Koss, Mary P., and Dinero, Thomas E. "Discriminant Analysis of Risk Factors for Sexual Victimization among a National Sample of College Women." *Journal of Consulting and Clinical Psychology,* 57 no. 2 (1989): 242–250.

Marini, Zopito A., and Dane, Andrew V. "Direct and Indirect Bully-Victims: Differential Psychosocial Risk Factors Associated with Adolescents Involved in Bullying and Victimization." *Aggressive Behavior,* 32 no. 6 (2005): 551–569.

Miniwatts Marketing Group. "Internet Usage Statistics." Last modified December 12, 2013. http://www.internetworldstats.com/stats.htm.

Mohammed, Rafi, Fisher, Robert J., Jaworski, Bernard J., and Paddison, Gorden. *Internet Marketing: Building Advantage in a Networked Economy*. New York: McGraw-Hill, 2007.

Testa, Maria, and Livingston, Jennifer A. "Alcohol Consumption and Women's Vulnerability to Sexual Victimization: Can Reducing Women's Drinking Prevent Rape?" *Substance Use & Misuse* 44 (2009): 1349–1376.

Veenstra, Rene, Lindenberg, Siegwart, Oldehinkel, A. J., De Winter, Andrea F., Verhulst, F. C., and Ormel, Johan. "Bullying and Victimization in Elementary Schools: A Comparison of Bullies, Victims, Bully/Victims, and Uninvolved Preadolescents." *Development Psychology* 41 no.4 (2005): 672–682.

Yu, Szde. "Email Spam and The CAN-SPAM Act." *International Journal of Cyber Criminology* 5 no.1 (2011): 715–735.

Yu, Szde. "Behavioral Evidence Analysis on Facebook: A Test of Cyber-Profiling." *Defendology* 16 no. 33 (2013): 17–30.

Child Victim Recruitment

Comparisons and Contrast in Domestic and International Child Victim Recruitment

6

RYAN J. ALEXANDER

Contents

Major Issues

1. Gain an understanding of what is commercial child trafficking.
2. Understand the differences in commercial exploitation on an international scale.
3. Obtaining information and knowledge about facilitation factors relating to commercial child sexual exploitation (CCSE) helps identify and understand how to curb or combat it.

4. Understand how personal and social factors influence where CCSE recruiters target children.
5. CCSE is not only an international issue but is domestically important as well, as the United States is part of the global CCSE community.

Introduction

Child sexual exploitation (CSE) takes shape in many forms, and those that victimize children use varied techniques and target children through a variety of ways. These techniques and coercion can share similarities globally and locally. They can also be divergent, and traffickers as well as abusers can manipulate local customs, take advantage of economic hardships, or prey on victims of conflict when targeting children. Recruitment of child victims does not imply a voluntary action taken by abused and trafficked children; rather this term is used to illustrate coercion and manipulation. Advertising for employment in different countries is a frequent tactic employed by traffickers to dupe children and their guardians that more conventional employment awaits them in far off lands. Certainly other more direct approaches are taken by traffickers, where some children are sold by parents or children are coerced into child prostitution through other means. Those looking to abuse or traffic children must know where to look or recruit victims, as not all conditions are favorable for recruitment.

Child sexual exploitation is usually referred to as "practices by which a person, usually an adult, achieves sexual gratification, financial gain, or advancement through the abuse or exploitation of a child's sexuality" (Estes and Weiner, 2005, p. 95). This type of exploitation usually occurs in one of two ways. Whether the exploitation takes place through coercion such as kidnapping or subtler ways such as deceptive techniques, a constant appears to be an inherent imbalance of power that exists between children and adult. This imbalance both exists physically and intellectually. The influence of the cultural status of children can either exacerbate or hinder abuse and trafficking opportunities. Understanding these implicit and explicit nuances can help authorities shape policy and overall strategy.

Types of Child Sexual Exploitation

There are various types of child sexual exploitation (CSE) such as contact offenses, like rape and molestation, and noncontact offenses, such as viewing and distributing child pornography. For our purposes CSE will be split into two categories. The first is commercial child sexual exploitation (CCSE). Estes and Weiner (2005) describe this as sexual exploitation of children for financial or economic reasons. There can be either an exchange of money or children can be bartered away permanently or for brief abusive encounters. Either way the crime is instrumental in nature. It satisfies a commercial demand. Therefore when considering law enforcement and social welfare remedies it may be best to understand supply and demand.

The second type of CSE is noncommercial. In this situation there is no exchange of money or services for this exploitation. Rather this crime can be classified as expressive in nature. The offender is satisfying their prurient interest in the child. An example would be a person sharing child pornography with another or an abuser molesting a family member.

The focus here will pertain mostly to commercial exploitation of children, as trafficking is usually done because there is some type of exchange, either monetary or otherwise, between parties. This exchange can occur where children are an uninvolved third party or where the child is involved in the transaction such as street prostitution. In some instances the child can or might have some autonomy in the transaction decision in street prostitution or in a brothel.

Scope of the Problem

The numbers of trafficked children are notoriously difficult to estimate due to the nature of the crime, the people involved, the difficulty in detecting and prosecuting those involved as well as getting victims to assist or become involved in data collection. Therefore as with most crime data collection, official and unofficial numbers need to be seen as part of the overall crime picture. Richard (2000) estimates that approximately 50,000 children are trafficked into the United States each year and approximately one-third of those children come from Latin America. Domestically Estes and Weiner (2005) estimate that nearly 300,000 children within the United States are at serious risk of being commercially sexually exploited.

Beyond the United States the problems of CCSE is just as severe. CCSE occurs on every continent on the globe (note none has been recorded in Antarctica). Certain regions of the world are more advantageous for recruitment and exploitation to occur. Asia certainly appears to be an area that experiences a great deal of not only international trafficking but also domestic trafficking. Certain countries in this region experience more trafficking than others and that certainly should not go unnoticed. ECPAT (End Child Prostitution and Trafficking) (2003) found that China (200,000 to 500,000 children subjected to CCSE) had many more children subjected to commercial exploitation than another Asian country, Bangladesh (10,000 to 29,000 children). Thus hotspots for CCSE may require more attention and resources than other places.

The United States and other nations have attempted to address the issue of CCSE for a number of years. More recently nations have banded together to create international agreements to try to limit CCSE on a global scale. Domestically the United States has sought to curb trafficking within its borders as early as the 1910 Mann Act, which prohibited the transportation of individuals in interstate or foreign commerce for the purpose of engaging in prostitution. Later in 1978, the Mann Act was modified to where children were specifically granted more protection. Certain technological advances have made the inclusion of protection from children pornography or facilitation of abuse necessary. As events transpire more legislation will surely be adopted to address contemporary problems.

On a global scale the Convention on the Rights of the Child has addressed a number of child-related issues such as labor along with CCSE. Other global responses have been more CCSE specific such as the First World Congress against Commercial Sexual Exploitation of Children, 1996. Still others have specifically addressed CCSE specifically on a more regional scale such as the African Charter on the Rights and Welfare of Children.

Child Victim Recruitment

Children are commercially sexually exploited for a number of different reasons. They can provide income to families that are severely economically distressed, they can be perhaps more easily manipulated or duped by pimps or others looking to exploit them, or they can be perhaps more easily coerced due to their physical size and social status. To be sure, recruitment is multifaceted and complex. The National Institute of Justice (2007) advised that CCSE takes place at three different levels: local exploitation by one or a few people, small regional networks involving a number of adults and possibly children, and a large national/international network. All tiers involve children being bought and sold or traded as a commodity. Each level or tier seems to satisfy the demand.

Children as Prostitutes

Children can be considered viable sources or pools of prospective prostitutes for many reasons. First, some children are prized sexual objects by those who are attracted to children. Pedophiles are considered as such because of this unconventional attraction. Therefore there is a market based on the wants of those people. Also, in some societies children are not viewed as children or adolescents but as small adults. As such the chronological age of a prostitute may be distressing to Western sensibilities but not met with as much disdain as the country of origination. Sex with a child can be viewed as a rite of passage for a child (Holmes and Holmes, 2009). Thus the societal opinion of children's social status as well as cultural attitudes toward and about sex may not mesh well with Western ideals about children and sex. An understanding of these regional or cultural specifics about children and sex would be beneficial for law enforcement, social welfare, and policy makers.

The introduction to prostitution can be immediate or occur due to prolonged and repeated trauma. Although both roads toward prostitution can take place no matter the social and economic condition of the country, it appears that chronic trauma or abuse is more of a facilitating factor for children in Western countries (James and Meyerding, 1977; Slibert and Pines, 1982). Here the abuse often begins in the victim's home at the hands of a family member or acquaintance (Estes and Weiner, 2001; Greenfeld, 1997). As a result of victimization at home those children may wish to escape the abuse by leaving or running away from home or they may be forced to leave. Either way this change can expose the child as a vulnerable person to future victimization. Facilitation toward prostitution in developing countries appears to be more direct. Children in developing countries are more apt to be sold to traffickers, leave home to pursue work that ultimately ends in CCSE, or be taken for the explicit purpose of CCSE. Higher rates of CCSE take place more in developing countries or countries in economic transition (Bales, 1999; Hughes, 2000).

Recruitment

Children are recruited into CCSE through several different ways. Overall they share similarities no matter the economic condition of the country or the culture in which the abuse takes place or from where the child originates. Recruitment methods are not mutually exclusive to certain parts of the globe or culture. However, there are apparent differences in recruitment inside and outside of the United States. These differences are dependent upon cultural views of the child, social status of the child, cultural views about sex, and economic distress to name a few.

Children outside the United States are often lured into CCSE with the promise of a conventional job. They leave guardians and loved ones behind because the economic distress pushes them out of familiar surroundings while also pulling them toward the promise of a better life. This can and does happen domestically but it is more likely to occur in developing countries (Rigi, 2003). Those outside the United States are more easily forced or even kidnapped into CCSE than their American counterparts due to the inability or unwillingness of law enforcement to provide support. In some countries child labor and alternatively child prostitution are not seen as aberrations. Thus it becomes important to consider cultural sensitivities and contemplate

Western ethnocentricity when viewing issues facilitating CCSE in countries outside the United States. Also marriage by the age of 12 or 13 is not frowned upon in many other countries; indeed U.S. history proves that early marriage often occurred there too. In some societies it may not be considered immoral or perverted to have sex with children (Leth in Cooper, Estes, Giardino, Kellogg, and Veith, 2005). All the more necessary to understand others, we may not agree with but understand nonetheless.

A potentially universal recruitment method is simple blind obedience of the child to one's parents, whereby the child freely follows or is docile in their own victimization as a result of cultural social forces. This obedience surely vacillates and can be culturally deponent in the amount of reverence paid to adults or parents, which allows buying, selling, and bartering to more easily occur. This is where the adult-to-child power ratio is certainly important when considering recruitment in societies with higher rates of CCSE. Children may be able to be seen as capable of doing adult labor and performing adult sexuality, but in the United States they still are considered underclass. Overall attitudes about sex and gender must be dealt with, for instance, in certain areas of Latin America rape is not seen as reprehensive as stealing a cow (Jordan, 2002). This attitude about sex or coercive sex can impede authorities combating CCSE.

Latin America

In many Latin American countries women do not have much political, economic, or social power. They may equal or exceed males in numbers, but they often do not have the same political clout as males (Spangenberg, 2001). Male supremacy is often reinforced through religion where males dominate religious administration and practice. Government further reinforces male dominance as females are exempt from political office either explicitly or culturally implicitly. Finally, education further emphasizes male dominance by not allowing or discouraging females from postsecondary education or other educational opportunities. This easily translates into atmospheres where females, especially female children, are easily made docile and where coercion is acceptable. This docile population is much more readily conditioned to participate in CCSE. Once a female is sexually active outside of marriage the concept of rape does not apply (Leth in Cooper, Estes, Giardino, Kellogg, and Veith, 2005).

Latin America offers CCSE recruiters plenty of opportunity to find and exploit children. It is estimated that nearly 40,000 children are victims of CCSE each year. The balance of the children come from Mexico and the Dominican Republic (ECPAT, 2003). This illustrates that certain regions of the globe may have comparatively higher rates of CCSE, but it becomes vastly more important from a law enforcement standpoint to identify hotspot countries and even areas within countries when examining recruitment.

Southeast Asia

Prostitution and child sex trafficking are much more closely linked in Southeast Asia (Foundation for Women, 1988). The supply of available children for CCSE is more readily available, but the market or demand is located in major urban areas away from remote villages where many CCSE victims come from. Thus domestic trafficking and international trafficking occurs at higher rates here (Economic and Social Commission for Asia and the Pacific [ESCAP], 2000). Children are sold by parents for as little as $100 to $150 (Leth in Cooper, Estes, Giardino, Kellogg, and Veith, 2005). An ESCAP (2000) study investigating child sex trafficking in Asia found that children between the ages of 11 and 15 were most susceptible to coercion or lured into the sex trade. This age range is most desirable because they are suitable targets, in as much as they are old enough to leave home yet dependent enough to need an older caretaker. Also emotional dependence is exploited. Children can and do enter the workforce early in many Asian countries. The conventional labor force often does not pay wages comparable to the sex industry. Their emotional and economic dependence are easily manipulated as their naiveté is as easily exploited. Peer pressure to enter the trade can also occur, thus pushing children into prostitution (Foundation for Women, 1988). Still, others are born into the trade. Such recruitment while surely occurring in Western culture is more acceptable and occurs more frequently in Asia. There are fewer resources to help children of prostitutes leave or refrain from entering commercial sex trade. Culture dictates that these children of prostitutes are "throw away children" not worthy of resources (Leth in Cooper, Estes, Giardino, Kellogg, and Veith, 2005). These children who are raised in brothels become desensitized to abuse, while at the same time culture resigns them to sex trade.

Eastern Europe

The fall of communism in the late 1980s and early 1990s opened Eastern European countries to the promise of many things. It also brought with it issues such as CCSE that it did not have to deal with previously. Some former Eastern Bloc countries have flourished in newfound or created wealth, whereas other countries, such as Romania, have not fared as well. Just as in other regions of the world, such as Asia and Latin America, Eastern Europe has seen a rise in not only adult trafficking but also CCSE. As was the case with other regions, the entire region is not a hotspot per se, but individual countries could be called such. Romania is one example.

Romania appears to be an advantageous place to recruit children for CCSE. When considering areas more suitable for recruitment than others, one must consider social and individual-level variables. Socially, it is the poorest country in Europe, so the conditions are ripe for locating those that wish to leave for a better life elsewhere. There are also those who cannot afford the children they have or see children as a form of economic solvency. Romania is also surrounded by nations much better off. This relative deprivation enhances the pull for young people to leave and seek a better life while also experiencing a push realizing that opportunities may lay just over the border, if only they can get there. As a result of poor economic opportunity domestically, men have emigrated looking for work, leaving a high percentage of females (International Organization of Migration, 2001). With few marriage prospects left in many villages, girls (often being married by age 16 is preferable) will marry someone relatively unknown. These men can end up trafficking and exploiting their new young bride (Leth in Cooper, Estes, Giardino, Kellogg, and Veith 2005). The Italian Mafia has also been helping to facilitate international trafficking (Renton, 2001). They provide easy connections and act as a conduit to traffic children internationally. Thus there exists a vulnerable population of children and those who can exploit the economic troubles and cultural proclivities that make Romania an opportune place to recruit children into the sex trade.

On an individual-level basis Romania may be a preferable place to recruit children because children, especially girls, may be more docile than other European counterparts. Domestic violence rates are high in Romania, thereby creating an atmosphere of male dominance instilled at an early age (Renton, 2001). Girls are often retrafficked here too. Once they have left their villages, locals often discover the children are abused, and instead of empathy they are chastised and met with hostility. With few options for economic prosperity many re-enter the sex trade.

Africa

Africa as a whole experiences less CCSE than other previously mentioned regions. CCSE occurs across the whole of the continent and recruitment hotspots are still identifiable. These places appear to share the same characteristics with other regions. Specifically, children are more susceptible due to major armed conflicts in the region that separate children from parents or necessitate selling of children. Children being used for domestic labor away from their home is more readily acceptable here too, thereby increasing the social acceptance that a child must leave the house to gain sustainable employment. Children can much more easily be lured away with the promise of gainful employment beyond parental supervision (Leth in Cooper, Estes, Giardino, Kellogg, and Veith 2005). The result of conflicts that tear children away from guardians coupled with feeble economic prospects make conditions in certain parts of West and Central Africa favorable to recruiters of CCSE.

Western Africa is a well-used child trafficking zone. Children are in constant transition across the border of Mali, Benin, and Niger making it difficult for authorities inclined to investigate trafficking to actually be successful (Leth in Cooper, Estes, Giardino, Kellogg, and Veith 2005). This constant flux of children and street prostitutes as opposed to organized brothels further complicates investigation thus making this area an attractive place to recruit children into the commercial sex trade.

International Recruitment

International recruitment of children into CCSE shares some similarities with children recruited domestically in the United States. However, there are some stark differences that make children in certain regions or even countries or sections of countries more vulnerable than elsewhere. These set(s) of unique circumstances can be areas of focus for law enforcement and social welfare experts. Azola (2000) identified several risk factors that authorities may wish to key in on in order to curb CCSE. Some individual-level factors help facilitate either exposure to individuals that would do them harm or propel children into CCSE due to a lack of economic choices where street prostitution or work in brothels is a matter of survival. Issues of substance abuse or addiction can occur after or before involvement in CCSE. Addiction prior to involvement can facilitate the slide into it, or addiction after involvement can cement the child's continued involvement in CCSE. Also, children with developmental, mental health, or physical disabilities are at greater risk simply due to the nature of their condition. Again few opportunities and little social or governmental support may make the "choice" of entering CCSE much easier.

Social factors appear to be even more numerous and more significant than individual-level factors when assessing recruitment opportunities. Social atmosphere creates an environment that may in essence welcome or turn a blind eye to CCSE domestically and concerning international trafficking. The economic impact of CCSE can be economically important for some countries and be a factor in assessing GNP (Renton, 2001). With such economic importance, enforcement against CCSE is a difficult task. Other factors not directly related to CCSE impact law enforcement and welfare agencies. If too much is made out of a country as being a hotbed for CCSE, tourists with legal intentions can be scared away. Cultural considerations need to be made also. Some children are seen as throw away or unimportant as children of prostitutes are often considered. Other children such as orphans or those released from institutions are often considered as "other" and thus more susceptible to CCSE recruiters. Where there are large populations of street children the pool for recruitment is extensive.

Economic opportunities also play a huge role in recruitment. The simple geographical proximity that Mexico shares with the United States and considering the relative deprivation in economy is very enticing grounds for recruiters. Trafficking a child or children a couple of hundred miles across a relatively porous land border is much easier than the logistics it would take to traffic a child or group of children from overseas. This most certainly is the case for children in Romania (Renton, 2001). The countries in close proximity are some of the wealthiest in the world. As stated organized crime both in Romania and abroad has been very effective at moving children across borders. In some areas where prostitution is legal and law enforcement does not effectively police CCSE it can become difficult to identify children from adults, especially where there is poor documentation relating to birth certificates and personal identification.

CCSE recruiters often manipulate local customs to identify and coerce children and families into giving up their children, luring them away with false hopes of work, or simply using brute force to take children away from families. Some countries with armed conflict have orphaned children or separated children from guardians making them a vulnerable population for CCSE either domestically or for trafficking. These variables separate CCSE internationally from domestic CCSE in the United States.

United States

CCSE recruiters in the United States share some commonalities in how they recruit child victims with their international counterparts. Primarily recruiters prey on children in areas that are favorable toward recruitment. In as much as it is difficult to sell ice in the Arctic it is difficult to recruit children for CCSE in areas that are economically secure, where collective efficacy among the population is strong, and where law enforcement is effective and motivated to pursue offenders.

In the United States CCSE is everywhere but it is important to consider the areas that it occurs at higher rates when considering where to target resources. CCSE is concentrated in large coastal cities and resorts or vacation spots where there are large transient populations. Cities near the border of Canada and Mexico also provide more opportunities for CCSE and trafficking (Estes and Weiner in Cooper, Estes, Giardino, Kellogg, and Veith 2005). Transient areas offer offenders easy ways of obtaining illicit services without too much fear of exposure by unintentional contact with known others as well as a minimum of surveillance from others who might dissuade illegal behavior. The close proximity to borders allows traffickers to move children from one side of the border to the other when appropriate. Close proximity to the border can also "try" or "strain" cooperation among nations.

Medium and small U.S. cities are starting to serve as training grounds before trafficked children are move to larger venues (Estes and Weiner in Cooper, Estes, Giardino, Kellogg, and Veith 2005). By trying out trafficked children in these small venues traffickers can control new recruits more easily as there are fewer places to escape through as well as serving as a place wholly unfamiliar to the child, in essence removing them from a place they are not familiar with. For those children recruited from Midwestern locales, traffickers have been known to initiate children into CCSE in smaller or medium-sized cities as a way to ease them into CCSE. Once the child is a known commodity they are transported to larger venues.

Recruitment of children can be broken into two different categories: individual-level risk factors and social risk factors (Estes and Weiner in Cooper, Estes, Giardino, Kellogg, and Veith, 2005). These factors may not be mutually exclusive and often intermingle. For instance mental health issues such as depression impact decisions to run away from home. Being exposed to others on the streets is a risk factor facilitating CCSE. If the child had proper resources their mental health condition could have been rectified. Thus personal mental health issues intermingle with social aspects of socioeconomic levels.

Personal Factors Contributing to Commercial Child Sexual Exploitation

Many personal factors relating to risk of CCSE begin with family dysfunction (Cauce, Paradise, and Ginsler, 2003), where substance abuse by the parent(s) or guardian can cause the child to leave home, be neglected or learn habits or adopt unconventional behaviors and attitudes about sex or acceptance, and become docile when abused. Prior physical and sexual abuse by parents and guardians can be a key factor for a child who runs away from home (Briere and Runz, 1988; Ryan, Kilmer, Cauce, Watanabe, and Hoyt, 2000). Running away from home exposes children to a number of different potential dangers, CCSE being one of them.

Runaways represent perhaps the greatest risk of being involved in CCSE. They present a number of factors that not only expose them to nefarious people but also further increase their susceptibility of CCSE involvement. Runaway children most definitely lack financial resources to secure even the barest of life essentials. Oftentimes they have to resort to CCSE, as their employability is at a disadvantage to more skilled and mature people, especially in a job market that further demands levels of education usually not attained by children. Children may resort to other types of criminal behavior outside of CCSE but eventually find their way into it by being introduced to it through peer pressure or as a result of other criminal activity that introduced them to a CCSE recruiter or pimp (Azola, 2001; Loeber and Farrington, 1998; U.S. Department of Justice, 2003).

Emotional and mental immaturity is often taken advantage of by pimps, who tend to lurk at bus stations or shelters and other areas where runaway and homeless children tend to congregate. Pimps will often condition a new recruit through a series of gifts in which no payment is initially demanded but when dependence begins to form pimps take advantage of these situations. Often trauma bonds develop where a pimp gives gifts or shows affection only to punish or abuse the child later (Reid and Jones, 2011). These trauma bonds in essence have the appearance of creating a willing victim (Herman, 1992).

Social factors in the United States also help to contribute to CCSE recruitment opportunities. For instance, as previously mentioned, CCSE takes place at greater rates in coastal cities, border cities, and resort destinations (Azola, 2001). These environs all have transient populations. These hubs of activity attract recruiters because they draw runaways and other vulnerable populations. Recruiters or pimps are able to operate on familiar ground, which is a disadvantage to someone who does not know the area and has few means from which to operate. There often tends to be a large adult market for prostitution where children can easily be folded into CCSE involvement. Gangs have begun to exploit these areas as a new source of revenue (Moore and Hagedon, 2001). Just as Italian mobs are drawn to Romanian CCSE opportunities, American gangs have begun to capitalize on CCSE.

Estes and Weiner (2005, in Cooper, Estes, Giardino, Kellogg, and Veith) found that certain macrocontextual variables facilitated recruitment into CCSE. These social level variables did not directly result in CCSE but made recruitment much easier. Again, opportunity and accessibility to vulnerable targets attract CCSE recruiters. The large presence of those in lower socioeconomic strata produces a push–pull toward CCSE. The push may be to leave the area because there does not appear to be any economic opportunity where one currently resides. It is well documented that few financial resources breed a host of other social issues such as poor health, lack of education, and crime. Thus the push. The pull is the opportunity one sees in another area pulling them to leave. Relative deprivation is a motivating factor, whereby leaving at least creates opportunity for success.

The idea of social anomie can further solidify the push–pull. This normlessness can yield a number of contributing factors that assist CCSE recruitment. Anomie can create lax social attitudes about child victims of crime, or a denial of CCSE problems help to conceal from the public any targeted and effective response. Indeed, an admission of this type of social problem can result in further economic damage. Overall social attitudes about crime and response, or lack thereof, by authorities create attitudes that may be unfavorable toward policing.

Conclusion

CCSE is a global problem. CCSE recruitment of child victims is as varied as the countries and cultures that the victims originate from. They however share similarities such as poverty, social acceptance or ignorance of the issue, dysfunctional families, and limited or no response to core issues that result in easily exploited children, and as collateral damage from armed conflict. No matter what geographic area one is in the creation of a susceptible population of already susceptible people attracts those that would do them harm. These children are easy targets or low hanging fruit. By identifying how CCSE recruiters target children and where they focus their attention, law enforcement and social welfare advocates can begin to triage the damage and act in a more efficient and effective manner.

Key Terms

child sexual abuse
child trafficking
child victim recruitment
commercial child sexual exploitation

Review Questions

1. How is child victim recruitment different in the United States compared to other nations?
2. Explain how children are a susceptible population for the commercial sex trade.
3. Explain how culture or a child's status can affect recruitment into commercial sexual exploitation.
4. Why is it important to identify hotspots for child victim recruitment into CCSE within regions or countries?

References

Azola, E. (2001). *Stolen Childhood: Girl and Boy Victims of Sexual Exploitation in Mexico.* Mexico City, Mexico: UNICEF Report.

Bales, K. (1999). Disposable People: New Slavery in the Global Economy. Berkeley, CA: University of California Press.

Boyer, D., and Fine D. (1992). Sexual Abuse as a Factor in Adolescent Pregnancy and Child Maltreatment. *Family Planning Perspectives* 24: 4–11, 19

Briere, J., and Runtz, M. (1988). Symptomology Associated with Childhood Sexual Victimization in a Non-Clinical Sample. *Child Abuse and Neglect* 12: 51–59.

Cauce, A. M., Paradise, M., and Ginzsler, J. A. (2000). The Characteristics and Mental Health of Homeless Adolescents; Age and Gender Differences. *Journal of Emotional and Behavior Disorder* 8: 230–239.

Cooper, S., Estes, R., Giardino, A., Kellog, N., and Vieth, V. (Eds.). (2005). *Medical, Legal, and Social Science Aspects of Child Sexual Exploitation—A Comprehensive Review of Pornography, Prostitution, and Internet Crime*. St. Louis, MO: GW Medical Publishing.

Economic and Social Commission for Asia and the Pacific. (2000). *Sexually Abused and Sexually Exploited Children and Youth in the Greater Mekong Sub-Region: A Qualitative Assessment of their Health Needs and Available Services*. New York, NY: United Nations.

End Child Prostitution, Child Pornography and Trafficking of Children for Sexual Purposes (ECPAT) (2003). ECPAT International website. http://www.ecpat.net/eng/Ecpat_inter/projects/monitoring/online_database/index.asp.Retrieved Feb. 23, 2013.

Estes, R. J., and Weiner, N. A. (2001). *Commercial Sexual Exploitation of Children in the NAFTA Countries*. Philadelphia: University of Pennsylvania.

Foundation for Women. Report of the Kamala Project. (1988). Bangkok, Thailand: Women's Information Center.

Greenfeld, L. (1997). Sex Offences and Offenders: An Analysis of Data on Rape and Sexual Assault. Bureau of Justice Statistics Report, NCJ 163392.

Herman, J. L. (1992). Complex PTSD: A Syndrome in Survivors of Prolonged and Repeated Trauma. *Journal of Traumatic Stress* 5(3): 377–391.

Holmes, Stephen T., and Holmes, Robert M. (2009). Sex Crimes: Patterns and Behavior, 3rd edition. Los Angeles: Sage.

Hughes, D. M. (2000). The "Natasha Trade": The Transnational Shadow Market of Trafficking in Women. *Journal of International Affairs* 53: 625–652.

International Organization for Migration (IOM). (2001). Return and Reintegration Project—Counter Trafficking—Situation Report in Kosovo. IOM: Tirana.

James, J., and Meyerding, J. (1977). Early Sexual Experience and Prostitution. *American Journal of Psychiatry* 134: 1381–1385.

Jordan, M. (2002). In Mexico, Rape Often Goes Unpunished. *Washington Post.*

Lalor, K. J. (1999). Street Children: A Comparative Perspective. *Child Abuse and Neglect* 23(8): 759–770.

Loeber, R., and Farrington, D. (1998). *Serious and Violent Juvenile Offenders: Risk Factors and Successful Interventions*. Thousand Oaks, CA: Sage.

Moore, J., and Hagedorn, J. (2001). *Female Gangs: A Focus on Research*. Washington D.C.: US Dept. of Justice, Office of Justice Programs, Office of Juvenile Justice and Delinquency Prevention. NCJ 185234.

National Institute of Justice. (2007). *Special Report: Commercial Sexual Exploitation of Children: What We Know and Don't Know About It*. Washington D.C.: US Dept. of Justice. Office of Justice Programs.

Reid, J. A., and Jones, S. (2011). Exploited Vulnerability: Legal and Psychological Perspectives on Child Sex Trafficking. *Journal of Victims and Offenders* 6(2): 207–231.

Renton, D. (2001). *Child Trafficking in Albania*. Save the Children report.

Richard, A. O. (2000). *International Trafficking in Women in the US: A Contemporary Manifestation of Slavery and Organized Crime.* DCI Report, United States Department of State.

Ryan, K. D., Kilmer, R. P., Cauce, A. M., Watanabe, H., and Hoyt, D. R. (2000). Psychological Consequences of Child Maltreatment in Homeless Adolescents: Untangling the Unique Effects of Maltreatment and Family Environment. *Child Abuse and Neglect* 24(3): 333–352.

Slibert, M. H., and Pines, A. M. (1982). Victimization of Street Prostitutes. *Victimology* 7(1–4): 122–133.

Spangenberg, M. (2001). *Prostituted Youth in New York City: An Overview.* ECPAT-USA.

U.S. Department of Justice (USDOJ). (2003). *Juvenile Offenders and Victims: 2002 National Report.* Washington D.C.: US Department of Justice Office of Juvenile Justice and Delinquency Prevention.

Investigation of Human Trafficking

7

BRIAN F. KINGSHOTT

Contents

Major Issues

What is a criminal investigation?
Objectives of an interview/interrogation
Cognitive interview
Witness evaluation
Interviewing a witness
What is evidence?
Elements and characteristics of human trafficking
Awareness and understanding of the problem

Victims: Identifying and controlling
Challenges of the investigation
Addressing the problem

What Is a Criminal Investigation?

The general process of a criminal investigation is complex (Gilbert, 2010; Lasley and Guskos, 2014; Lyman, 2014), but it may be summarized as the systematic and thorough inquiry into an individual or an incident in order to ascertain the truth. There must also be a comprehensive report, since investigators must always have an end product, particularly if the case goes cold (Brown, 2001; Dempsey, 2003). Criminal investigation has an anticipated end product of bringing someone to justice; that is, arresting, prosecuting, and convicting perpetrators of crimes. However, it must not usurp the role of prosecutor, judge, and jury. That enormous responsibility is why ethics must be the first and foremost characteristic of criminal investigation (Weston and Lushbaugh 2003).

An equitable and effective criminal investigation process is an integral part of an efficient criminal justice system that underpins the state's constitution. The criminal justice system comprises a number of agencies and has both process and procedures that have been established by governments to control crime and impose penalties on those who violate laws (National Center for Victims of Crime, 2008). Although criminal justice systems will vary across the globe, most will have five components: law enforcement, prosecution, defense, courts, and corrections, each playing an integral role in the criminal justice process.

In essence, the investigation is the process by which the perpetrator of a crime, or intended crime, is identified through the ethical gathering of evidence in accordance with the law. A criminal investigation can be reactive (i.e., applied to crimes that have already taken place), or proactive (i.e., targeting a particular criminal or forestalling a criminal activity planned for the future) (United Nations Office on Drugs and Crime, 2006, p. 1).

There are two basic approaches to the management of a criminal investigation. The first approach relates to jurisdictions with a civil law tradition, the responsibility for an investigation lies with a prosecutor or judicial officer (*juge d'instruction*). Within this model the investigators work under the direction and management of the prosecutor or investigating judge. In the second approach, primarily found in jurisdictions with a common law tradition, investigations are conducted by the law enforcement agency independently of prosecutors until the case, and the charged suspect, is handed over for prosecution in the courts. There are, however, many variations within both basic systems, but regardless of the system of criminal investigation that has been developed or been adopted, there is one universal value that remains paramount in any criminal justice system. It is that the evidence is based upon an objective evaluation of the evidence presented and that suspects are innocent until proven guilty (United Nations Office on Drugs and Crime, 2006, p. 1).

Objectives of an Interview/Interrogation

The objectives of an interview or an interrogation are the same: to establish the truth. An interview is simply a meeting at which information is obtained or exchanged. Therefore, within the context of criminal investigations interviews are conducted for the purpose of gathering information from people who have or may have information that is pertinent to the investigation. That information may come from a victim, a suspected offender, or from a person who has no other relationship to the criminal activity other than being where he or she was at a specific time. To recall the incident the witness's memory can be enhanced by effective interview techniques (Fisher and Geiselman, 1992, 2010; Geiselman, Fisher, MacKinnon, and Holland, 1985; McLeod, 2010).

The term *interrogation* is often used when dealing with suspected offenders. The term interrogation comes from the Latin *interrogates* but has a negative connotation and suggests undue verbal aggression. For that reason the term interrogation should not be used when dealing with suspects as the term *interview* is inclusive and does not have negative connotations. It is acknowledged that within many criminal justice systems the term interrogation is used when interviewing suspects.

Having established that interviewing is the process of obtaining information from victims, suspected perpetrators, and witnesses to the particular offense under investigation, there comes a time when the perpetrator moves from being a witness to a suspect. At that time the questioning moves from interview to interrogation, but the author posits that the goal remains the same: to objectively gather information (evidence) in order to secure a conviction in a court of law.

It may be argued that an interrogation is designed to match acquired information to a particular suspect to secure a confession. However, despite the commonsense belief that people do not confess to crimes they did not commit, 20% to 25% of all DNA exonerations involve innocent prisoners who had confessed (Kassin, 2008). A national study found that 84% of false confessions occurred after interrogations of 6 hours or longer and that the average duration was more than 16 hours (Drizen and Leo, 2004). The literature identifies that a confession is not required to obtain a conviction and that many confessions are false or obtained illegally through unethical procedures employed by the interviewer.

However, this is a problem for all criminal investigators because the unreliability of witness evidence through faulty memory recall is a problem, especially as it relates to eyewitness testimony. The literature review concerning the unreliability of eyewitness accounts has led to a United States Supreme Court ruling (*Perry v. New Hampshire* 10-8974) and in the United Kingdom by the decision of *Regina v. Turnbull* (1977). Bartlett (1932), Yuille and Cutshall (1986), Duke (2006), Liptak (2011), Vallas (2011), and Clare (2012) confirm the unreliability of eyewitness accounts and that "many factors that affect the accuracy of the eye witness identification are unrelated to police conduct" (*Perry v. New Hampshire*, 10-8974, p. 5).

Bartlett's (1932) theory of reconstructive memory is crucial to the understanding of the reliability of eyewitness testimony because memory recall is subject to personal interpretation dependent upon learned or cultural values. This problem has led researchers to attempt to devise methods for improving retrieval of memory. One of these methods relies upon cognitive psychology, a term that came into use with the publication of the book *Cognitive Psychology* by Ulric Neisser in 1967.

Cognitive psychology revolves around the notion that knowledge is required of the internal mental processes that allow an individual to survive in the social environment. Cognitive psychology focuses on the way humans process information, looking at how dissemination of information comes to an individual (stimuli), and how this dissemination process leads to various responses. Whereas psychologists are interested in the variables that mediate between stimulus/input and response/output, cognitive psychologists study internal processes including perception, attention, language, memory, and thought process (Neisser, 1967). Then it follows that all these factors are important when obtaining memory recall from a witness or suspect.

Interviewing of a Witness: The Cognitive Interview

The cognitive interview technique is a questioning technique used by the police to enhance retrieval of information from the witnesses' memory and involves a number of techniques (Fisher and Geiselman, 1992, 2010). There are a number of interviewing techniques that may be used however; the author argues that cognitive interviewing is one of the most effective interviewing methods although all interviewing techniques have proven benefits. In the cognitive interview a number of techniques are used to mentally stimulate the witness to recall events that may appear to be trivial but are of investigative value when used in conjunction to support other witness statements. The interviewer tries to *mentally reinstate the environmental and personal context of the crime* for the witnesses, perhaps by asking them about their general activities and feelings on the day. This could include sights, sounds, feelings and emotions, the weather, or anything that appears important to the witness. In addition, the witness will be asked to describe the incident from a *different perspective*, describing what they think other witnesses (or even the criminals themselves) might have seen.

Witnesses are encouraged to *report every detail*, even if they think that detail is trivial. In this way, apparently unimportant detail might act as a trigger for key information about the event. An effective technique is for the witness to recount the incident in a *different narrative order* because Fisher and Geiselman (1992, 2010) argue that people tend to recall recent events more clearly than others. Therefore, to exploit this trait witnesses should be encouraged to change the narrative order, and change of perceptive techniques aid recall because they reduce the witnesses' use of prior knowledge, expectations, or schema (McLeod, 2010).

The purpose of the interview is to obtain the truth, which will include evidence both for and against the accused suspect, and much of that evidence will be obtained from witnesses.

Witness Evaluation

Witnesses may be classified as enthusiastic, reluctant, passive, or aggressive, and each has different motivations and perceptions that influence his or her responses during an interview including nonverbal (body language) responses. The interviewer must understand that personality and character traits may be reflected in the person's response to questioning. Some witnesses may be reluctant or suspicious of the motives of the interviewer until such time as an empathetic rapport can be established. The information that is provided may be affected by other factors that influence all witnesses, such as age, physical characteristics, ethnicity, religion, and emotions. Whereas some witnesses may refuse to provide any information in an interview regardless of what they may know, due to real or perceived fears of retribution. There may be other barriers faced by the interviewer that must be overcome in order to successfully interview someone who has information that may be of value to the investigation. A potential witness will have their perception of events altered if they were under the influence of alcohol or drugs when they witnessed the alleged offense. In evaluating information provided by juveniles, consideration needs to be given not only to chronological age but also to the level of schooling and their understanding of right and wrong. The interviewing of an older person may also present a unique set of challenges, which may include cultural influences as well as the physical changes that can occur with aging which may affect memory and perception, as well as impairment of visual and auditory capabilities.

Changes in vision that are related to aging vary widely from person to person. These changes are not strictly dependent upon chronological age or general health. The eye is so constructed that excellent vision without glasses is sometimes maintained even in extreme old age. However, this is an exception. About three-fourths of all older women and over half of all older men experience moderate to severe changes in visual functions. Those 65 or older account for half of all legally blind persons in the United States. It is important to establish whether the witness was wearing glasses when describing the events they witnessed due to the unreliability of eyewitness accounts.

Often what a person genuinely believes they saw is the result of an auditory perception that made them look in a certain direction. What they then see is a resultant action. The brain rationally computes that certain actions must have occurred to produce that result. Eyewitness testimony is always questionable and very often totally unreliable although the witness is not intending to deceive the interviewer but to assist them. Hearing loss associated with a witness may also present the interviewer with a challenge. When interviewing someone with a hearing loss, investigators should gain the person's full attention, be at the right distance, and speak slowly and clearly. It may be appropriate to have another person to support that witness, either by being able to sign what you are saying or simply to support them through what can be a traumatic experience.

Language could also be a barrier that would require the use of an interpreter. The interpreter could advise upon the culture associated with that language, as that too may limit meaningful interaction between the interviewer and interviewee. In addition to the language, and the nuances of cultural and nonverbal communication (body language) from the ethnocentric view of the investigator may be misinterpreted (e.g., lack of eye contact). The interviewer must also judge the credibility and competency of a witness.

Credibility relates to that quality of a witness that renders his or her testimony worthy of belief. Credibility is distinguished from competency in that the latter is based on the assumption that a witness is qualified and will be permitted to testify. The competency of a witness describes a witness's personal qualifications to testify in court. Among the factors an investigator must evaluate in determining the competency of a witness include, but are not limited to, age, gender, ethnicity, religion, level of intelligence, mental state, relationship to individuals involved in the case, and background characteristics that might preclude the testimony of the witness from being heard in court.

What Is Evidence?

The question raised is what constitutes evidence. All evidence will be presented for the "due process of law," which is "a fundamental principle of fairness in all legal matters, both civil and criminal, especially in the courts. All legal procedures set by statute and court practice, including notice of rights, must be followed for each individual so that no prejudicial or unequal treatment will result" (Hill and Hill, 2002, p. 1).

Generally speaking, there are two main categories of evidence: *inculpatory* (causing blame to be imputed to) and *exculpatory* (applied to evidence that may justify or excuse an accused defendant's actions, and will tend to show the defendant is not guilty or has no criminal intent). Inculpatory evidence can be defined as evidence that has the power to be incriminating to the defendant. It is very powerful due to the fact that inculpatory evidence establishes guilt. Exculpatory evidence is opposite, having the power to clear a defendant of the blame. Both state and federal courts require exculpatory evidence to be presented to the defending counsel because the defendant's attorney can call for a rule of discovery. A rule of discovery allows the defendant's attorney to examine information possessed by the police and the prosecution. Both exculpatory and inculpatory evidence are important in criminal cases.

Direct and *indirect* are two more types of evidence. Direct evidence tends to prove facts without support and is usually gathered from sensory perceptions. An example of direct evidence would be to say, "I saw that man rob the bank at gunpoint." Indirect, or circumstantial, evidence does not directly prove the truth of a fact but may strongly point to a truth. An example of circumstantial evidence would be to say, "That man was talking about robbing the bank this morning. I heard him at the coffee shop." These two types of evidence have two very different meanings, but both are important.

Physical and documentary evidence are two more important types of evidence to understand. Physical evidence is any kind of real object associated with an investigation. Physical evidence is required to be physical, tangible items. Documentary evidence is different in the fact that it need not be the exact item. Documentary evidence is evidence that is of physical nature, but needs only to be an acceptable representation of the item. For example, an item considered to be physical evidence may be a murder weapon. The documentary evidence for the same item may be a forensic lab report or a picture of the weapon at the scene. Both physical and documentary evidence can be representing the same object, but the way in which the evidence is presented is different.

Evidence must be admissible in court. For this reason, tests of suitability exist to determine if it is admissible or not. The requirements for evidence to be considered admissible in court include that the evidence must be competent, relevant, and material. Evidence that would be considered competent means that it is sufficient to prove a fact and that it was obtained legally. Relevant evidence can be defined as evidence that is directly related to the problem under consideration. It deals with the event, the time of the event, and the people involved. The last requirement for admissible evidence is that it is considered material. This means that the evidence carries a bearing on the determination of the truth. Evidence must meet these requirements except when evidence is said to have been inevitably found lawfully.

Types of Evidence and Limitations

Evidence is simply every type of proof (verbal, written, charts, maps, models, photographs, and video) legally obtained and presented at a trial against an accused person. The totality of the evidence presented by the prosecution and the rebuttals of the defense attorney at the trial are intended to convince the judge and jury of alleged facts material to the case, beyond a reasonable doubt. The evidence must survive objections of opposing attorneys that it is irrelevant, immaterial, or violates rules against hearsay (statements made by a party not in court), and other technicalities (such as violations of *Miranda v. Arizona* [1966], exclusionary rule, and fruit of the poisonous tree).

The *Miranda warning* is an explanation of rights that must be given before any custodial interrogation, stemming largely from the Fifth Amendment privilege against self-incrimination. Without a Miranda warning or a valid waiver, statements might be inadmissible at trial under the exclusionary rule (e.g., they cannot be used as substantive evidence of guilt in criminal proceedings). (See *Miranda v. Arizona*, 384 U.S. 436 [1966].) This requirement, also called the Miranda rule, states that prior to the time of arrest and any interrogation of a person suspected of a crime, he/she must be told that he/she has the right to remain silent, the right to legal counsel, and the right to be told that anything he/she says can be used in court against him/her. Further, if the accused person confesses to the authorities, the prosecution must prove to the judge that the defendant was informed of these rights and knowingly waived them before the confession can be introduced in the defendant's criminal trial.

The *exclusionary rule* prevents the use of evidence gathered in violation of the United States Constitution. It applies to evidence gained from an unreasonable search or seizure in violation of the Fourth Amendment [see *Mapp v. Ohio*, 367 U.S. 643 [1961]), to improperly elicited self-incriminatory statements gathered in violation of the Fifth Amendment, and to evidence gained in situations where the inquiry violated the defendants' Sixth Amendment right to counsel (see *Miranda v. Arizona*, 384 U.S. 436 [1966]). The rule does not apply to civil cases, including deportation hearings (see *INS v. Lopez-Mendoza*, 468 U.S. 1032 [1984]).

If evidence that falls within the scope of the exclusionary rule led law enforcement to other evidence, which they would not otherwise have located, then the exclusionary rule applies to the evidence found subsequent to the excluded evidence as well. Such subsequent evidence has taken on the name of "fruit of the poisonous tree." Evidence secured by illegal means and in bad faith cannot be introduced in a criminal trial. The technical term is that it is "excluded" upon a motion to suppress made by the lawyer for the accused. It is based on the constitutional requirement that "no [person] can be deprived of life, liberty, or property, without due process of law" (Fifth Amendment to the Constitution, applied to the states by Fourteenth Amendment). A technical error in a search warrant made in good faith will not cause exclusion of the evidence obtained under that warrant.

The *fruit of the poisonous tree* is an extension of the exclusionary rule established in *Silverthorne Lumber Co. v. United States*, 251 U.S. 385 (1920). This doctrine holds that evidence gathered with the assistance of illegally obtained information must be excluded from trial. Therefore, if an illegal interrogation leads to the discovery of physical evidence, both the interrogation and the physical evidence obtained may be excluded, the interrogation because of the exclusionary rule, and the physical evidence because it is the "fruit" of the illegal interrogation and is therefore tainted evidence. This doctrine is subject to three important exceptions. The evidence will not be excluded (1) if it was discovered from a source independent of the illegal activity; (2) if its discovery was inevitable; or (3) if there is attenuation between the illegal activity and the discovery of the evidence.

The evidence presented can include written and oral testimony of witnesses, including experts on technical matters. It may be documentary, including public records, physical objects, and photographs or video evidence. However, the totality of the evidence presented must demonstrate the components of *mens rea* (guilty mind or criminal intent in committing the act) and *actus reus* (as an element of criminal responsibility, the wrongful act, or omission that comprises the physical components of a crime). Criminal statutes require proof of both *actus reus* and *mens rea* on the part of a defendant in order to establish criminal liability.

Direct or real evidence is tangible or evidence of a fact, a happening, or an action that requires no consideration to prove its existence, as compared to circumstantial evidence; whereas with *indirect evidence* this may be a photocopy, photograph, or model of an item that is no longer in existence and therefore cannot be produced to the court as direct evidence.

Circumstantial evidence is evidence that is intended to create belief by identifying one or more surrounding circumstances that logically lead to a conclusion of fact.

Demonstrative evidence relates to aids used to demonstrate or illustrate "real" evidence. These may be actual objects, illustrations (scene plan or photographs), and models used to clarify the facts for the judge and jury. The trial judge will determine the type of aid so that the impartiality of the evidence is balanced between legitimate aids and evidence intended to impact a juror's emotions, either for or against an accused person.

Hearsay evidence is second-hand evidence in which the witness is not telling what he/she knows personally, but what others have said to him/her, which is in effect simply gossip. The exception to hearsay evidence would be a *dying declaration*. This is the statement of a fatally injured person who is aware he/she is about to die, and verbally states the cause of the injuries sustained and the circumstances of such injuries. Although such evidence is hearsay, since the deceased person cannot testify in person, it is admissible based upon the theory that a dying person has no reason not to be truthful in recounting such circumstances.

An *exhibit* relates to any document or object (including a photograph) introduced as evidence during a trial. It may include a copy of a paper attached to a pleading (any legal paper filed in a lawsuit), declaration, affidavit or other document, which is referred to and incorporated into the main document.

Expert witness relates to an individual who is a specialist in a subject, often technical, who may present his/her expert opinion without having been a witness to any occurrence relating to the lawsuit or criminal case. It is an exception to the rule against giving an opinion in trial, provided that the expert is qualified by evidence of his/her expertise, training, and special knowledge.

Documentary evidence relates to any document (paper) that is presented and allowed as evidence in a trial or hearing, as distinguished from oral testimony.

Incompetent evidence relates to testimony, documents, or other items that one side attempts to present as evidence during trial, which the court finds (usually after objection by the opposition) are not admissible because they are irrelevant or immaterial to the issues under review.

Insufficient evidence relates to a decision by a trial judge, or an appeals court judge, that the prosecution in a criminal case, or a plaintiff in a lawsuit, has not proved the case because the attorney did not present enough evidence intended to convince the judge or jury of alleged facts material to the case, beyond a reasonable doubt.

Preponderance of the evidence relates to the weight of the evidence required in a civil (noncriminal) lawsuit for the trier of fact (jury or judge without a jury) to decide in favor of one side or the other; the meaning is somewhat subjective. This preponderance is based on the more convincing evidence and its probable truth or accuracy, and not on the amount of evidence.

Search warrant relates to a written order by a judge that permits a law enforcement officer to search a specified location, and may identify individuals (if known) and any articles intended to be seized (often speci-fied by type, such as "weapons" or "drugs and drug paraphernalia") that will be material evidence for a criminal prosecution. A search warrant can only be issued upon a sworn written statement of a law enforcement officer (including a prosecutor). The Fourth Amendment to the Constitution speci-fies: "no warrants shall issue, but upon probable cause, supported by oath or affirmation, and particularly describing the place to be searched and the persons or things to be seized." The Fourteenth Amendment applies the rule to the states. Evidence unconstitutionally seized cannot be used in court, nor can evidence traced through any illegal evidence.

Search and seizure relates to where there is an examination of a named individual's premises (residence, business, or vehicle) by law enforcement offi-cers looking for evidence of the commission of a crime. In that search the law enforcement officers are authorized to the taking (seizure and removal) of articles of evidential value (such as controlled narcotics, a pistol, or counterfeit bills). The basic question is whether the search and seizure were "unreasonable" under the Fourth Amendment to the Constitution, which provides: "The right of people to be secure in their persons, houses, papers, and effects, against unreasonable searches and seizures, shall not be violated." Therefore, searches and seizures must be under the authority of a search warrant or when the officer has solid facts that give him/her "probable cause" to believe there was evidence of a specific crime on the premises but no time to obtain a warrant. *Probable cause* is a "reasonable belief" that a crime has been committed or that evidence of a crime exists at the place being searched or that a suspect has committed a crime. Because a reasonable belief is a relatively nebulous con-cept, probable cause determinations are based, in part, on a judge's common sense as applied to the totality of the circumstances.

A definition of human trafficking has been given in an earlier chapter but it is important to understand what is required to identify, in domestic and international law, what constitutes a crime under that definition. It is traffick-ing of persons that has three constituent elements:

1. The act (what is done)—The act of human trafficking is the recruit-ment, transportation, transfer, harboring or receipt of persons.
2. The means (how the act is done)—Human traffickers coerce their victims through threats or use of force, violence, coercion, abduc-tion, fraud, deception, abuse of power, or the victim's vulnerability, or giving payments or benefits to a person who is much like a pimp and is in control of the victim.
3. The purpose (why it is done)—It is done for the sole purpose of exploitation, which would include exploiting the prostitution of oth-ers, sexual exploitation, forced labor, slavery or similar practices, and the removal of organs.

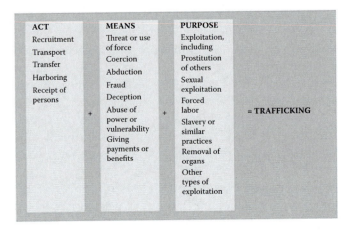

ACT	MEANS	PURPOSE	
Recruitment	Threat or use of force	Exploitation, including	
Transport	Coercion	Prostitution of others	
Transfer	Abduction	Sexual exploitation	
Harboring	Fraud	Forced labor	
Receipt of persons	Deception	Slavery or similar practices	= TRAFFICKING
+	Abuse of power or vulnerability +	Removal of organs	
	Giving payments or benefits	Other types of exploitation	

Figure 7.1 Criminal elements of human trafficking.

To ascertain whether a particular circumstance constitutes trafficking in persons, consider the definition of trafficking in the Trafficking in Persons Protocol* and the constituent elements of the offense, as defined by relevant domestic legislation. A reference to Figure 7.1 and the constituent components of the Act, means, and purpose will quickly identify a trafficking offense.

Elements and Characteristics of Human Trafficking

The Trafficking Victims Protection Act of 2000 (TVPA) defines "severe forms of trafficking in persons" as follows:

- Sex trafficking—The recruitment, harboring, transportation, provision, or obtaining of a person for the purpose of a commercial sex act, in which a commercial sex act is induced by force, fraud, or coercion, or in which the person forced to perform such an act is under the age of 18 years.
- Labor trafficking—The recruitment, harboring, transportation, provision, or obtaining of a person for labor or services, through the use

---

* The Trafficking in Persons Protocol refers to a UN document titled the U.N. Protocol to Prevent, Suppress, and Punish Trafficking in Persons, Especially Women and Children, Supplementing the United Nations Convention against Transnational Organized Crime, published by the Organization for Security and Co-operation in Europe (15 November 2000).

of force, fraud or coercion for the purpose of subjection to involuntary servitude, peonage, debt bondage or slavery. (U.S. Committee for Refugees and Immigrants*)†

A major investigative dilemma that is apparent with human trafficking is that any person could be a participant (Beck, Cohen, and Kyckelhahn, 2009). Those involved in human trafficking are legal immigrants who maintain close contacts with their country of origin and are often family members or members of the victim's own ethnic or national community. The trafficker may be fluent in both their national language as well as the source or destination country language and that allows them an advantage. The common language and ethnic background initiates a relationship with the potential victim. The Federal Bureau of Investigation (2006, p.1) listed the following as criterion for traffickers:

- International criminal syndicates with "diversified trafficking portfolios" that smuggle drugs and guns along with people and use the same routes for all three.
- "Mom-and-pop" family operations that often have extended family on both sides of the border and lure victims by striking up romantic relationships.
- Independently owned businesses with contractors/agents who provide laborers for menial jobs; and individuals, such as diplomats or foreign business executives who arrive with "servants," and sometimes even neighbors and friends of the victim.

The major cities where human trafficking is most prevalent have identifiable characteristics in that they are close to international borders, they have extensive highway routes for victim dispersal, a growing immigration population, a proximity to large universities, and international corporations (Davis, 2006). That profile identifies cities, such as Detroit, that have been identified as a source, destination, and transit point for human trafficking incidents. According to Detroit Free Press, Metro Detroit is becoming a

---

* The U.S. Committee for Refugees and Immigrants (USCRI) has been helping people flee war and persecution since 1911. The USCRI addresses the needs and rights of persons in forced or voluntary migration worldwide by advancing fair and humane public policy, facilitating and providing direct professional services, and promoting the full participation of migrants in community life. Through its network of resettlement field offices and partner organizations, USCRI provides refugees and immigrants across the United States with the support, services and opportunities they need to rebuild their lives and enrich their communities. (Source: See http://www.uscrirefugees.org/2010Website/2_About%20Us/2_2_1_Albany/USCRI_Albany_Internships_2011_12.pdf.)

† United Nations Office on Drugs and Crime, "Human trafficking," http://www.unodc.org/unodc/en/human-trafficking/what-is-human-trafficking.html?ref=menuside.

major hub for human trafficking. Authorities have stated that the frequency of incidents of human trafficking in the area is increasing at nearly the same rate as the illegal drug trade (Evans, 2014). Major conferences and sporting events attract human traffickers and their victims, who are forced into prostitution at these venues (Zezima and Henry, 2014).

Awareness/Understanding of the Problem

A major challenge that law enforcement faces in the wake of human trafficking is the hidden nature of the crime, making it very difficult to identify victims. Public education is important, because at present victims are not recognizable as victims thorough their social interactions within their communities. The support of the victim is important because their personal information will complement the circumstantial evidence that will support a prosecution.

There is a duty of care for the victim to prevent secondary victimization through the legal process. Many of the international victims of human trafficking are brought into the United States legally and illegally. Their documentation, passport, and visa may be legal, but many are false. The trafficker will control access to all personal documentation, thereby controlling the victims' movement and denying them their human rights. The illegality associated with the victims of human trafficking provides for a clandestine existence for the victims, who are often hidden within their own ethnic community.

In many victims' country of origin, the government and government agencies, including law enforcement, are corrupt. The victim often believes that their destination country also has a corrupt government and associated agencies, and these fears are reaffirmed by the victim's captors as a control mechanism (Bales and Soodalter, 2009). Victims become afraid to turn to authority figures or anyone for help for fear that their perpetrators will seek retribution against them or their family members, or that they will be deported. There is a lack of trust because of what victims may have experienced in their own countries or within their own ethnic community in which they assumed they would be supported and helped. The lack of language skills relating to the destination country or the opportunity to learn that language is also a controlling mechanism because the victim will have to rely upon their captors for survival. The physical and mental control of the victim will be a barrier to their rehabilitation because of low self-esteem, their limited movement within society, and their compliance to obeying their captor's demands. In some instances this interdependency initiates a psychological phenomenon known as Stockholm syndrome.

Many communities do have the potential to come in contact with victims of this clandestine business because victims of trafficking are at risk of injuries as victims of domestic violence, assaults, rape, and associated health issues that may prevent their captor's selling, or exploiting, the victims' services. Victims frequently contract sexually transmitted infections or become pregnant. Therefore, health clinic workers or emergency room personnel are often first responders and should be trained to assess whether someone is a victim of human trafficking. In addition, victims could potentially be identified if they gain admission to homeless or battered women shelters. Many victims are initially identified by federal and local law enforcement personnel (Caliber Associates, 2007), and are referred to nongovernment organizations and other service providers as social victims, but not as trafficked victims.

A significant challenge to identifying victims of human trafficking is that many have been historically identified as undocumented immigrants. They may have come to attention through prostitution or other illegal activity, and are liable to arrest, detention, and possibly deportation. Law enforcement personnel may also come into contact with victims of human trafficking through the investigation of other crimes (Clawson, Dutch, and Cummings, 2006). Victims of sex trafficking have the greatest chance of being identified through arrests made by law enforcement pursuant to state prostitution and vice statutes (Clawson and Dutch, 2008).

It has been identified through data that the general public is skeptical that human trafficking exists in today's society and, in particular, in their communities. There is a need for greater public awareness and a comprehensive understanding of the crime of human trafficking and its victims. Even when there have been many attempts to raise awareness, the confusion of who is a victim still remains, along with the lack of belief that it happens in the United States domestically and that not all of human trafficking is overseas (Clawson and Dutch, 2008). The literature identifies that estimates of human trafficking have focused almost exclusively on international trafficking victims (Laczko and Gozdziak, 2005), and this creates a diversion from the problem of domestic trafficking especially in the United States.

It is necessary to also focus on domestic victims (e.g., U.S. citizens, legal permanent residents, or illegal immigrants), male victims, and labor trafficking (especially single-victim domestic servitude cases) is recognized as a continuing contributing factor to the misconceptions surrounding this crime. Working within the community policing paradigm, public awareness is a key factor for the investigator because the public can provide the evidence to support the prosecution.

Identifying Victims

Although the clandestine nature of human trafficking and the illegal activities the victims are forced to undertake minimize the social interactions of the victims with their geographic community, many sectors within those communities have the potential to come in contact with a victim of human trafficking. Victims of sex trafficking are at risk for the same types of injuries suffered by victims of domestic violence and rape. The victims frequently contract sexually transmitted infections or become pregnant. Those victims of labor trafficking may experience injuries during their employment, physical abuse by their traffickers, and health issues caused by their environment. These may include, but are not limited to, poor nutrition, hygiene, dental problems, diabetes, and other ailments that require medical intervention and help. Therefore, law enforcement and service providers identify health/dental/clinic workers and emergency room personnel as sources of victim referrals. Other referral sources include domestic violence and sexual assault shelters, crisis hotlines, social workers, community- and faith-based organizations, religious/community leaders, good samaritans/citizens, school personnel, business owners, postal workers, and neighbors. These represent individuals within the community who are able to provide interdiction for the victim, but often with little training or experience (Clawson and Dutch, 2008).

It is acknowledged that law enforcement is recognized as the group with the greatest chance of identifying victims. Law enforcement is continually introducing new strategies, such as Innocents Lost, Internet Crimes Against Children, and Anti-Trafficking Task Forces, in order to identify cases. It has been found that victims are identified through the investigation of other crimes associated with human trafficking, such as kidnapping, prostitution, assault, domestic violence, and homicide (Clawson and Dutch, 2008).

Controlling the Victim

"Too often, police, prosecutors, judges, and policymakers assume a victim has free will if she has the physical ability to walk away. This assumption is wholly inconsistent with what is known about the nature of pimping and sex trafficking. The use of force, fraud, and coercion is pervasive but often overlooked" (U.S. Department of State, 2011, p. 1).

The literature identifies that a large percentage of victims of human trafficking are for the purposes of commercial sexual or labor exploitation (Thomas-Whitfield, 2011). That exploitation is maintained through the use of fear, violence, sexual assault, fraud, or coercion to control the victim. Many victims, including minors, of human trafficking are forced to work in prostitution or the sex entertainment industry. In addition, the Trafficking Victims Protection Act, 22 U.S.C. 7101(11), identifies that sex trafficking exposes victims to serious health risks. Women and children trafficked in the sex industry are exposed to deadly diseases, including HIV and AIDS. It is acknowledged that trafficking also occurs in forms of labor exploitation, such as domestic servitude, often in industries such as restaurant, janitorial, factory, or agricultural work. Traffickers use various techniques to instill fear in victims and to control and keep them enslaved. That fear can impede a criminal investigation with the victim being noncompliant with law enforcement personnel.

The Polaris Project (2010) identifies human trafficking as a form of modern-day slavery where people profit from the control and exploitation of others. As defined under U.S. federal law, victims of human trafficking include children involved in the sex trade, adults aged 18 or over who are coerced or deceived into commercial sex acts, and anyone forced into different forms of labor or services, such as domestic workers held in a home or farmworkers forced to labor against their will. The factors that each of these situations has in common are elements of force, fraud, or coercion that are used to control people. Then, that control is tied to inducing someone into commercial sex acts, or labor or services. Human trafficking is considered to be one of the fastest growing criminal industries in the world on a par with drug trafficking.

The Federal Bureau of Investigation (2006) identified that victims are recruited primarily by fraud, enforced with violence. The commonality with victimization is a vulnerability that attracts the perpetrator to the individual. This allows for victims to be lured away from family and friends by the promise of a better life, often in another country. For traffickers, there is never a shortage of victims especially when economic hardships allow for people to become eager for higher paying jobs that may lead to additional opportunities in distant cities and nations. The majority of victims are found to be women and children who seem to be the most vulnerable in trying to better themselves.

The various types of work that victims may be forced to do are potentially both legal and illegal. Many victims have been found doing everything from prostitution to exotic dancing, street peddling, housekeeping, childcare, construction, and landscaping. Some victims are forced to work in restaurants and factories, and are drawn into servile marriages and various criminal activities due to control of their handlers, guardians, or traffickers.

Victims are controlled in many different ways ranging from physical assaults that can include, but are not limited to, beatings, burnings, rapes, and starvation. The psychological control is through emotional abuse to destroy self-esteem, through isolation, as well as their introduction to drugs and subsequent drug dependency. There may be threats against family members in the victim's home country; and financially through debt bondage, and the ever-present threat of deportation back to the environment from which they fled. That deportation also holds the threat of becoming a secondary victim of trafficking. Victims are made to feel inferior because of the psychological control of their handlers; they are not treated as a human being but simply as a saleable commodity. Many victims are proficient in their native language but lack of other language skills limits their self-esteem, and provides additional control for their handler who will control their documentation (passport, birth certificate, and personal papers) and all aspects of their lives. As has already been acknowledged this psychological manipulation is fertile ground to initiate Stockholm syndrome.

That total control makes it difficult for victims to take the initiative to escape from their environment because they are often invisible within the society they are placed. In their home country often the police and other agencies are corrupt and that will be the victim's perception of the destination countries police and other agencies. Therefore, with the fear of deportation and in a country where the victim may not speak the language, victims are helpless to improve their personal situation unless there is law enforcement interdiction on their behalf. One aspect associated with deportation of victims is that upon their repatriation, to the same environment they fought to leave, there is the possibility that they may once again become a victim of human trafficking.

Challenges of the Investigation

The primary challenge to combat human trafficking is to attempt to contest the view that the patriarchal paradigm is an appropriate societal model for the 21st century. A patriarchal society is one whereby men are the decision makers and hold positions of power and prestige, and have the power to define reality and common situations. Patriarchy can be enforced in a variety of ways, including intimidation of women through violence, sexual assault, and other forms of harassment, and the discrediting of their efforts to organize and resist. Patriarchal societies are typically more authoritarian and rely heavily on rational-legal modes of organization, show stronger military implication, and more reliance on police repression to impose authority. It is a society that tends to hold contempt for women and for her attempts to emancipate herself. The patriarchal paradigm allows for women to be viewed as second-class citizens, devoid of any human rights, and therefore females from such a society are viewed simply as a commodity to be traded. Therefore, there has to be an educational program to target source, transit, and destination countries to change that patriarchal society into a more inclusive society that acknowledges and values the women's role in their society.

There has to be domestic and international interagency cooperation for any criminal investigation. The literature has identified that the community has a role to play in identifying victims. Often that information identifies that more than one agency (e.g., law enforcement, medical, schools, social services, and religious organizations) is involved, either directly or indirectly, with the victim so there has to be effective protocols to share information for the benefit of the victim.

One of the most common challenges law enforcement faces in the wake of human trafficking is the hidden nature of the crime, making it very difficult to identify victims. The support of the victim is important because their personal information will complement the circumstantial evidence that will support a prosecution. There is a duty of care for the victim to prevent secondary victimization through the legal process. Many of the international victims of human trafficking are brought into the United States legally and illegally. Their documentation, passport, and visa may be legal, but many are false. The trafficker will control access to all personal documentation, thereby controlling the victims' movement and denying them their human rights. The illegality associated with the victims of human trafficking provides for a clandestine existence for the victim.

A significant challenge to identifying victims of human trafficking is that many have been historically identified as undocumented immigrants. They may have come to attention through prostitution or other illegal activity and are liable to arrest, detention, and possibly deportation.

When it comes to investigating human trafficking, law enforcement in order to be effective in its response cannot merely rely on the application of law in individual cases but it has to depend upon all of the complicated avenues of human trafficking (Clawson and Dutch, 2008). The literature review identifies that victims are the primary source of evidence in human trafficking investigations; therefore, securing victim cooperation is critical. However, studies that examined law enforcement responses to human trafficking identified victim cooperation as one of the most common challenges faced by law enforcement (Clawson et al., 2006; Farrell, 2011; Farrell, McDevitt, and Fahy, 2010; Farrell et al., 2012). The Federal Bureau of Investigation estimates that 70 percent of victims fail to cooperate with the investigation. However, it is the noncooperation and fearful behavior of the victim that can be one of the most important indicators of the possibility of a human trafficking offense. It is believed that victims do not cooperate with law enforcement agencies due to either the fear of retaliation directed at them or their family, and a distrust of the criminal justice system (Bales and Lize, 2007). It is important that trust is established for the victim and witnesses during an empathetic interview in order to obtain a full and comprehensive factual account. Issues to be addressed include culture and language, but these can be overcome. However, overcoming gender issues can be problematic. As with many victims of sexual crimes, women and child victims may be emotionally traumatized and experience shame, embarrassment, or a belief that they will be considered socially unacceptable to the rest of society because of their experience. Males, particularly those from a patriarchal society and associated culture, may not want to admit their victimization because they fear that their disclosure of losing control of their lives may lead to perceptions of diminished masculinity. It is for these reasons that the victims may prefer to confide to law enforcement personnel and service providers of the same gender (Bales and Lize, 2007).

Foreign Governments: Denial or Complicity

Dishonest government officials in some source, transit, and destination countries add to the growth of the human trafficking industry and provide a sanctuary for the criminals involved. While most governments do not promote trafficking, they often fail to initiate the domestic or international laws. The full force of the law due is not implemented due to the fact that human trafficking ties in with many of the other industries of the nation such as sex tourism. In order to fully deal with the problem of human trafficking within specific countries, the social and economic issues must be addressed. The Protocol* is an avenue and can achieve greatness when it comes to providing clear definitions of terms and aspects of human trafficking, but these definitions contain within them many powerful terms that can be interpreted differently by varying legal agents and states (Kuersten, 2011). The differentiation can be seen in the beginning of Article 3, Paragraph a, as defined in an earlier chapter. The various terms being used such as recruitment, harboring, and deception can be considered loaded and each term should be then broken into one concise definition and meaning. These problems when it comes to defining will lead to a much broader problem of interstate coordination (Kuersten, 2011). One of the key limitations for the Trafficking Protocol is the underlying fact that each state may vary in their definitions and reactions to what it contains or should contain.

Human trafficking is a global problem. Samant (2013) identifies the top 10 countries for human trafficking (source, transit, and destination) as Bangladesh, Brazil, Haiti, Pakistan, India, Sri Lanka, Nepal, Uganda, Ghana, and China. The United Nations has identified every country in the world as an origin country (i.e., source), a transit country, or a destination country for human trafficking. United Nations Office on Drugs and Crime (UNODC) data identifies trafficking of human beings from 127 countries to be exploited in 137 countries. The regions that are main source areas have been identified as Africa, Asia, Central and Eastern Europe, former Eastern Bloc and Soviet

* This refers to the Protocol to Prevent, Suppress, and Punish Trafficking in Persons, Especially Women and Children, Supplementing the United Nations Convention against Transnational Organized Crime (2000). "The States Parties to this Protocol: Declaring that effective action to prevent and combat trafficking in persons, especially women and children, requires a comprehensive international approach in the countries of origin, transit and destination that includes measures to prevent such trafficking, to punish the traffickers and to protect the victims of such trafficking, including by protecting their internationally recognized human rights" (preamble; see http://www.uncjin.org/Documents/Conventions/dcatoc/final_documents_2/convention_%20traff_eng.pdf).

Union countries, Latin America, and the Caribbean. The data identified that the highest origin countries include Albania, Belarus, Bulgaria, China, Lithuania, Nigeria, Republic of Moldovia, Romania, Russian Federation, Thailand, and the Ukraine. All these countries are also transit and destination countries, but the main destination areas are identified as Western Europe, Western Africa, Asia, Arab Nations, and North America. The highest destination countries are identified as Belgium, Germany, Greece, Israel, Italy, Japan, Netherlands, Thailand, Turkey, and the United States (Freedom Project, 2013). The global problem identifies the failure of countries to address the problem and put in place investigative protocols that transcend cultural, religious, and political obstacles in the search for justice for the victims.

There are other countries involved, as the U.S. State Department's 2011 Trafficking in Persons Report assessed efforts by 184 governments worldwide to fight sexual exploitation, forced labor, and modern-day slavery (Zhang, 2007). The report identified that human trafficking is flourishing in the Democratic Republic of Congo, North Korea, Saudi Arabia, and Iran, with the countries' governments doing little to combat it (Dougherty, 2011). In 2013 the U.S. State Department identified China, Russia, and Uzbekistan as among the worst offenders when it comes to human trafficking, joining Iran, North Korea, Cuba, Sudan, and Zimbabwe on the bottom tier of the U.S. human trafficking rankings (Khazan, 2013).

Addressing the Problem

There has to be an agreed national and international methodology in order that intelligence-sharing protocols can assist in national and multinational planning to provide strategies for effective international interdiction and prevention initiatives. Training is a key area and several recommendations have been identified.

1. The creation of training courses in human trafficking for government personnel. This will increase their ability to recognize human trafficking indications while engaged in their employment.
2. Increase the awareness of local, state, and federal officials of their requirement to notify Health and Human Services when they discover that a foreign national under the age of 18 may be a victim of human trafficking.
3. The training of local and state law enforcement agencies and personnel to recognize the indications of human trafficking. In addition, provide training with guidance on beginning a human trafficking investigation and get cooperation from other agencies that may have involvement.

4. Provide human trafficking training to other agencies and nongovernmental organizations who come into contact with vulnerable persons, crime victims, immigrants, runaways, and homeless in order to recognize the indicators of human trafficking.

Prosecution

There is a need to identify obstacles that slow or prevent the identification, investigation, and prosecution of human trafficking. In addition, there is a requirement for national and international governments and agencies to develop strategies to overcome identified obstacles (LeBlanc, Valdes, and Helber, 2011).

Trafficking Victims

1. There is a need to identify and address any barriers to victim identification during the investigative process.
2. There has to be agreed protocol in order to meet the needs of human trafficking victims regardless of national origin.
3. One aspect often overlooked is the requirement to increase the support for reunification efforts for the victims and their families. This includes victims who have family in their country of origin and want to be reunited with them in the United States and for those who want to be repatriated to their country of origin.
4. The U.S. Department of Health and Human Services Unaccompanied Refugee Minor program capacity needs enhancing. This includes bed space availability, language, culture, and supporting foster care placements.

Summary

The U.S. State Department has published a detailed examination of the issue, ranking every major country across the globe (Dougherty, 2011). The literature review has identified that human trafficking provides for myriad forms of enslavement, and that provides a challenge for investigators due to the numbers involved (Banks and Kyckelhahn, 2011; Rogers, 2011; Zhang, 2007). Over a decade ago estimates by the United Nations identified that up to 200 million women and girls are demographically "missing" (Diamantopoulou, 2000). The same literature review also identified that issues relating to culture and the place of women and their real and perceived role within some societies remain problematic for investigators. If the predominately patriarchal society and ensuing culture identifies women as property of males and does not see their treatment of women as inappropriate and against human rights issues, it will be difficult to obtain a consensus of opinion that condemns such treatment. The global problem identifies the failure of countries to address the problem and put in place investigative protocols that transcend cultural, religious, and political obstacles in the search for justice for the victims.

This chapter has reviewed aspects of human trafficking from the perspective of a criminal investigation. That investigation will have a global component because of the movement of victims across national and international borders. The primary focus will be to obtain evidence from the identified victim primarily through empathetic cognitive interviews. The additional evidence required has been identified and the problems associated with obtaining that evidence in an ethical manner, without causing secondary victimization through the criminal justice system, remains a challenge. This will require an understanding and awareness of the problem of human trafficking and the associated crimes that control the victim allowing them to often become invisible within their community. The challenges of the investigation are numerous and include, but are not limited to, the failure of intelligence sharing protocols, cultural and language barriers, fear of the investigative procedures, lack of forensic evidence, and often the psychological barrier provided by the victim adhering to the Stockholm syndrome.

The literature review identified that human trafficking was a global problem (Territo and Kirkham, 2010), but that it was not delineated by culture, religion, or ethnicity (United Nations Development Program, 2005). The literature review identified that human trafficking is a global problem and therefore must be acknowledged and addressed by the global community. The primary evidence comes from the victim so the investigative process must focus upon the victim. There will have to be interagency cooperation to assist victims in their rehabilitation into society without them being stigmatized or deported to their country of origin and the environment they were attempting to escape. The secondary focus must be to present evidence of the offense of human trafficking. In addition, evidence must be presented to include the other crimes, for example, conspiracy, assault, rape, and associated crimes used to control the victims of human trafficking. The law, both domestically and internationally, must have serious consequences for all those involved in trafficking if it is to act as deterrent.

Key Terms

cognitive interview	human trafficking
criminal investigation	interview/interrogation
evidence	witness evaluation

Review Questions

1. How can a criminal investigation be categorized?
2. What stated case in the United States concerns the unreliability of eyewitness accounts?
3. What is the objective of a cognitive interview?
4. What are the two main categories of evidence?
5. What were the four witness classifications identified by the author?

References

Banks, D., and Kyckelhahn, T. (2011). *Characteristics of Suspected Human Trafficking Incidents, 2008–2010* (NCJ 233732). Retrieved January 28, 2014, from http://www.bjs.gov/index.cfm?ty=pbdetail&iid=2372.

Bales, K., and Lize, S. (2007). *Investigating Human Trafficking: Challenges, lessons learned, and best practices.* Retrieved November 2, 2011, from http://findarticles.com/p/articles/mi_m2194/is_4_76/ai_n19039324/pg_2/?tag=content;col1.

Bales, K., and Soodalter, R. (2009). *The Slave Next Door: Human Trafficking and Slavery in America Today.* London, England: University of California Press.

Bartlett, F. C. (1932). *Remembering: A Study in Experimental and Social Psychology.* Cambridge: Cambridge University Press.

Beck, A. J., Cohen, T. H., and Kyckelhahn, T. (2009). *Characteristics of Suspected Human Trafficking Incidents, 2007–2008.* Retrieved September 15, 2011, from http://bjs.ojp.usdoj.gov/index.cfm?ty=pbdetail&iid=550.

Brown, Michael F. (2001). *Criminal Investigation: Law & Practice.* New York: Butterworth Heinemann.

Caliber Associates. (2007). *Evaluation of Comprehensive Service for Victims of Trafficking: Key Findings and Lessons Learned.* Final report submitted to the National Institute of Justice, U.S. Department of Justice.

Clare, Aileen P. (2012). Is eyewitness testimony inherently unreliable? American Bar Association. Retrieved November 18, 2013, from apps.americanbar.org/litigation/committees/trialevidence/articles/winterspring2012-0512-eyewitness-testimony-unreliable.html.

Clawson, H., and Dutch, N. (2008). *Identifying Victims of Human Trafficking: Inherent Challenges and Promising Strategies from the Field.* Retrieved December 5, 2011, from http://aspe.hhs.gov/hsp/07/humantrafficking/IdentVict/ib.htm.

Clawson, H., Dutch, N., and Cummings, M. (2006). *Law Enforcement Response to Human Trafficking and the Implications for Victims: Current Practices and Lessons Learned.* National Institute of Justice. Washington, DC: Government Printing Office.

Davis, K. Y. S. (2006). *Human Trafficking and Modern Day Slavery in Ohio.* Washington, DC: Polaris Project.

Dempsey, J. (2003) *Introduction to Investigations.* Belmont, CA: Wadsworth/Thompson.

Detroit Free Press. (2014). Super Bowl on guard for human trafficking criminals. Retrieved January 28, 2014, from http://www.freep.com/article/20140118/NEWS07/301180069/Super-Bowl-on-guard-for-human-trafficking-criminals.

Diamantopoulou, Anna. (2000). Violence against women: zero tolerance. International conference. Closing of the European Campaign Lisbon, Centro de Congressos de Lisboa, May 4–6. http://europa.eu/rapid/press-release_SPEECH-00-161_en.htm.

Dougherty, Jill. (2011). State Department report ranks countries on human trafficking. Retrieved February 13, 2014, from http://www.cnn.com/2011/POLITICS/06/27/human.trafficking/.

Drizen, Steven A., and Leo, Richard A. (2004). The Problem of False Confessions in the Post-DNA World. *North Carolina Law Review,* pp. 841–1004. Retrieved January 13, 2014, from http://web.williams.edu/Psychology/Faculty/Kassin/files/drizenl.leo.04.pdf.

Duke, Steven B. (2006). Eyewitness testimony doesn't make it true: A commentary by Steven B. Duke. Retrieved November 18, 2013, from www.law.yale.edu/news/2727.htm.

Evans, Vanessa. (2014). Human trafficking becoming a growing issue in Metro Detroit. Retrieved January 28, 2014, from http://news.yahoo.com/human-trafficking-becoming-growing-issue-metro-detroit-201900282.html.

Farrell, Amy. (2011). Improving law enforcement identification and response to human trafficking. In John Winterdyk, Phillip Reichel, and Benjamin Perrin (eds.), *Human Trafficking, International Issues and Perspectives.* New York, NY: Taylor & Francis.

Farrell, Amy, McDevitt, Jack, and Fahy, Stephanie. (2010). Where are all the victims? Understanding the determinants of official identification of human trafficking incidents. *Criminology and Public Policy* 9(2): 201–233.

Farrell, A., Owens, C., McDevitt, J., Dank, M., Pfeffer, R., Adams, W., and Fahy, S. (2012). *Identifying Challenges to Improve the Investigation and Prosecution of State and Local Human Trafficking Cases.* Washington, DC: National Institute of Justice. Retrieved December 15, 2012, from https://www.ncjrs.gov/pdffiles1/nij/grants/238795.pdf.

Federal Bureau of Investigation. (2006). Human Trafficking: An Intelligence Report. Retrieved November 18, 2013 from http://www.fbi.gov/news/stories/2006/june/humantrafficking_061206

Fisher, R. P., and Geiselman, R. E. (1992). *Memory Enhancing Techniques for Investigative Interviewing: The Cognitive Interview.* Springfield, IL: Charles C. Thomas.

Fisher, R. P., and Geiselman, R. E. (2010). The cognitive interview method of conducting police interviews: Eliciting extensive information and promoting therapeutic jurisprudence. *International Journal of Law and Psychiatry* 33:321–328.

Freedom Project. (2013). Human trafficking affects every country in the world. Retrieved February 13, 2014, from http://www.thefreedomproject.org/human-trafficking/.

Geiselman, R. E., Fisher, R. P., MacKinnon, D. P., and Holland, H. L. (1985). Eyewitness memory enhancement in the police interview: Cognitive retrieval mnemonics versus hypnosis. *Journal of Applied Psychology* 70(2): 401–412.

Gilbert, James N. (2010). *Criminal Investigation,* 8th ed. Upper Saddle River, NJ: Prentice Hall.

Hill, Gerald N., and Hill, Kathleen T. (2002). *The People's Law Dictionary*. New York: Fine Communications Publisher. Retrieved November 24, 2013, from http://dictionary.law.com/.

INS v. Lopez-Mendoza, 468 U.S. 1032 (1984).

Kassin, Saul M. (2008). False Confessions Causes, Consequences, and Implications for Reform. *Current Directions in Psychological Science* 17(4): 249–253.

Khazan, Olga. (2013). A fascinating map of the worst countries for modern slavery. Retrieved February 13, 2014, from http://www.theatlantic.com/international/archive/2013/06/a-fascinating-map-of-the-worst-countries-for-modern-slavery/277037/.

Kuersten, A., (2011). *Prosecuting human traffickers*. Retrieved December 2, 2011, from http://www.ungift.org/doc/knowledgehub/resource-centre/The_Beaver_Online_Prosecuting_human_traffickers.pdf.

Laczko, F., and Gozdziak, E. (eds.). (2005). *Data and Research on Human Trafficking: A Global Survey*. Geneva, Switzerland: International Organization for Migration.

Lasley, James, and Guskos, Nikos. (2014). *Criminal Investigations*. Boston: Pearson.

LeBlanc, S., Valdes, M., and Helber, S. (2011). Differing laws on human trafficking impede U.S. crackdown. *The Charleston Gazette*, December 1. Retrieved December 3, 2011, from http://wvgazette.com/News/201112010178.

Liptak, Adam. (2011). In case of eyewitness vs. alibi, a question of lawyers' competence. *New York Times*, May 2. Retrieved December 15, 2012, from http://www.nytimes.com/2011/05/03/us/03bar.html.

Lyman, Michael. (2014). *Criminal Investigations*. Boston: Pearson.

Mapp v. Ohio, 367 U.S. 643 (1961).

Miranda v. Arizona (1966) 384 U.S. 436, 10 Ohio Misc. 9, 86 S. Ct. 1602, 16 L. Ed. 2d 694 (1966).
  Brief fact summary—The defendants offered incriminating evidence during police interrogations without prior notification of their rights under the Fifth Amendment of the United States Constitution. Synopsis of rule of law—Government authorities need to inform individuals of their Fifth Amendment constitutional rights prior to an interrogation following an arrest. http://www.casebriefs.com/blog/law/criminal-procedure/criminal-procedure-keyed-to-israel/police-interrogation-and-confessions/miranda-v-arizona-2/.

McLeod, S. A. (2010). *Cognitive Interview*. Retrieved November 24, 2013, from http://www.simplypsychology.org/cognitive-interview.html.

National Center for Victims of Crime. (2008). The criminal justice system. http://www.victimsofcrime.org/help-for-crime-victims/get-help-bulletins-for-crime-victims/the-criminal-justice-system.

Neisser, Ulric. (1967). *Cognitive Psychology*. East Norwalk, CT: Appleton-Century-Crofts.

Perry v. New Hampshire, 10-8974, Supreme Court of the United States. Retrieved November 18, 2013, from http://www.americanbar.org/content/dam/aba/publishing/previewbriefs/Other_Brief_Updates/10-8974_petitioneramcuapa.pdf.

Polaris Project. (2010). Human trafficking. Retrieved October 1, 2011, from http://www.polarisproject.org/human-trafficking.

Regina v. Turnbull and another PNLD REF NO C1417 CASE YEAR1976 REPORTING REF (1977) 1 QB 224

Rogers, Simon. (2011) Human trafficking: How the US State Department ranks your country. *The Guardian: London*. Retrieved February 13, 2014, from http://www.theguardian.com/news/datablog/2011/jun/27/human-trafficking-us-state-department.

Samant, Shreya. (2013). Top 10 countries infamous for human trafficking. Retrieved February 13, 2014, from http://listdose.com/top-10-countries-infamous-for-human-trafficking/.

Silverthorne Lumber Co. v. United States, 251 U.S. 385 (1920).

Territo, L., and Kirkham, G. (2010). *International Sex Trafficking of Women & Children: Understanding the Global Epidemic*. Flushing, NY: Looseleaf Law Publications.

Thomas-Whitfield, Chandra. (2011). Justice Department report sheds light on human trafficking stats. Retrieved January 28, 2014, from http://jjie.org/justice-department-report-sheds-lights-on-human-trafficking-stats/.

United Nations Office on Drugs and Crime. (2006) *Policing: Crime Investigation, Criminal Justice Assessment Toolkit*. New York: United Nations. http://www.unodc.org/documents/justice-and-prison-reform/cjat_eng/3_Crime_Investigation.pdf/

United Nations Development Program (UNDP). (2005). Cultural liberty in today's diverse world. *Human Development Report*.

U.S. Department of Justice. (2005). Assessment of U.S. activities to combat trafficking in persons. Washington, DC.

U.S. Department of State. (2011). Trafficking in persons report. Office to Monitor and Combat Trafficking in Persons, Washington, DC. Retrieved December 18, 2012 http://www.justice.gov/eoir/vll/country/trafficking/2011_report/TIP_report_2011.pdf.

Vallas, George. (2011). A survey of federal and state standards for the admission of expert testimony on the reliability of eyewitnesses. *American Journal of Criminal Law* 39(1): 97–146.

Yuille, J. C., and Cutshall, J. L. (1986). A case study of eyewitness memory of a crime. *Journal of Applied Psychology* 71:291–301.

Weston, P. B., and Lushbaugh, C. A. (2003). *Criminal Investigations: Basic Perspectives*. New York: Prentice Hall.

Zezima, Katie, and Henry, Samantha. (2014). NJ works to curb sex trafficking before Super Bowl. Associated Press, January 6. Retrieved January 16, 2014, from http://m.apnews.com/ap/db_289563/contentdetail.htm?contentguid=bhLN3oYN.

Zhang, S. X. (2007). *Smuggling and Trafficking of Human Beings: All Roads Lead to America*. Westport, CT: Praeger.

What Does Human Trafficking Look Like in the Midwest? It Can't Happen Here?

8

JEFFREY W. WEIBLE

Contents

Major Issues

- Collaboration and communication between social services and law enforcement is essential to combating human trafficking.
- Human trafficking, both sex and labor, does not reside in the Midwest alone.
- Why is it important to examine the similarities between cases of human trafficking?

Many people think human trafficking is an issue for other countries or, domestically, large cities. However, this is not just an issue on a national and global scale but for every small town across the country. This chapter specifically deals with the issue of domestic minor sex trafficking, or DMST. Although many people will think of this issue in terms of "prostitution" or as a victimless crime, it is not. This becomes clearer when you realize the average age of entry to this world is 12 to 13 years of age, from what I have seen in the middle of the country in Wichita, Kansas.

As long as there is a demand for underage sex, someone will be there to exploit and provide the supply. As an investigator, it would be an asset to have a profile of those individuals who fall in the demand category. Unfortunately much like physical and sexual abuse cases, you cannot paint a profile on where the next case or suspect will come from. As noted, this is not just a global or national issue; this is a hometown issue. The same techniques used to groom victims of sexual abuse are used to lure victims into the cycle of abuse related to human trafficking. As I heard our local Sedgwick County District Attorney Marc Bennett say, "This issue boils down to abuse." I would have to agree with this assessment. These are the same issues related to human trafficking that fall into other crimes related to abuse (i.e., emotional, physical, and sexual). In the realm of human trafficking, whether it be sexual or labor related, there is still an element of someone controlling and exploiting another human being. The control or abuse can be in the form of sexual, physical, financial, or emotional, used to exploit their victims for a profit by their perpetrators.

In the Midwest there has been a paradigm shift for law enforcement in how we look at these crimes. As a young beat cop, I saw many victims walking the streets but I looked at them as criminals violating local ordinances. Since that time, I have come to realize that in this world they are victims, though they may not identify themselves as such. They are the supply, females or males, used to make a profit by selling themselves for another or labor in a never-ending world of paying a debt. We will focus on the sex trafficking aspect throughout this chapter. When I would patrol areas of our city known for prostitution, we as law enforcement would focus our efforts on the supply side not realizing that those we could see, had been doing this work for quite some time and were only a small part of the total problem. Yet we spent little time focusing on the demand side of the equation or the profiteers. Over the years, locally, we began focusing on the demand side as well through coordinated john stings.

In the 1990s, the issue of prostitution along one of our downtown streets became such an issue we used the SARA (scan, analyze, respond, assess) problem-solving model used in community policing to address it. These methods included education, awareness, and enforcement. In addition to the enforcement piece were additional ordinances to map individuals from a geographical area to help displace the problem. This helped in curbing the problem in the downtown area, but it did not solve the overall issue.

Since those days, I have come to realize that this was just the visible problem. The public perception would say that these "criminals" were doing this for their own benefit. However, when you look at the issue at the deeper level, there were people making a profit for themselves by victimizing or exploiting others. The "pimps" have taken this issue from the streets to the world of technology, which we will examine later in this chapter. As mentioned earlier, this is a business with a supply, demand, and a need for marketing, but there is an aspect of abuse at every level.

As the director of operations for the Wichita-Sedgwick County Exploited and Missing Child Unit (EMCU), I have learned much about emotional, physical, and sexual abuse of children. Additionally, I have seen the various aspects of domestic minor sex trafficking that seem to overlap each of these categories. Wichita, Kansas, sits along major highways going north, south, east, and west across the country. Throughout my career, I have seen these routes used for gang and drug activities. However, while with the EMCU, I have seen that these routes are also used for domestic minor sex trafficking. Victims have been transported along the Interstate 35 corridor to the Interstate 70 corridor to cities from San Antonio, Dallas, Oklahoma City, Tulsa, to Wichita and beyond. We have recovered local victims in Atlanta, Dallas, New Orleans, and Chicago. If one were to look on a map, you would see the major highways involved.

Similarities among Victims

In the last several years, I have learned and adapted from each case I have come across. Though the majority of victims that have identified are female, there have been a few male victims as well. Many of the male victims have gender identification issues. We have used the theory of if it walks like a duck, and talks like a duck, it is probably a duck. There are some commonalities among those who have been identified over the years. The age range for local victims is from 13 to 17. The common denominator is exploitation and abuse. These cases are extremely difficult to investigate and prosecute. As we look at these issues, we will paint a picture that makes this a little more understandable.

Most of the victims have a history of running away from home wherever it may be. Many have been victims of physical or sexual abuse, or have been placed in state's custody. Some have turned to domestic minor sex trafficking in the past. Yet, they all have one thing in common: they are looking for stability in their lives regardless of where they can find it. This warped stability is in the form of someone who will claim to take care of their needs. Much like any other "grooming" process, those who will exploit them will groom them to provide something they are missing. These same techniques are used by gangs or sexual predators to appeal to what the juvenile is missing in their lives. This has become easier for these predators to accomplish with the use of social media and the Internet. There have been cases where the victims were recruited on various social media websites and in turn exploited on the Internet.

As noted, this is not just a criminal issue but a social and community issue as well. Community awareness is key in addressing this issue because most public perception is that this cannot and does not happen in our community.

Yet, the general public has the same perception of physical and sexual abuse cases. To address this issue holistically, we must identify there is a problem and attack it through awareness, education, enforcement, and services to the victims much like we have for domestic violence. We cannot identify this as a problem unless we are looking for it collectively in our communities. This is similar to someone who wants to find a four-leaf clover. You will not see it unless you are really looking for it.

At the end of this chapter, I will share a couple of case examples to show these dynamics as they appear in the Midwest. There has been a trend where gangs have realized that it is more lucrative to participate in domestic minor sex trafficking than selling drugs. Humans are a commodity that can be sold over and over or even traded as currency as opposed to drugs that are sold and used one time. Humans can be recruited, brought into this lifestyle, and used for profit. As cases have developed, the trend of gang involvement has increased.

As noted, recruitment can be through personal contact or virtual on the Internet. Suspects prey on those who have low self-esteem or something missing in their lives. Additionally, many victims have been exploited in various ways prior to getting involved in this world. Victims come from single-parent homes, broken homes, prior victimization, or are thrown away/homeless youth that run and are never reported missing.

Although there is a perception that individuals are stolen off the street and taken into this life, this perception is not accurate. After the initial grooming and recruitment, victims are generally sold locally. Victims from my jurisdiction have been recovered in larger cities like Atlanta, Chicago, Dallas, and New Orleans, but the majority of the victims remain in the Midwest. I have seen a trend where traffickers run a loop between Dallas, Oklahoma City, Wichita, Topeka, and Kansas City, Missouri.

You Can't Find What You Are Not Looking For

The first case study that we will examine is a case involving a 15-year-old girl whose ads were online for several weeks. Investigators first noticed her on one of the popular websites known for escort ads. A sting was attempted to identify and recover the victim with no success. Our police department had just finished holding training to help in recognizing that there are victims to this crime of prostitution, many of whom are juveniles.

It started as a routine suspicious character call at a local motel. An alert clerk who had seen several stories in the local media about trafficking recognized two females who came to a rent a room. The clerk remembered these females as renting rooms in the past. Shortly after the room was rented, a young female went to the room followed by a much older male. The clerk realizing something else was going on and called 911. Officers contacted the two females that rented the room and realized something was amiss. They observed the young female and male exiting the motel while they were still in the parking lot and stopped them asking what they were doing. When the stories did not match, the officers contacted EMCU. As we kept everyone separated, we learned that the young female had placed several ads online.

As the investigation continued, the runners were identified as the pimp's sisters. They had been pimped out as well. One sister was talking and the other was not. The pimp was a known gang member who was currently on house arrest; let's call him Steve. As things unfolded, investigators were able to put probable cause to arrest the other male (john) and the gang member (pimp). Though the electronic evidence was there as well as confessions, the victim did not see herself as a victim. In fact, even at the time of trial, the 15-year-old victim said that she was a businesswoman and the only thing the pimp was guilty of was having sex with her.

The victim was asked in court whom she gave her money to and she said Steve. When asked who arranged the dates and the ads, she said Steve. When asked who protected her when she had problems, she said Steve. When asked who quoted prices and got the money, she said Steve. What does Steve sound like to you? The pimp. The jury thought so too. In fact, due to his criminal history, Steve was sentenced to 640 months. Again, if it looks like a duck, walks like a duck, and talks like a duck, it is probably a duck.

Self-Esteem Goes a Long Way

To give an example of the recruitment process, there was a case with a self-proclaimed second-generation pimp, who we will call Money Mike. He was in town going to local high school parties to meet prospective girls. He would flirt with them at the party and exchange social media information. At one such party, he met a 17-year-old girl. They began chatting online after the party. After several conversations, Mike solicited the girl to travel to New Orleans with him to get into the game and make money nationwide.

Our victim in this case thought Mike was creepy and turned him down. He then began to talk bad about her on social media. Because this girl was not running from other issues and had a good support network and family, she decided to tell someone. The victim contacted her school resource officer and reported this incident. The school resource officer contacted EMCU and the Internet Crimes Against Children Task Force (ICAC), which began an investigation.

ICAC investigators went online undercover and contacted Mike with the persona of a 15-year-old runaway much like the television show *To Catch a Predator*. After several days of online conversation, an undercover officer agreed to meet Mike to travel to New Orleans and Florida to make money in the game. Mike came to meet the undercover persona and was greeted by law enforcement. Mike was federally indicted by the U.S. Attorney's Office in the District of Kansas. Mike was convicted and is serving a 10-year sentence in federal prison.

The preceding case examples illustrate the dynamic difference between the two victims in these cases. In the first, you have a victim with little stability at home that appeared to be running from something to something. They thought they found what they were lacking in their life, a sense of belonging and family. They did not identify as being victims. In the second case, you see a victim that has a solid support network with self-esteem that felt the need to report predatory behavior.

These dynamics are not unique to Wichita or any other city across the country. This can be seen in any city or town in the country. Just like any predator, the pimp will prey on the weak and vulnerable, those who are looking for something they are missing or running from something in their lives. In my opinion the abuse cycle is similar to that of the domestic violence abuse cycle.

In the cases that EMCU and ICAC have worked, the majority of the victims were active runaways when they were identified. Many are also in the custody of social services based on their dysfunctional family lives, physical abuse, or sexual abuse. They are running from something and running to those who exploit them. I can't emphasize this point enough: this trend can happen anywhere in any city. I have had the opportunity to talk to law enforcement across the country and they are seeing the same trends that I have mentioned throughout this chapter.

In the Kansas state statutes, it is easier to prove criminal cases where the victim is under the age of 18. Despite this, without victim cooperation it is difficult to obtain successful prosecutions even when law enforcement has changed its perceptions related to the victims. As noted, the victims will not self-identify themselves. They will protect their pimp at all costs because they are in love, scared, or feel that they are in control. Again, in my opinion this mirrors the cycle of domestic violence.

Things to Ponder

I have given examples of two successful cases based on the recovery of the victims and the prosecution of the offenders. However, not all cases are successful if your priority is safety of the child. Many cases EMCU has investigated have not reached criminal prosecution because of the difficulty in developing probable cause. If the child is recovered and given resources to move in a positive direction, then that investigation was successful as well.

The next case will examine a win–lose scenario that I think was not successful based on the fact the victim did not want to be saved. Much like a recovering addict, the victim had not hit rock bottom and returned to this hidden world of exploitation.

When "Suzy" was a child, her father horribly abused her. Her father was put in prison and due to complicity, her mother had her rights to Suzy removed. Suzy was sent to foster care but was not given the resources to cope with the abuse. Suzy began to run away from one home to another. Eventually, Suzy became involved in a sexual relationship with a person of authority, who was suppose to protect and guide her, in a group home where she had been placed. This led Suzy into the world of human trafficking. Suzy had done this before and was coerced to get involved in this activity, again by someone she trusted. We recovered Suzy and again we were able to proceed with a successful prosecution. Yet, Suzy began the cycle of running away again. She had told investigators during one interview that this world and activity was the only thing she was good at.

Additional intervention was tried with Suzy, but she was resistant because she felt the "system," courts, law enforcement, and social services, had failed her. Suzy could not see that the system was trying to help but like an addict she could not see that and was still resistant. Suzy went so far as to recruit others into this life to work for the particular pimp she had at the time.

Since this time, we have investigated more cases involving Suzy. Each time, Suzy would tell us about her dreams of getting into the medical field but would say she could not do it because she did not deserve it. In every investigation involving Suzy, therapy and services were put in place and yet she would not take advantage of them. So, the philosophical question is, at what point does she become a criminal rather than a victim? If this rebranding does occur, who makes that call? The courts? Law enforcement? Social services? Prosecutors?

Due to Suzy's age, the multidisciplinary team made the decision to prosecute Suzy to allow the juvenile court to have additional control over her. Suzy told us she wanted to live independently and that recommendation was made to the court system. Her wish was granted. Therapy continued. Resources were shared. Yet, within months, Suzy had left the independent living program, failed to report for court, and was advertising online within a week. Suzy became the recruiter instead of the recruited. In each case she had a pimp, yet she felt as if she was the one in control.

Would this case study be a success or a failure? If an agency judges success by arrest, then it was a success multiple times. If an agency judges success by prosecutions and convictions, then it was a success multiple times. If an agency judges success by the "Child First" doctrine, where the child was recovered safely and placed in a safe place, then one could argue it was successful multiple times. However, if you judge the success of a case is when a victim is not only recovered but changes their behavior, then this was a systematic failure.

If you judge this case as a failure, then we must ask ourselves what went wrong and when. In speaking with a therapist that deals with these victims, our discussion has turned to the fact that each victim of human trafficking shares similarities with abuse victims and addicts combined. Each victim must have services and therapy individually tailored to them, much like law enforcement and social services must investigate with an open mind and see each case individually.

I have seen many investigations come through EMCU. Each one is as unique as the victim that is involved. Though the moving parts are the same—victim, pimp, and john—each case is individually unique.

The aforementioned scenarios are repeated across the state as well as the country. I feel that no community is immune from this activity as long as there is a demand. We in law enforcement must address the demand while focusing on identification of the victims. But we cannot find what we are not looking for. Therefore, we must focus on similarities and patterns as we have discussed.

- Does the juvenile have numerous runaway cases?
- Where was the juvenile located?
- Whom was the juvenile with?
- Is the juvenile a prior victim of sexual abuse?
- Is the juvenile a prior victim of human trafficking?

How Communities Can Combat Human Trafficking

There are several things a community can do to address human trafficking. First, the community needs to realize that "it can happen here." Much like other forms of abuse, many communities do not want to realize that these bad things can happen in their hometowns. Additionally, there needs to be a coordinated effort to address it. This can occur through education, awareness of the issue, signs to identify victims, and education of social services and law enforcement on what to look for.

This coordinated effort must include communication. As with any social issue, if there is no dialogue to identify a problem, then a plan to address it cannot happen. As with any form of abuse, one discipline cannot address it. Therefore, once the dialogue starts it must continue in a multidisciplinary effort to have success. We are fortunate that in the state of Kansas, we have a state statute that requires collaboration and communication between social services and law enforcement. This helps, but bringing in additional partners will make a recipe for success. These partners include the following:

- Social services
- Nonprofit agencies that assist with advocacy
- Prosecutors and the juvenile justice system
- Medical providers
- Community organizations

By bringing everyone to the table to discuss human trafficking, a solid foundation to create public awareness can be developed. Once this occurs, each case can be addressed in that holistic way we discussed earlier. A game plan to create public awareness without creating hysteria can be developed. In doing so, there can be success as discussed in the first case study. Individuals will report suspicious activity that can be investigated.

Any community that has Internet access and local motels can be vulnerable to human trafficking. As noted, with any other business if there is a demand for a commodity, then someone will step up to provide a supply. To verify this, one only needs to look online for sites that sell items, adult chat rooms, and so on. Additionally, a community can have success in addressing this issue through collaboration. By the aforementioned services working together, then there is less of a chance that a victim will slip through the cracks.

Once a potential victim is identified, each discipline cannot work in a vacuum. The collaboration must continue. Each partner must have input as to the services offered to the victim. If the collaboration and communication are not maintained throughout the investigation, court process, and aftercare, then during each phase there will be an opportunity for the victim to run or relapse. If this occurs, then this continues not only the cycle of abuse and exploitation but the cycle of investigating additional crimes.

Discussion among the partners through a multidisciplinary team concept can assist in dealing with these cases individually. Will this make every investigation a success? No, but it will improve the odds of overall success regardless of how your agency or community measures success.

In our community, we have been able to identify more victims each year. Does this mean there is more of a problem? Does this mean that awareness works? Does this mean we are getting better at the identification of victims? I would say yes to the last two questions, simply because this issue is still underground though advertised on the Internet. I cannot tell you the scope of the problem in the Midwest, Kansas, or even the Wichita metro area. Yet, if there is one child being sold and exploited, I think that is one child too many.

Whether law enforcement uses intelligence-based policing, predictive crime analysis, or proven community policing problem solving methods, there must be a collaborative effort of multiple disciplines to truly have impactful success.

Summary

As I have said, there is no community immune from human trafficking, child abuse, and exploitation. Regardless of the size of the community, these issues exist whether we want to acknowledge them or not. Through thoughtful dialogue, collaboration, and awareness efforts, an impact can be made. One-sided investigations will not be successful. Where there are runaways, homeless youth, child physical and sexual abuse, and online exploitation, then there is clearly a risk for human trafficking or domestic minor sex trafficking.

Additionally, a network of professionals, whether it be law enforcement, social services, medical, or advocacy, must share trends, best practices, successes, and failures collaboratively so techniques may be tailored for others. I have seen this work through my involvement with the Internet Crimes Against Children Task Force. Nationally task forces share best practices so that those techniques may be adapted and tailored for your community.

Finally, more academic study is needed on this issue. Though this is still considered a taboo or underground problem, additional analysis is needed to truly understand the scope and magnitude of the issues.

Key Terms

"Child First" Doctrine
domestic minor sex trafficking (DMST)
Exploited and Missing Child Unit (EMCU)
Internet Crimes Against Children Task Force (ICAC)
multidisciplinary team
SARA (Scan, Analyze, Respond, Assess)

Review Questions

1. What is the typical profile of a DMST victim?
2. Explain why human sex trafficking cases are difficult to prosecute.
3. Explain how the community can help to combat the issue of human trafficking.
4. What differences in the case studies led to their individual outcomes?
5. Why does the line between victim and criminal become difficult to distinguish?

Sex Trafficking in Sexually Oriented Businesses

9

D. G. OBLINGER

Contents

Major Issues

- Many lawful, sexually oriented businesses readily conceal sex trafficking and victimization.
- Culture and language can make investigating sex trafficking challenging for local investigators.
- Prostitution is often a red herring in sex trafficking cases when it comes to public opinion.
- A collaborative approach to combating trafficking requires public awareness that sex trafficking has true victims and the community is harmed.

Introduction

Maria is 15. She was a runaway from her home when she met her pimp. He is violent and abusive toward her, but he is also a form of protection and source of shelter and drugs. She has been involved in prostitution for over a year, traveling from hotel to hotel in large Midwestern cities.

Li Guo is 43. She came to the United States on a tourist visa that she obtained under false pretenses with the aid of a shell company in China. She was able to find work at a massage parlor on the West Coast. Li quickly found she must commit acts of prostitution to continue in employment. She was afraid, because the bosses took her passport and visa, and explained that the neighborhood was dangerous. When she resisted providing sexual services, the patrons complained to the manager and she was chastised and threatened with deportation. She gladly escaped China and does not want to return.

Sizing Up the Problem

Although Maria and Li are fictional examples, their stories echo the nightmares of real women in modern America. The Federal Bureau of Investigation (FBI) cited research in a March 2011 Bulletin that estimated that victims of human sex trafficking number in the millions, making this criminal enterprise "the most common form of modern day slavery" (Walker-Rodriguez and Hill 2011). The driving force in this sordid industry is the same as any other: money.

Sex trafficking is a specific variety of human trafficking wherein the victim is valued by the offenders for their usefulness in performing sex acts for hire. It is not rare. The United Nations Office of Drug Control's (UNODC) 2012 *Global Report on Trafficking in Persons* estimated that "trafficking for the purpose of sexual exploitation accounts for 56% of all trafficking cases detected globally" (p. 11). Sex trafficking is big business and getting bigger. The United Nations notes that it is the fastest growing enterprise of organized crime, and the revenue is measured in the billions of dollars (p. 5). To understand sex trafficking, it is important to begin with a basic understanding of the inner workings of a criminal sex-for-hire enterprise, usually called a prostitution ring. *Prostitution* refers to any sexual contact between parties in exchange for something of value.

Sex trafficking is a complex problem. The size and scope of the social and global forces that facilitate the trading of humans for commercialized prostitution can be intimidating for a policy maker or criminal investigator. In order to gain an understanding of how to dismantle this type of criminal enterprise, it is critical to understand the ancient practice of prostitution itself, the operation of typical sexually oriented businesses, and modern sex trafficking practices. Armed with this knowledge, members of the criminal justice community are positioned to think strategically about combating the scourge of sex trafficking.

Sex Workers

The vast majority of prostitutes are women (Siegel 2011, 485). It should be no surprise that the vast majority of sex trafficking victims are also women and children (UNODC 2012, 5). A prostitute is properly referred to as a *sex worker* and in the case of a woman, a female sex worker. Depending on the jurisdiction, individuals who promote prostitution with these sex workers are classified as a *pimp* or *panderer* under criminal code. Pandering includes a wide range of activity and is not necessarily linked to acts of prostitution alone. It can entail many ways of appealing to the crass desires of clientele. Pimping is a specific type of pandering that procures prostitutes for those willing to pay. Not all prostitutes work for pimps, but prostitutes are more likely to work under a pimp in jurisdictions with a lot of demand or competition, when they are younger sex workers, and when fear of violence from johns is acute. The independent prostitute operates at her own peril. Without the protection afforded by a pimp, she faces intimidation and violence by johns, competitors, and pimps who may recruit her to work for them.

Acts of sex-for-hire between sex workers and their clients, universally known as *johns* by police and pimps alike, require proper advertising and a certain degree of vetting by both parties. A "date" or *trick* is arranged at the street level or more commonly now over the Internet. The traditional "streetwalker" model features pimps and prostitutes operating in areas with high volumes of vehicle and foot traffic, and easy access to apartments or hotels that cater to hourly customers. This model has many variations. One version features the prostitute, known as a "lot lizard," working the parking areas of interstate truck stops to capitalize on demand from the truck operators. In any iteration of the traditional model, sex workers put in the time to loiter in the area widely known by all involved to be the spot for tricks to be turned.

The traditional model has its obvious flaws for the offenders. Time is money in any business. Time spent loitering without dates means lost revenue for the pimp. Likely hangouts for prostitutes are not a tightly guarded secret, and the local constabulary invariably intervenes. With the wide availability of the Internet, the traditional model has been supplanted by a high-tech version (Siegel 2011, 486). By posting advertisements to Internet sites, prostitutes gain anonymity to a degree. Popular sites include Craigslist, Backpage, and USA Sex Guide. Many Internet sites cater to the commercial sex industry by allowing johns to post what sex acts were available from sex workers in the shops, and how much they paid. Direct advertising and Internet communications allows prostitutes to compress their work into a shorter shift, limiting wasted hours walking streetside. The convenience of the Internet permits greater control of the business by pimps, who can create and edit postings and monitor the electronic communication between their workers and the johns.

The Blade

By advertising in different cities and booking in advance, a pimp can take a stable of prostitutes on a tour of lucrative locations. Such a prostitution group tends to work in a circuit. This model of prostitution is often referred to as "the blade," and the participants are said to be "on the blade" or "working the blade."

The Internet also opens greater opportunity for freelancing by sex workers. They can handle their own advertising and limit their contact with the general danger from working curbside. Even with this protective action, the particular danger of robbery, rape, or assault from clients is ever present in the more discreet liaisons afforded by Internet bookings. In fact, pimps or their bottoms are known to exploit this danger by responding to the advertisements to recruit these independent workers.

A pimp is essentially the general manager of a prostitution business. The pimp ensures that the business operates smoothly. This means establishing methods of recruiting and training sex workers, collecting the proceeds from acts of prostitution, arranging the liaison between his employees and clients, protecting the assets of the enterprise by force or threat, and transporting and harboring the sex workers. Most prostitution rings feature a high level of control by the operator over the workers.

Roles within the Prostitution Ring

Many pimps delegate some of their duties to a manager. This is commonly an experienced sex worker who has the closest relationship to the pimp. The industry term for this role is "bottom bitch" or "bottom girl," usually shortened to "bottom." The bottom could collect money, assess discipline for girls who get out of line, train new workers, and serve as a buffer for the pimp from law enforcement. In such an arrangement, the pimp still receives the benefit of the proceeds of the prostitution and is protected from legal jeopardy.

The culture of sex-for-hire has its own language. For the uninitiated observer, the industry terms and acronyms can be mind-boggling. The Internet advertising posted by prostitution rings commonly uses abbreviations to telegraph to clients what is available. Sexual acts are frequently referred to using coded words to veil the criminal act of prostitution from law enforcement.

The parallels between this commercialized prostitution and legitimate enterprises may be shocking, but this is a business after all. The principal difference is the goods that are being sold. The basic structure of a prostitution ring is unsophisticated. The strict control of the sex worker is a crude means of keeping "overhead," business expenses, low for the pimp. The importance of advertising and marketing is clear for prostitution just as in the retail world. Pimps cater to the desires of the clientele to generate repeat business. Many erotic massage parlors offer punch cards for repeat patrons to earn free massages. Like any good modern business, contemporary prostitution enterprises make extensive use of Internet resources to promote and expand their market share.

Generally, the culture of the sex-for-hire trade is one of violence and degradation for the prostitute. The clinical term "sex worker" is preferred by academics. Most patrol officers utilize "prostitute" or "working girl." The pimp will speak strictly in terms of "bitches," "hoes," or any other name designed to establish a clear sense of power and control. Acts of violence against sex workers by pimps, other members of the criminal organization, their competition, and even clients is commonplace.

Prostitutes are frequent victims of rape, robbery, assault, and aggravated assault. They are also frequently the victims of homicide and premature, unnatural death (Potterat, 2003). The threat for violence comes from within the prostitution ring and from their clientele. The nature of their business means they work alone, frequent high-crime areas, work through the night, interact with criminal elements, and exchange cash for service. Moreover, since they are engaging in illegal activity, they are likely to avoid police reports or decline prosecution as a victim (Siegel 2012, 485).

Prostitution in Sexually Oriented Businesses

Contemporary investigations of sex trafficking require a working knowledge of sexually oriented business practices. These operations serve to conceal the actual sexual exploitation and related offenses behind the appearance of legitimate commerce. Understanding key terms related to sexually oriented businesses is critical to learning about these various schemes to capitalize on the big business of sex trafficking.

Sexually oriented businesses are commercial enterprises that are legal per se, advertise services of a sexual or romantic nature, and usually serve as thinly veiled fronts for commercialized prostitution. Examples include strip clubs, escort services, and massage parlors.

The importance of understanding how these businesses exploit sex workers to make money is important in the investigation of sex trafficking. There is a clear nexus between sexually oriented businesses and human sex trafficking. By trafficking sex workers, the operators have a constant source of new "talent," limit the workers' ability to access resources or police assistance, and can operate with very little overhead to cut into the profit of the business.

Escort Services

One example of a sexually oriented business is an *escort service*, sometimes called a valet or companion service. Escort services are, in most cases, lawful businesses that are regulated by local jurisdictions. The business itself may be licensed, as well as all its employees. Ostensibly, the escorts are hired by clients to accompany them out on the town. Most regulatory ordinances state as much. Escorts in reality are almost exclusively engaging in prostitution. Because these companions are paid to accompany their client, if any sexual relations occur there is an exchange of value and prostitution occurs. A common defense by the escort service is that the money paid for the escort is only for their actual accompaniment of the client. In this line of argument, the sex act is artificially separated from this escorting activity. In reality, the acts of escorting and sex are inseparable.

The escort service is merely prostitution with a legal veneer. Escorting, a lawful activity when merely going out for an evening of companionship, is a ruse to put johns and prostitutes together. This appearance of legality is the entire purpose of a sexually oriented business. It merely bears the appearance of a cleaner and more professional model of prostitution compared to streetwalking.

There are clear advantages for the operators of a sexually oriented business. They are insulated from the prostitution act itself. Most such businesses will claim that any sexual acts performed by the sex worker are prohibited and the fault of the worker. The money derived from the prostitution appears to come from a legitimate commercial enterprise, allowing it to flow into the economy without being laundered. The front company allows marketing and advertising to build a client base in a way not available to streetwalkers.

Escort services generally offer their services in two formats known as "out-call" and "in-call." An out-call occurs when the client orders the escort and meets the escort away from the escort business. In-calls occur when the date takes place inside the escort business. The out-call often occurs at motels or hotels. Many escort services will employ "escort runners" or "drivers." These predominantly male employees escort the escorts. They may collect the money and ensure the escort's safety. In-calls occur in private rooms at the business set up for that purpose. The escort business owners walk a fine line in this case. They control the environment for the date and take the money directly from the client, but they run the risk of having direct knowledge of the acts of prostitution.

The similarity in roles between a pimp and the owner or runner in the escort business model is undeniable. This likeness should reinforce the fact that escorting is merely prostitution in disguise. The escorting business model is flexible enough to spawn niche enterprises. Examples include *dust bunnies*, escorts that will clean patron's home or office in sexually suggestive outfits; or shoe shine girls, offering in-call services with topless or nude women to polish one's boots.

Strip Club

A *strip club* is a bar that features entertainment for patrons by women dancing in various stages of undress. Within the industry, such establishments may be called nudie bars, bikini bars, go-go clubs, or the euphemistic *gentlemen's club*. Usually a licensed drinking establishment, the strip club caters to mostly male clientele with nudity to the extent allowed by local custom.

The establishment retains the female strippers or exotic dancers, and generates revenue from cover charges, mandatory drink sales, and tips for the dancers. Depending on the jurisdiction, lap dances, private booths, and secluded VIP lounges contribute to the sexual orientation of the business by providing the opportunity for prostitution acts between patrons and dancers. In more restrictive legal environments, the club may actively discourage sex on the premises but will redirect such lucrative activity to a nearby motel. Not all exotic dancers engage in prostitution, but the enticement of patrons in a sexual fashion is part and parcel of the stage persona. The constant mix of pandering, patrons, and performers seeking money through a sexually charged show has always linked the so-called gentlemen's club to sex-for-hire. Once again, the club through its doormen, managers, wait staff, and house rules, serves in the controlling, exploitative, and protective role of a pimp. The basic model of prostitution is still evident behind the glitz and neon of a modern strip joint. The insulating legal protection and attractive financial benefits of the lawful status of a gentlemen's club are much the same as an escort business.

Massage Parlors

Another popular sexually oriented business is the *massage parlor*. Here, unlike escorts and strip clubs, there is even more cover for the establishment offering sex-for-hire. Many massage therapists offer professional and therapeutic massages to clients needing relaxation and health benefits. Concealing themselves in this industry are parlors that offer sexual favors for a fee, with little in the way of professionalism or therapy. For the purposes of this text, these illicit businesses that offer prostitution along with massage services are referred to as massage parlors.

A massage parlor is often regulated by local or state law under the auspices of being a member of the healing arts community or for purposes of public health. Massage workers maintain office hours and perform massage services in half-hour or hour increments. For parlors, their clientele are strictly male and mostly a cash customer. Independent operators do exist, usually local masseuses and masseurs who advertise in the same manner as escorts in unsavory online postings. These same sexually oriented postings often single out Asian-themed parlors as a preferred location for johns to seek pleasure. Certainly on the coasts with their ports of entry but even in smaller centrally located cities like Wichita, Kansas, and Omaha, Nebraska, parlors can be found operating with women from all over the world.

In keeping with the veneer of legitimacy, parlor patrons will receive a massage for the majority of the time allotted for the visit. Many of the workers will have some documentation indicating they have been trained in massage therapy, whether domestically or in their country of origin. What makes the business sexually oriented and places it firmly in the realm of a parlor as opposed to a legitimate medically based massage office is what is available "off-menu."

A massage in a parlor begins with the patron face down. During the initial massage, the patron or worker may send signals with suggestive touch or vague remarks to signal that the sex act is available or desired. On "the flip," when the patron is turned over for the massage to continue on the front of the body, negotiations will begin over what act is to be performed and how much the patron should tip for this extra, off-menu service. Once an agreement is made, the massage will end with these extra services, before the patron will pay the tip and leave.

In a busy parlor, there may be more than one girl working. In more established operations, there may be an on-site manager who is usually a woman and thus referred to as the madame. Although she might also perform massages when volume is high, the madame runs the show and ensures customers are satisfied and pay completely. Again, the madame's role reprises that of the pimp. The massage parlor sexually oriented business model is thinly veiled commercial prostitution.

Workers in the Asian-themed massage parlor work 12- to 13-hour shifts, seven days a week, with no holidays off. Many will live in the parlor itself or at a nearby "flophouse" with other massage workers. The isolated nature of the massage worker's life and the market demand for Asian massage makes massage parlors a natural conduit for sex trafficking.

In keeping with the theme of variation within each segment of the sexually oriented services industry, massage parlors have evolved to face stiff competition, law enforcement, and threats of robbery and violence. Some move from storefronts to apartments or homes, requiring johns to book appointments and meet runners in public parking lots to be driven to the engagement. Others offer "out-call" massage on portable massage tables in homes or hotels. Some businesses keep the exotic allure of Asian-themed massage and remove the massage pretense. An example of this is the hostess bar, popularized in Japan and now finding traction in American markets. In these businesses, patrons find women in the bar who will attend to their needs while inside the establishment. The hostesses will serve food and drink, converse, dance, and in many cases engage in sex acts in private areas of the building—all for a fee. Many such bars identify with women of a specific nationality, which varies from hostess bar to hostess bar. Much like massage parlors, providing women from exotic locales can be a marketing tool and lends itself to sex trafficking.

In summation, prostitution is an ancient method of exploiting the charms of women to make money. Although in some instances the woman is the sole member of the enterprise, in the vast majority of instances the prostitute is merely a pawn in a large commercial endeavor. Pimps, bottoms, sex workers, and johns all contribute to the colossal industry of sex-for-hire. Sexually oriented businesses merely provide sophistication, designed to build insulation around the basic prostitution model to derive greater profit and reduced legal liability. These goals naturally lead the owner of a sexually oriented business engaged in prostitution to seek another level of control over labor, profit, and risk. Sex trafficking caters to this need.

Sex Trafficking

Since sex trafficking is merely a specific motivation for human trafficking, there are many similar features. Victims of trafficking, sexual or otherwise, tend to be significantly vulnerable. Examples of these vulnerabilities include victims who tend to be women and children, those without legal residence, and individuals who bear considerable debt related to immigration or other expenses. These vulnerabilities put the victim in a position of weakness to demand fair labor practices, fair wages, and humane treatment.

To a sexually oriented business owner already committed to the practice of pimping or pandering, a woman in this predicament makes the ideal employee. The trafficked woman is transplanted in a location that is unfamiliar. Many do not speak the language or know the local laws or customs. They are not inclined to seek out law enforcement due to perceived risk in their own actions or immigration status. They are easily intimidated by misinformation about the parlor's host city.

One major obstacle for gaining a clear understanding of the sex trafficking problem is the shadowy nature of the characters and activities involved. It is challenging to get hard data on the number of victims, participants, or revenue. All criminal industries have this feature, but the sophistication and transnational nature of sex trafficking compounds this problem.

Within the definition of sex trafficking, there are two broad categories of this crime. The origin of the trafficking victim, either domestic or international, can change the complexion of the investigation. Domestic trafficking often targets juveniles. Their immigration status is not an issue of vulnerability, but youth, naiveté, drug use, or being a runaway can be. With international sex trafficking, the victim has often entered into a hard bargain with organized crime to enter the United States illegally or by fraud (Palmiotto and Unnithan 2011, 273). This debt makes the victim a slave to the traffickers and she often finds herself in forced labor, including prostitution.

When the motive for human trafficking is sexual exploitation, the traffickers operate similarly to pimps in prostitution rings and sexually oriented businesses. Operators of sex trafficking organizations tend to maximize control by force and fear. The business is profit driven and ensures the workers remain vulnerable to maximize revenue and suppress overhead costs.

The Law

The vast majority of cities and states outlaw prostitution and promoting prostitution, and criminalize acts that further the crime by transporting or harboring women or benefiting from the business proceeds. Prosecutions for prostitution and pimping are simple and occur routinely across the country. Once the underlying network of criminal activity causing sex trafficking is unearthed, prosecutions can occur for federal violations of the Mann Act (USAO 9-29), harboring aliens for sexual purposes, peonage, money laundering, wire fraud, and potentially RICO. RICO, Racketeer Influenced

Corrupt Organization Act, allows serious penalties for operating a criminal enterprise that used corruption and violence to engage in a list of crimes that include prostitution. Many states also have mirroring statutes for RICO to allow local prosecutions (USAO 9-110.000, 2014).

Investigating Sex Trafficking Organizations

Armed with an understanding of prostitution, sexually oriented businesses, and sex trafficking, the criminal investigator charged with investigating these types of offenses is ready to begin. Investigating a sex trafficking organization is a monumental task. Best practices emphasize a collaborative approach that focuses on methodical investigative techniques.

Building a Team

Sex trafficking is predominantly a complex conspiracy. An international trafficking ring in particular will be geographically dispersed and present a challenge for investigation. It is best to work in partnership with every available agency that has a stake in the investigation. Examples include local and state law enforcement, prosecutors, social service agencies that specialize in supporting victims of trafficking like women's shelters, and federal law enforcement agencies with mandates to combat organized crime and human trafficking. The Federal Bureau of Investigation (FBI) and Homeland Security Investigations (HSI), formerly Immigration and Customs Enforcement, are two such examples. The FBI or HSI can sponsor cases for federal charging and forfeiture actions and provide investigative capabilities wherever the case leads.

The impetus for a successful investigation and prosecution of sex trafficking can begin with something quite innocuous. A prostitution complaint, a concerned citizen making a tip to their beat officer about suspicious activity at a massage parlor, or an informant could all turn police attention to a potential trafficking situation. No matter the origin, a competent investigator begins with gathering exhaustive information while focusing on the natural vulnerabilities of the operation itself.

Sex trafficking is predicated upon regular and reliable activities to ensure profits flow into the criminal enterprise. Sex workers must be recruited, transported, trained, harbored, and put to work. The business itself must advertise, conduct financial transactions, and maintain its physical assets. The operators must communicate and travel. Each of these particular activities is an investigative avenue. When an investigator examines enough of these sources of insight, a clear path to a prosecutable case should appear.

Information Collection Plan

Before any actual evidence collection occurs, smart investigators plan. They anticipate the technical and meticulous nature of a trafficking case. This planning should focus initially on document control. An information collection plan is critical to maintaining control of knowledge of the criminal activity and relevant supporting documents. The investigative team must maintain a single database of the involved people, locations, financial accounts, phone numbers, and electronic data sources. Each key person, place, and thing should have a unique identifier. Now data can begin to flow into the plan and be shared by all the members of the team.

An example would be in the case of a complaint about a single massage parlor. By checking licensing through the local jurisdiction, the owner, operating manager and some employees can typically be identified. The shop's phone number and address should be recorded. Using these various points of information, a broad search of the Internet and other local resources can be conducted to locate Internet advertising, postings to john review websites, and any other open sources that can shed light on the potential for criminality at the parlor. Each person known to be involved in the operation of the parlor should have a thorough background investigation. Consider involving federal agencies that can verify immigration status and check databases for suspicious financial activity. Physical surveillance should begin to verify hours of operation, develop demographic information on the clientele, and look for delivery or pickup of workers or visits by managers or couriers. If money pickups and worker exchanges between multiple parlors occur, the information collection plan must expand to these new targets. The plan should also include any residential locations where workers could be harbored.

Supporting documentation for the information collection process should not be overlooked. The collection plan can serve as a source for unexplored leads and an easy method of preparing for trial and the discovery process, but only if all supporting documentation is complete and orderly. It is not enough to know the identity of the escort service owner; the copy of the license application should be obtained. As information is collected and investigative milestones are achieved, the story of the complex will begin to become clear. While information can be gathered throughout the entire investigation, once a critical mass of intelligence is obtained on the target organization, the active investigation can proceed in earnest.

Active Investigative Techniques

Investigators use a variety of techniques to establish probable cause for the underlying crimes of prostitution and pimping. When humans are trafficked for sexual purpose, these underlying crimes are important to establish the motives of the organization, to use as a tool for developing cooperative witnesses, and in a federal proceeding to use as a *specified unlawful act* for asset forfeiture. The choice to use these techniques alone or in concert should be made in partnership with the prosecutor who must ultimately try the case in court.

One simple technique exploits the requirements for licensed sexually oriented businesses. Uniformed officers making a routine business check for license compliance can gain some insight into the operation of the business and the identity and origin of the workers. If the local jurisdiction does not regulate the industry of the particular business, this technique is less effective.

Patron Debrief

Another effective intermediate tactic for actively gaining knowledge of criminal activity in sexually oriented businesses is consensual debriefs of patrons. During surveillance, investigators can identify likely patrons of the sexually oriented business, and follow them away from the business. When they arrive at their next destination, the investigator simply makes a request for information. During the surveillance, care can be given to find patrons who are more likely to discuss the activity inside the salon. By running vehicle registration queries, investigators may prefer to contact out-of-town visitors less likely to know the business operators, pick patrons who have a spouse on their vehicle registration, or identify patrons who are on probation or supervised release who must cooperate with law enforcement under terms of their release.

A motivated john can provide a wealth of information about the internal workings of these businesses and might even divulge signs of human trafficking in the business. Good investigators always interview multiple patrons for each location to ensure the information is accurate and actionable. A variation of this technique can be contacting the john at a later time or even by phone. A more extreme option is to pose as a quality assurance agent for the business and remove the direct knowledge of police interest in the shop. John debriefs are not likely to generate probable cause for a warrant or arrest of the shop workers but can be invaluable to prepare undercover officers for more direct operations.

Buy-Bust

The backbone of investigative operations against commercialized prostitution is the *buy-bust*. Undercover officers contact the business by phone, or in the case of a massage parlor or in-call, enter the business posing as a patron. Once a deal is made between a sex worker or manager and the undercover officer, an act of prostitution has occurred. In some cases, the undercover might be asked by the sex worker to engage in conduct that would compromise their integrity. In many cases, an adept investigator can work around these requests. Alternatively, investigators can use confidential informants as a go-between if the prosecutor prefers to keep an officer from testifying they had to disrobe or were groped during the investigation by the defendant.

Once probable cause for an arrest has been established, other officers can enter the business or motel room and effect an arrest. If local ordinances allow "right of entry and inspection" for a licensed business, officers can immediately search the shop for evidence of prostitution, money to be seized, or signs of human trafficking. Otherwise, they would have to apply for a search warrant.

Reverses

In cases where pimping is suspected, some jurisdictions have used a *reverse buy-bust*. In reverses, the officers pose as the seller of illegal goods to turn the tables on criminals who might make a purchase. In the case of pimping, if a female officer poses as a prostitute, a case can be developed against a pimp who attempts to recruit her into his ring or groom her for human sex trafficking. These operations are more risky than the other techniques due to the inherent danger faced by the officers who pose as sex workers. A greater degree of security could be maintained if the recruitment and enticement occurs via the Internet after officers post an ad as a ruse.

Advanced Techniques

By their nature, sex trafficking organizations are shadowy networks that quickly adapt to threats to their business from competition, market fluctuations, and law enforcement. Antiprostitution investigators frequently note countersurveillance and changes to business operations with each successive arrest for prostitution in a sexually oriented business. When buy-busts, informants, or even a reverse is unsuccessful, investigators may need a more intensive method to document the sex trafficking and identify other participants in the network.

Title III of the Omnibus Crime Control and Safe Streets Act of 1968 allows law enforcement officers to use wiretaps to investigate these complex crimes (U.S. Department of Justice, 1). Officers must exhaust more traditional and less invasive techniques, and there are many extraordinary requirements for officers to comply with this law while electronically eavesdropping. Wiretaps are excellent for documenting complex conspiracies, and sex trafficking is vulnerable for wiretapping since it usually requires the prostitution ring and traffickers to communicate over great distances. The information collection plan can be invaluable for identifying the likely phone numbers that would qualify for tapping.

Sneak-and-Peaks

With more sophisticated sexually oriented businesses using in-call settings, there can be a high level of countersurveillance and vetting of patrons to ensure they are not police. This vigilance on the part of the offender makes it difficult for undercover officers to operate. Some jurisdictions have used warrants to obtain judicial permission to enter businesses overnight and additional court orders to install video cameras with no audio. These so called "sneak-and-peak" warrants permit the investigators to watch the cameras remotely, witness the acts of prostitution in real-time, and then make arrests of johns leaving the business. Eventually, the operators and sex workers are arrested too. These operations are resource intensive and depending on the jurisdiction may be impractical. They can have a serious impact in creating a perception of risk for the johns.

A major vulnerability for sex trafficking conspiracies and commercial prostitution rings is the money they generate. Patrons often pay cash. Much of the income is tied to acts of prostitution. Money laundering is often associated with these criminal enterprises. Investigators should always consider financial inquiries by subpoena as an investigative technique. These inquiries and the resulting bank records and account transfers can help identify new conspirators and additional targets for surveillance or arrest. Once the operation reaches its conclusion, these accounts and their assets can be seized and forfeited. Phone records are also available through this method.

Challenges for Investigators

The investigator in a sex trafficking case faces daunting challenges. Prostitution, the underlying crime for the trafficking itself, is often viewed by the public as being a victimless crime and a waste of police resources. In some cases, this disdain for prostitution enforcement can extend to elected officials and even police administrators. Education regarding the true nature of violence, vulnerability, exploitation, and public health risks from exotic sexually transmitted disease must be provided to policy makers.

As investigators make arrests and build their evidence, organizations will change their tactics and may even move their operation to a different jurisdiction. Having partners with broad authority, including federal agencies, is vital.

Prostitution and other complex criminal enterprises have an ancient tradition of surviving through graft and corruption of law enforcement. Investigators must take great pains to keep their work confidential, and only provide intelligence and preoperational briefings on a need-to-know basis. This includes other officers, prosecutors, and support staff.

By far the greatest challenge to investigators in these cases is the fragile relationship between sex workers and the police. Sex workers traditionally mistrust the police, and police likewise harbor a disdain for prostitutes. Investigators must make a heroic effort to convince the sex workers that they are victims of crimes, even as they are committing and perhaps being arrested for the prostitution acts. There is a constant debate about how sex workers should be treated by the criminal justice system. It is clear that most are truly victims. It is also true that the motivation for their involvement in earning money for sex is often complex and plays poorly through the lens of public perception. The uncomfortable reality remains that arrests for prostitution have been useful in the past to break the cycle of violence and exploitation against a sex worker and convince them to assist in the prosecution of pimps and traffickers.

Trafficking victims engaged in prostitution are even more likely to be afraid of cooperating in the investigation. They are conditioned to see the criminal organization as their source of shelter, protection, and means. They are often far from home and told the police will not help. Their constant vulnerability instills mistrust and paranoia. Even when assured by investigators that they can be sheltered from retribution, many sex trafficking victims will chose to take their chances with the "devil they know."

The challenge of mistrust of the investigator can be compounded in international sex trafficking. Investigators must plan for the challenge of language and cultural barriers with victims. If the sex worker hails from a country where the police are corrupt and violent, they may fear the investigator. If the investigator is unable to interview and communicate in the sex worker's native language, the process of earning trust to gather evidence is undermined. One way to plan for success in this arena is to obtain access to trusted and technically competent translators. Consideration for cultural norms means finding the appropriate gender, age, and cultural competence for a translator to make the victim comfortable to tell their story. In many cases, the investigator might have to resort to a phone translation service, but this is not ideal. In any case, the translator must be able to transmit empathy and accurately pass on the plea of the investigator for the victim to trust and cooperate. This process can take time. Good investigators will not rush to evidence gathering.

A good practice is preparing a safe house or bank of hotel rooms that can be secured. The victims will have time to decompress in a comfortable setting. This allows the investigators to build rapport and obtain more detailed statements. Throughout the interviews of the victims of human sex trafficking, investigators should be prepared for the chilling effect on cooperation that can come from the victim's immigration status, incarceration, and threats to their family back in their home country.

The importance of cooperating victims in sex trafficking cases is critical. Investigators wisely spend their time building trust and thoroughly documenting what they know of the organization's activities. Questioning should cover

- How the victim was recruited into the trafficking organization
- How they entered the United States
- What they were told by members of the trafficking organization about their obligations and duties to the organization
- Any threats or acts of violence they have witnessed or suffered
- How they obtain food, shelter, and other necessities
- How they were transported within the United States
- Who paid for their travel and lodging
- Where their identification documents are and whether they can obtain them
- If they engaged in prostitution, questioning should extend to these activities, including training and instruction in their role as a sex worker

Commercial prostitution, sexually oriented businesses, and sex trafficking are not innocuous institutions in society. The activities of these organizations have true victims and demand justice. Competent investigators should look for evidence of these activities in their jurisdiction, plan for a detailed collection of evidence, and intelligently match modern investigative techniques to the problem at hand. Above all, they should keep the care and welfare of the victims in mind.

Summary

To understand the increasing business of sex trafficking, it is important to consider the sex-for-hire enterprise. Often called prostitution, the sex-for-hire enterprise is a complex business with a language of its own. In the traditional model, clients known as johns solicit sex acts from prostitutes whose pimps maintain control through various acts of violence and intimidation or protection. These traditional models have obvious flaws, however, which has led to the use of Internet advertisements as a way to maintain a degree of anonymity. In addition, the use of Internet-facilitated prostitution allows workers to shorten their shifts, limits wasted time walking the streets, and allows pimps to book dates in other cities in advance. Online advertising further permits freelance prostitution, though it entails a higher risk of rape, violence, and robbery.

Special kinds of prostitution include sexually oriented businesses such as strip clubs, escort services, and massages parlors, which provide fronts for commercialized prostitution. Sex trafficking victims often provide ideal employees for such businesses since many are vulnerable, without legal residence, and are unfamiliar with their surrounding environments. Though business practices vary, most employ policies indicating that any sexual act is the fault of the worker and as such businesses can remain insulated from legal liabilities. This makes prosecution difficult but not impossible.

Using several different investigation techniques, law enforcement officials in corroboration with other agencies work to prosecute these sex trafficking and prostitution rings. Techniques such as patron debriefs, routine business checks for license compliance, buy-busts, reverses, and sneak-and-peaks help law enforcement officials gather evidence for prosecution of prostitution and sex trafficking. With the assistance of an information collection plan, investigators maintain control of knowledge and documents key to the investigation. The greatest investigation challenge is the relationship between sex workers and police. Victims are often slow to trust and easily afraid of cooperating in any investigation. As such, it is essential that good investigators take time to build a solid relationship with victims if there is any hope of cooperation.

Key Terms

"A" file—Alien file maintained by the U.S. Citizenship and Immigration Service to document an alien's permission to enter, remain, and work in the United States.

alien—Someone in a country who is not a lawful resident of that country.

the blade—In the context of commercial prostitution, a circuit of locations frequented by a pimp and sex workers.

bottom—In the context of commercial prostitution, the manager who trains and regulates workers on behalf of the pimp.

escort—A worker for an escort service who accompanies clients for a fee. Often a sex worker.

exotic dancer—An employee of a strip club who dances on stage.

harboring—In the context of commercial prostitution and sex trafficking, housing a sex worker in furtherance of prostitution.

hostess bar—A sexually oriented business that allows patrons to pay for a woman to entertain them while inside the business.

in-call—Services offered by a sexually oriented business inside its physical storefront.

john—Client of a sex worker.

lot lizard—A sex worker who operates in parking lots, often of interstate truck stops.

Mann Act—Federal code prohibiting interstate prostitution.

massage parlor—Specific type of sexually oriented business that offers massage as its lawful service and prostitution for an additional fee.

money laundering—The process of introducing ill-gotten gains into legitimate financial markets by concealing the source of the income.

out-call—Services offered by a sexually oriented business away from the physical storefront.

panderer—Anyone who profits by catering to the base desires of their clientele.

pimp—A criminal who operates a prostitution organization and profits from its activities.

prostitution—Sexual contact between people in consideration for something of value.

sneak-and-peak—A slang term for court orders allowing law enforcement to enter locations surreptitiously to search or install surveillance equipment.

sex-for-hire—Alternate term for prostitution.

sex trafficking—A specific variety of human trafficking wherein the victim is valued by the offenders for their usefulness in performing sex acts for hire.

sex worker—Proper name for anyone who engages in sex-for-hire.

sexually oriented business—A lawful business that incorporates products or services of a sexual nature in its business plan, and often serves as a front for commercial prostitution.

streetwalker—A sex worker who works near streets.

Title III—Shorthand for the federal law allowing law enforcement agents to conduct wiretaps and electronic surveillance with a court order.

trick—Slang term for an act of prostitution.

Review Questions

1. Discuss the similarities between sexually oriented businesses and legitimate business practices.
2. Define the major aspects of the three special kinds of prostitutions mentioned.
3. Briefly explain the different investigation techniques associated with investigating sex-trafficking organizations.
4. What types of challenges do investigators face in dealing with human trafficking cases?
5. Why is the relationship between sex workers and law enforcement officers so important to the handling of cases?

References

"9-79.100 Mann Act." U.S. Department of Justice, United States Attorney General. http://www.justice.gov/usao/eousa/foia_reading_room/usam/title9/79mcrm.htm. Accessed February 16, 2014.

"9-110.000 Organized Crime and Racketeering." U.S. Department of Justice, United States Attorney General. http://www.justice.gov/usao/eousa/foia_reading_room/usam/title9/110mcrm.htm. Accessed February 16, 2014.

Global Report on Trafficking of Persons. New York, NY: United Nations Office of Drug Control, December 2012.

Hess Orthmann, Christine, and Karen Matison Hess. *Criminal Investigation,* 10th ed. Belmont, CA: Wadsworth Cengage Learning, 2013.

Palmiotto, Michael J., and N. Prabha Unnithan. *Policing and Society: A Global Approach.* Clifton Park, NY: Delmar Cengage Learning, 2011.

Potterat, John J., and Devon D. Brewer et al. "Mortality in a Long-term Open Cohort of Prostitute Women." *American Journal of Epidemiology,* 159, 8, 778–785, 2003.

Siegel, Larry J. *Criminology,* 10th ed. Belmont, CA: Wadsworth Cengage Learning, 2012.

Walker-Rodriguez, Amanda, and Rodney Hill. "Human Sex Trafficking." *Federal Bureau of Investigation Law Enforcement Bulletin.* March 2011.

U.S. Department of Justice, Office of Justice Programs. "Title III of the Omnibus Crime Control and Safe Streets Act of 1968 (Wiretap Act)." https://it.ojp.gov/default.aspx?page=1284. Last revised September 19, 2013.

Street Gangs and Human Trafficking

10

JOSEPH STEARNS

Contents

Major Topics

- Brief history of street gangs and human trafficking
- Modern street gang activity and human trafficking
- Parallels between gang members and human trafficking victims
- Roadblocks faced by law enforcement
- Recommendations from a law enforcement perspective

Introduction

In this chapter an exploration will be made into how human trafficking has become more prevalent among localized street gangs. A dynamic change within both nationally recognized and locally identified street gangs has resulted in an overall lack of organization from the top down. Traditional rules and "street law" generally followed by these organizations have become a thing of the past. The lack of leadership coupled with an absence of rules to follow has caused gang members to commit crime on an individual level instead of typical group activities. Human trafficking has come to the forefront as the crime of choice for these gang members to make money. We will also look at a few of the factors affecting both the gang members taking part in human trafficking, as well as the victims involved, including mental conditioning and modern social behaviors. The roadblocks for law enforcement regarding human trafficking investigations and prosecution will be addressed and solutions will be offered, as we examine street gangs and human trafficking from a law enforcement perspective.

Brief History of Street Gangs and Human Trafficking

In the law enforcement arena, gangs are generally in three classifications: outlaw motorcycle gangs, prison gangs, and street gangs. Although human trafficking has been shown to exist within each of these groups, we will focus on the street gang and their use of human trafficking. The street gang mentality has always boiled down to two main motivations: power and respect. Power and respect are directly affected by one another. One of the main methods a gang uses to enhance its power and respect is with the almighty dollar. Money is used to recruit new members, buy more weapons, and buy more drugs, all of which add to the gang's power and respect.

Traditionally, when we think about how a street gang makes money, we think of crimes such as robbery, auto theft, and narcotics sales, to name a few. The crime of human trafficking is oftentimes forgotten. The reason for this is because in the past it was referred to both in the law enforcement community and in the civilian community as prostitution. In many conversations, one is mostly likely to hear that prostitution is the world's oldest profession. Since prostitution has been around long before street gangs, it is only logical that gang members would figure out a way to exploit the world's oldest profession to benefit themselves and their gangs.

The world of prostitution gave society one of the earliest forms of a gangster: the pimp. Pimps were motivated by power and respect, and they did this by making money. Exploiting females to buy expensive clothes, cars, and drugs increased their power among the other criminals in their environment. These pimps were looked upon by the low-level street thug with envious eyes. A desire to emulate these early pimps, not only in criminal activity but with their style of dress, has had a lasting effect on the street gang culture. At some point it became socially acknowledged that being "a pimp" was to "be gangster" and vice versa. Both terms have now developed into common descriptors for something that is cool.

The idea that prostitution had much the same effect on how street gangs were shaped as did the rise of crack cocaine is definitely a topic that could be debated. The social devastation caused by crack cocaine since its creation often overshadows prostitution. So much so, that prostitution has not been the focus of the law enforcement community and lawmakers until recently. Street gangs have drastically changed their dynamic over the years. The crimes, including prostitution, are the same, but their methods are different.

Modern Street Gang Activity and Human Trafficking

Compared to street gang members of the past, the modern street gang member is a completely different specimen. Many factors over several decades have contributed to the extreme change in dynamic of the modern street gang. From their inception, many traditional street gangs were formed with a leadership hierarchy that could rival a Fortune 500 company including written bylaws and codes of conduct. As time has passed, so has the existence of most highly organized street gangs. Continued law enforcement efforts and an improved social awareness of street gangs have helped fracture these organizations from the top down. This has resulted in an extreme change in the dynamic of the traditional street gang.

Law enforcement agencies across the country are experiencing gangs with a total disregard for the traditional street rules. Gang members that traditionally feud with each other are now going into business with each other. Members of rival gangs are now riding in cars, committing crimes and, in some instances, living together. For veterans of law enforcement, this is often a difficult concept to understand and accept. The days of walking like a duck and talking like a duck type of identification are gone. The term *hybrid gangs* is one that has received a lot of press since it was officially recognized in the Federal Bureau of Investigation's 2011 National Gang Threat Assessment. Among gang professionals, this term is up for interpretation but has come to be the most accurate way to describe the type of gangs that are being encountered.

The traditional mob mentality has been replaced by a money over everything mentality, which contributes to the hybrid gang theory and leads to a more individualistic approach to gang crimes. When a gang member is acting on his own behalf, the level of risk is much higher. Traditional crimes of robbery, aggravated assaults, and even dealing narcotics have an increased risk associated with them. This has led to the increase in the low-risk, high-reward crime of human trafficking. Though the modern gang member still relies on traditional gang-related crimes, an increase in human trafficking cases has been reported nationwide.

When talking about human trafficking and street gangs, we are talking about the male exploitation of females, often juvenile females, for the use of sex. Much like the pimps of the past, the gang member facilitates a meeting between the victim and a client for the purpose of sexual activities. The gang member then reaps the monetary rewards from the activities of the victim. In most instances, we are talking about American-born victims and not the illegal immigrants that one commonly thinks of when human trafficking is discussed.

So how is it that these gang members are able to force a female into performing sexual acts on other gang members or, in many instances, complete strangers? What factors exist that prevent these girls from getting out or going to the authorities for help? Interestingly enough, many parallels exist between gang member recruitment and the victims of human trafficking that can help answer these questions.

Parallels between Gang Members and Human Trafficking Victims

Many similarities exist between how street gangs recruit new gang members and how they exploit their victims of human trafficking. Both types of individuals can be seen as victims and often have similar characteristics. The prospective gang member is often an at-risk youth with little to no adult supervision. These lost souls are looking for a sense of belonging, protection, and an overall identity. The human trafficking victim shares the same types of wants and needs. Oftentimes, these victims are prone to being habitual runaways, survivors of abuse, and are already using alcohol and drugs. Gang members target these victims making grand promises to meet these needs. With the use of increased social status, money, and a feeling of belonging to a family, the gang members place a stranglehold on these victims that often leads to a lifestyle much different than what is initially promised. The human trafficking victim is promised much the same but with the added influence of male acceptance.

The male gang member may begin an intimate relationship with the victim, immediately tapping into the emotional needs of the victim. With promises of being taken care of both emotionally and financially, the gang member begins his manipulation of the victim. Much like the new gang recruit is used to "put in work" or commit crimes on behalf of the gang, the female victim is put to work doing sexual acts for money. As was previously discussed, once these victims are part of the process, the gang members use fear and intimidation to keep these individuals involved in their respective activities. The thought of trying to remove themselves from their current situations seems impossible in the minds of the new gang member and the human trafficking victim.

In contrast, as with many gang members, there are some human trafficking victims that do not want to get out of the situation. A desensitization of our youth has contributed to these instances where the human trafficking victim is willing to go out and make money for their man and the man takes no issue with exploiting the female. A generation that is being influenced by popular culture and its support of gang activity and sexual exploitation of females creates a complicated situation for our society as a whole to combat. Popular culture in the form of movies, magazines, and music videos is full of images of females being paid to dance naked or have sex with men. Musical lyrics that degrade females to the point of being merely a sexual object are now being played on popular radio stations nationwide. A social acceptance of this type of material has conditioned a new generation both mentally and emotionally, making human trafficking difficult to address. Gang members have capitalized on this situation and it is now up to us, not only in law enforcement but as a society as a whole, to fracture this activity.

Roadblocks Faced by Law Enforcement

Law enforcement faces many roadblocks when it comes to the battle with human trafficking and its relation to street gangs. From the perspective of a veteran law enforcement professional that has specialized in street gangs for the better part of a decade, the main roadblock is denial. The denial that street gangs exist in a community has historically been the response by many law enforcement agencies outside of the larger well-known origins of street gangs. Street gangs, and the social stigma that accompanies them, add to the fear and intimidation that makes them powerful as criminal organizations.

Another factor that creates a roadblock for law enforcement but has also transformed how street gangs operate as an organization is the use of the Internet and social media. Social media outlets including, but not limited to, Facebook, Twitter, YouTube, and Snapchat allow gangs to conduct business that was traditionally handled in the street in the virtual realm. Unfortunately, these virtual beefs over newsfeeds, recruitment requests, and set tripping can end with very real results. These gang members are often more adept to the newer technologies than some of their law enforcement counterparts. The same social media outlets are being used by gang members to recruit new females to their team to begin the human trafficking process. Internet outlets make it easy for gang members to begin the relationships with these females and, if the relationship comes to fruition, just as easy to facilitate the human trafficking process.

Even when a law enforcement agency is able to arrest a gang member for human trafficking, the battle has not been won. Some jurisdictions do not have the ability to use sentencing enhancements for gang members or human traffickers. Similarly, some states do not have statutes allowing law enforcement to actively identify and track street gang members. However, even when jurisdictions have both the ability to identify gang members and the ability to prosecute using gang-related or human-trafficking-related enhancements, there is a lack of communication between those involved that creates the roadblock. Both parties will also inevitably deal with a lack of cooperation from both the victim and the perpetrator.

Recommendations from a Law Enforcement Perspective

With each roadblock comes many possible solutions. By no means do these recommendations guarantee success, but they will enhance the abilities of law enforcement and the communities they serve. When considering the fear and stigma that accompany the subject of street gangs, one has to think about why anyone fears anything. We often fear what we do not understand because it is unknown. The solution to the unknown, and the fear of such, is education. The education of our law enforcement and the communities affected by street gangs is a strong tool in the fight against street gangs and human trafficking. Specific education for law enforcement, school personnel, and community groups is necessary to improve the identification of those involved in gangs and human trafficking. An increase in knowledge will also lead to an increase in communication and trust between these entities. Everyone in the equation must take some of the responsibility for acquiring and maintaining this education. The education level must be group specific to be effective and must be updated as current trends develop and change.

A solution to the rise of social media and street gangs comes down to several factors. Law enforcement must be able to identify those gang members that are using the social media outlets, but then must also understand how the outlets work. A basic understanding of each outlet is often not enough. A department must have intelligence officers or analysts that monitor these sites on a daily basis. These individuals must know what to look for when looking for gang activity and the use of girls for human trafficking. Law enforcement must be aware of the legal red tape involved when requesting user information from these sites to assist in prosecution, as well as the time it takes to conduct a lengthy investigation. Parents of those involved in the gang activity, as well as the human trafficking aspect, must also be aware of the power of social media. Education on this topic should also be a part of the overall push against gangs and human trafficking.

What can be done to bypass the roadblocks that exist in the prosecution process involving street gangs and human trafficking? Many states have passed legislation that provides law enforcement the ability to identify and track street gang members. The ability to develop databases for names and criminal intelligence is a powerful tool for law enforcement during many investigations. These laws also allow prosecutors to use criminal enhancements when a gang member commits specific crimes. A gang enhancement clause, or a definition of a gang-predicated crime, could be used for longer sentences, bond restrictions, or parole and probation stipulations. With states that do have specific laws in place concerning gang crimes and human trafficking, they are often exclusive to their respective crimes, meaning that the ability is there to impose severe sentences and prosecution on gang members for human trafficking, but it is not used, in lieu of employing one or the other and not both. In some cases involving gang members and human trafficking, federal prosecution is available and must be considered, especially in jurisdictions that lack street gang legislation.

Summary

Law enforcement has been faced with the individual problems of human trafficking and street gangs for many decades. Only until recent years have the two come together to create a problem of epidemic proportions. Street gang members are employing the same tactics that they have traditionally used to recruit new members to recruit young girls into human trafficking. The further use of fear and intimidation by these gang members makes it difficult to not only get these girls out of the human trafficking arena but to also prosecute cases when arrests are made.

Law enforcement agencies and the communities that they serve must work in partnership with each other against street gangs and human trafficking. Proper education for all entities involved is necessary to create successful outcomes from the identification of street gangs, identification of human trafficking, and finalizing a prosecution. Lawmakers must also realize the detrimental impact both street gangs and human trafficking can have on a community and empower law enforcement with stricter penalties for the perpetrators and appropriate care for the victims. The fact remains that both gangs and human trafficking will always exist in some capacity, but with increasing awareness and strong law enforcement–citizen partnerships an impact can be made.

Key Terms

desensitization
fear
gang-predicated
hybrid gangs

intimidation
recruitment
social media

Review Questions

1. What are some of the reasons for the dynamic shift in street gang activity?
2. What are some of the tactics used by street gang members involved in human trafficking?
3. What are some of the roadblocks faced by law enforcement in regard to human trafficking and street gangs?
4. What are some solutions to the problems faced by law enforcement in regard to human trafficking and street gangs?

Forced Labor in the United States

11

MICHAEL J. PALMIOTTO

Contents

Major Issues

- Defining forced labor
- Overlooked prevalence of forced labor
- Victims' and offenders' education about forced labor

Introduction

In recent years human trafficking has received a great deal of attention, but defining and identifying human trafficking victims has been difficult. Before defining human trafficking the reader should recognize that human trafficking is often confused with human smuggling. The smuggling of humans has been identified as the facilitation, transportation, and entering of illegals across international borders. Smuggling requires the participation of two willing parties in a commercial transaction. Trafficking of persons involves a monetary profit by criminally exploiting people being trafficked. Human trafficking does not require that those being trafficked be transported across an international border. Human trafficking exploits individuals for labor and commercial sex. Those trafficked could be children or adult men and women (Wilson and Dalton, 2008, p. 297). There are four points that differentiate smuggling from trafficking (Bajrektarevic, 2000, p. 16):

1. Smuggled persons always travel voluntarily; trafficked persons can either begin their trip voluntary or may have been coerced or kidnapped.
2. Trafficked persons are used and exploited over a long period of time.
3. An interdependency occurs between the trafficked persons and organized crime groups.
4. Trafficked persons are eligible for further networking (recruitment for criminal purposes).

Human trafficking appears to occur in every country in the world. It could be the country of origin, transit, or destination. According to the International Labor Organization there are over 12 million people in forced labor. About 2.5 million are made to work for the government, rebel military groups, and the army. The remaining almost 10 million are forced to work in the private sector. Most of these are in forced labor with about 14 percent involved in the sex business. In the United States forced labor trafficking has not received much attention (Zhang, 2012b, pp. 469–470).

It may be difficult to comprehend for many Americans that forced labor does occur in the United States. Not only does it occur, but it is a serious problem in the United States. People are being forced to work against their will in cities, towns, and in rural America for minimum wages, if any at all. Generally forced labor is not visible and the general population does not recognize it. Most Americans would not know how to define the forced labor aspect of human trafficking. However, in recent years the media has frequently reported human trafficking in the United States. The reports are similar in the actions taken against the offenders against human trafficking victims. Traffic victims receive little or no pay for difficult and menial work, and are held in debt bondage. The traffickers confiscate government and identification documents such as immigration papers and passports. Without government documents the victims are at the mercy of the traffickers who are practicing not only a criminal act but also labor and human rights violations.

Definitions of Forced Labor

There are numerous definitions of human trafficking, but we will provide three definitions for this chapter. The definitions are from the International Labour Convention of 1930, the United Nations, and the United States Trafficking Victims Protection Act (TVPA). First to be examined is the International Labour Convention of 1930 (No. 29, Article 2 (1)), which states that "the term 'forced or compulsory labour' shall mean all work or service which is exacted from any person under the menace of any penalty and for which the said person has not offered himself voluntarily." The elements of the convention require a further explanation. First, "all work or service" includes all types of work, employment, or occupations. Forced labor can also take place in a private residence or household. Second, "any person" includes children as well as adults. The person held in forced labor could be a citizen of the country where the offense is occurring. Third, "menace of penalty" not only refers to criminal offenses but also to coercion, threats, violence, retaining government identity documents, confinement, or nonpayment for services or wages. The important point is that a person should be free to leave his job without losing his rights, privileges, or wages. Fourth, "voluntary" refers to the worker giving his consent to enter a relationship with an employer. The worker must be free to provide his consent to be employed by a specific employer (Andres, 2008, p. 4).

The United Nations (2000) definition of human trafficking is as follows:

> "Trafficking in persons" shall mean the recruitment, transportation, transfer, harboring or receipt of persons, by means of the threat or use of force or other forms of coercion, of abduction, of fraud, of deception, of the abuse of power or of a position of vulnerability or control over another person, for the person of exploitation. Exploitation shall include, at a minimum, the exploitation of the prostitution of others or other forms of sexual exploitation, forced labor or services, slavery or practices similar to slavery, servitude, or the removal of organs. (Article 3(a) Protocol)

The United Nations definition provides broad definitions of human trafficking from forcing sexual exploitation to forced laboring.

The United States Trafficking Victims Protection Act (TVPA) defines forced labor of human trafficking as, "The recruitment, harboring, transportation, provision, or obtaining of a person for labor or services, through the use of force, fraud, or coercion for the purpose of subjection to involuntary servitude, personage or bondage, or slavery" (U.S. Department of State, 2013, p. 8). Both the United Nations and the TVPA recognized that forcing people into prostitution should also be considered forced labor. The TVPA considers "sex trafficking in which commercial sex act is induced by force, fraud, or coercion, or in which the person induced to perform such an act has not attained 18 years of age" (U.S. Department of State, 2013, p. 8).

The TVPA holds that physical transportation is not necessary for a crime to fall under either of the two previous definitions. Victims may be those not born in forced labor, transported, or previously consented to work for a trafficker, or be involved in a crime resulting from trafficking. Generally, human trafficking is considered a federal crime and primarily dealt with by federal authorities.

Human trafficking requires several elements for it to be considered trafficking of humans. First, there has to be recruitment, transportation, transferring of people, housing, and receiving persons. Second, the means of obtaining people can involve the use of force or threat, coercion, abduction, fraud, deception, abuse of power, or providing monetary payments or benefits to control the victim. Third, the goal is exploitation, which may include prostitution, forced labor, slavery, or the removal of organs. An element in each of these sections must occur for human trafficking to occur. Children under the age of 18 are exempt of the requirement from the previous categories (Aronowitz, 2009, pp. 1–2). Labor trafficking is a modern form of slavery and a major violation of human rights as well as being criminal.

Causes of Human Trafficking

The cause of labor trafficking crosses economic, social, and cultural factors, and requires intensive study. There are a number of reasons for the causes of trafficking of people. In many cases those selected may be called "throwaway people." Those who find themselves in forced labor may be extremely poor and are raised in families with a history of poverty, struggling to survive. The victims are often illiterate, which goes along with their poverty. If they are economically deprived they may suffer from indebtedness or be unable to find decent employment. Those pushed to forced labor may be discriminated against, lacking opportunities, or not valued as human beings. Often this includes females and those of ethnic and racial minorities.

An increase in forced labor trafficking could be attributed to a lack of workers and the number of jobs available where the worker resides. The worker needs the opportunity to freely accept a job he desires. Forced labor frequently occurs when the employment is illegal, the person is not of legal age, or the working conditions are below the legally accepted standards, or the worker wants to migrate to a country illegally. Forced labor does occur when it is profitable for the offender doing the exploitation (*Stopping Forced Labour*, 2001, p. 53).

For human trafficking to occur there must be reasons and purposes. There seems to be no uniform answer to the specific causes of human trafficking, because it crosses a wide number of countries and geographical regions. Trafficking occurs because of criminal greed, economical needs, political instability of regimes or local or state governments, and cultural and social factors to specific areas. Often human traffickers are criminals involved in an assortment of crimes. Criminals get involved in human trafficking because it is low risk and highly profitable. Trafficking of people is relatively inexpensive and usually does not require a large amount of funds. The manipulation of adult men and women violates labor laws and human rights and lacks of human decency in the treatment of a human being. Human trafficking preys on those most vulnerable. This includes the poor, uneducated, young children, and the immigrant who is impoverished but hoping for a good life (Bales and Lize, 2005, pp. 8–9). Traffickers may offer victims jobs in restaurants or hotels, and as nannies. Offenders may advertise in newspapers, employment agencies, magazines, and on the Internet as a ploy to attract victims. Once victims are hooked they come under the control of the traffickers.

Contemporary forced labor holds several groups vulnerable to this inhuman form of bondage. Those vulnerable specifically include the poor, women, children, racial and ethnic minorities, and migrants. The inability to recognize human trafficking makes it difficult for law enforcement to locate victims, obtain evidence, and make arrests that can lead to prosecution. Many foreigners who may be victims of trafficking are arrested for violations of immigration laws and deported. This action results in the victim being penalized and the offender free from reprimand (Aronowitz, 2002, p. 271).

Forced Labor Found in Economic Sectors

Forced labor can be found in five economic sectors in the United States. Forty-six percent are found in prostitution and sex services, 27 percent in domestic services, 10 percent in agriculture, 5 percent in sweat shops, and 4 percent in restaurant and hotel work. These sectors are vulnerable to forced labor because there is a demand for cheap labor with workers receiving low wages and with little or no regulation of working conditions. Employers in these sectors gain control over the workers lives (Human Rights Center, 2004, p. 5). Forced labor in human trafficking can be divided into several categories, with different researchers and authors providing their own categories. For the purpose of this chapter the following categories of forced labor are submitted and reviewed:

- Slavery
- Public works projects
- Agriculture
- Domestic servitude

- Bonded labor
- Manufacturing
- Child soldiers
- Construction

Slavery

The League of Nations' Slavery Convention of 1926 in Article 1(1) defines slavery as "the status or condition of a person over whom any or all of the powers attaching to the right of ownership are exercised." Slavery simply means a human being owns another human being. The slave owner has control over an enslaved human being. Slavery can be traced to ancient times. The Babylonians had slaves as did the Romans, Greeks, and Mesopotamians. Slavery has existed in every part of the world, in every continent from Africa to the Middle East to Europe and Asia. Slavery has continued to exist throughout the centuries down to the first decades of the twenty-first century.

Throughout history different academic disciplines have speculated on the origins of slavery. They have identified common characteristics underlying the manifestation of slavery (Burke, 2013, pp. 27–30):

> First, societies that have practiced slavery have tended to dehumanize workers of the lowest and most graded social status by classifying them as chattels, or items of personal property capable of being bought, sold, hired, mortgaged, bequeath to heirs, and moved from place to place.
> Second, most societies with slaves marginalized the enslaved population.
> Third, a shared characteristic of ancient and modern slave system is that chattel status is typically a heritable condition passed from mother to child.

There are approximately 30 million people currently held in slavery. No country seems to be free of slavery, although some countries have a larger number of slaves than others. According to the *Global Slavery Index* (Walk Free Foundation 2013, p. 11) the operational index used for their study follows:

Slavery is the possession and control of a person in such a way as to significantly deprive that person of his or her individual liberty, with the intent of exploiting that person through their use, management, profit, transfer, or disposal. Usually this exercise will be achieved through means such as violence or threats of violence, deception, or coercion.

Modern slavery has as its main feature controlling one individual by another and depriving them freedom for the sole purpose of exploiting the slaved individual. Forms of slavery include forced labor, debt bondage, child and forced marriages, and the sale of children. Even in our contemporary world hereditary slavery exists, specifically in sections of South Asia and West Africa. Victims of slavery can be kidnapped or captured and sold as slaves. Modern slavery, as in some African countries, uses children as military combatants. In this decade slavery is rarely recognized or understood since it is hidden from view in homes, worksites, and communities (Walk Free Foundation 2013, 2013).

The *Global Slavery Index* ranked 162 countries having slavery (with number one being the worst). The United States ranked 134 out of 162 countries. In a superpower with a republican form of government claiming to support democracy this seems a poor record for America. The *Trafficking of Human Report* claims the United States has been found to be a source, transit, and a country for the destination of adult men and women and children from not only foreign countries but also from America as well. The victims are made to participate in forced labor, involuntary servitude, debt bondage, and sex trafficking. The victims are forced to work in brothels, message parlors, hotel services, agriculture, manufacturing, janitorial services, domestic service, and elderly health care.

In our contemporary world, slaves are hidden from view, and all races, ethnicities, and religious groups can be forced into slavery. American citizens are not immune from becoming slaves and victims in their hometowns and cities. Several examples of victims kept as slaves will be reviewed. In 2007 a Long Island millionaire couple was convicted of abusing two Indonesian women whom they brought to America. The prosecutor called the case an example of modern slavery. The victims were beaten with brooms and umbrellas and cut with knives and made to take freezing showers. One victim was forced to eat her own vomit (Eltman, 2007). Another example of slavery was Ariel Castro, who kept three females as slaves for his use over a decade. He abducted the first woman in 2002, the second in 2003, and the third in 2004. Castro abused them physically and sexually. The women were able to escape and Castro was arrested and later convicted of murder and kidnapping. Castro committed suicide while in prison.

Public Works Projects

In some countries of the world, natives of their countries are required to participate in public works projects. They usually do not have the right to refuse. Usually the compulsory participation in public works projects takes place in Asia and Africa. The author of this chapter did not find any cases of compulsory participation in public works in the United States.

Agriculture

Forced labor in agriculture takes place throughout the world. The United States is no exception. Forced labor in U.S. agriculture can be traced to slavery, which was a part of Southern culture for several centuries. After the Civil War with the adoption of the Thirteenth Amendment that eliminated slavery, a new form of servitude took its place. The outlawing of slavery did not change the culture of the South, which held on to its belief that the black man did not have the same or equal rights of the white man. The black community was terrorized and was relegated to the lowest and least desired positions. The state of Florida approved the convict-lease system as forced labor. Blacks were arrested on trumped-up charges and were then leased to farmers for a fee. Working conditions were dismal and the mortality rate was high (Sellers and Asbed, 2011, p. 34). The forced labor of the Florida agricultural industry has continued to the first decades of the twenty-first century.

Since the late 1990s the Civil Rights Division of the U.S. Department of Justice has prosecuted agriculture companies in Florida. The Justice Department found that workers were held against their will with the use of violence, including beatings, shootings, and pistol-whipping. The forced victims were undocumented immigrants, guest workers, permanent residents, and U.S. citizens (Sellers and Asbed, 2011, p. 38).

Yearly guest workers are brought to the United States under the guest worker visa program. Workers are recruited from Latin countries and they are promised housing accommodations and good wages. However, upon arrival the workers' passports are confiscated and are threatened if they run away. The guest workers' living conditions are extremely unhealthy and often will not receive medical attention when injured or ill. The guest workers are forced to work and receive poor wages, if any at all. With the frequency of forced labor in the agriculture industry, guest workers are vulnerable and exploited (Hager, 2010).

In a study of migrant laborers in San Diego County, it was estimated that 30 percent of the migrant workers were victims of labor trafficking, and 55 percent were victims of exploitation or abusive labor practices which were redundant. In San Diego County illegal immigrants were taken advantage of. Because of their illegal status they would maintain silence about any abuses received making them vulnerable to labor traffickers. Unauthorized immigrants are most likely to be victims of forced labor, but they are at a disadvantage since law enforcement considers them a criminal rather than a victim (Zhang, 2012a). There seems little doubt that legal immigrants and illegal immigrants are open to exploitation with the illegal immigrant, at least in San Diego County, receiving the greatest abuse.

Domestic Servitude

A form of forced labor that primarily affects females is domestic servitude. Women and girls primarily work in homes, performing a number of various household chores, including caring for children and the elderly, gardening, cooking, cleaning, and laundry. The women and girls performing domestic work usually are poor, have little or no skills, and are poorly educated. Frequently domestic workers are recruited from a foreign country with the expectation that they will be improving their lives. However, they often find themselves captives to their employers, not being allowed out of the house, physically, emotionally, and sexually abused, and made to sleep on the floor, given little to eat, and not receiving any compensation for their hard work. In addition, when they are sick or injured they are not allowed to receive medical attention. When arriving from a foreign country their passports and personal documents are taken from them. Many of the foreign domestic workers do not speak English and often are not given the opportunity to learn the language. Several examples of employers abusing domestic workers follow.

Jefferson Calimlim Sr. and his wife, Elnora, both medical doctors in Milwaukee, Wisconsin, were sentenced to 72 months in prison for forcing a woman to work as their domestic servant and illegally harboring her for 19 years in their Brookfield home (Federal Bureau of Investigation, 2013). In another case, two men took a 16-year-old cook from New York to Indiana and subjected her to sexual abuse, forced labor, and beatings during a 6-month ordeal, federal prosecutors said. Ya Niang Soe, 22, and Jonathan A. Sullivan, 23, were charged with forced labor and trafficking with respect to forced labor, and more chargers could come later, authorities said. Authorities say the girl was forced to cook for one of the men and babysit for the other man's children (Federal Bureau of Investigation, 2008).

The two previous cases are only examples of domestic abuse and how women are treated in an inhumane manner simply because of their position. There are many examples of abuse of domestic workers by their employers. Many of the domestic abusers are educated, hold prestigious positions, and are wealthy. It is difficult to locate abuse of domestic workers since it is a hidden workforce. The laws of America protect the right of privacy for homeowners, but these rights provide an opportunity to be a abuser and free from arrest.

Another example of domestic labor is child domestic labor, which includes girls under the age of 18. Children become involved in domestic labor because of poverty and it seems normal since they will become wives and mothers. Young girls become involved in domestic work through siblings and friends involved in this occupation. Similar to domestic labor of adult women, child labor of young girls is also ignored, and is hidden in the dwelling of their employers. The children like the adult domestic workers are dependent on the families that employ them for their needs (Blagbrough, 2008). Obviously, child labor should be eliminated, but when a child comes from a family in poverty it seems rather difficult for domestic work to be avoided.

Bonded Labor

Bonded labor is an old economic institution. Workers become bonded when they voluntarily make the decision to be bonded because they are extremely poor or even starving. Victims become bonded laborers when their labor becomes demanded as a means of repayment for a loan or service in which the terms and conditions have not been defined or in which the value of the victims' services as reasonably assessed is not applied toward the liquidation of the debt. The value of their work is greater than the original sum of money borrowed.

Bonded child laborers are often forced into bondage by their parents as payment of a debt or collateral on a debt. Generally, forced child labor is found in illegal sections of the economy, which are not regulated. Countries with bonded child labor include India and Pakistan. The United States imports products from these countries with goods produced by child labor (U.S. Department of Labor n.d.). The United States does not seem to have bonded labor; if it exists it is hidden and not well known. This includes bonded child labor as well.

Although America may not have bonded child labor there exists concerns on the hazards of the work the youth do in our society. The National Consumer League (2000) has rated the five most dangerous jobs as

- Delivery and other driving
- Working alone in cash-based business and late-night work
- Traveling youth crews (children are illegally recruited to sell candy, magazines, and other consumer items in neighborhoods or on street corners)
- Cooking (exposure to hot oil, and grease, hot water and steam, and hot cooking surfaces)
- Construction and work in heights

Obviously, actions must be taken to protect America's youth from serious injuries and harm. Child labor laws have to be enforced and new laws need to be adopted to correct possible harm to young people.

Child Soldiers

Young children under the age of 18 are forced to serve in government military or rebel military groups in many parts of the world, including Asia and Africa. A child soldier is any person under 18 years old who has been forcefully recruited in a government military service or any person under 15 who has voluntarily agreed to government military service, or anyone under 18 who has been used in hostilities distinct from government military (U.S. Department of State, 2013).

In the twenty-first century, Human Rights Watch (2008) reports child soldiers are serving in 21 armed conflicts throughout the world. The most likely child soldier comes from poverty, has limited contact to education, is separated from family, and lives in a combat zone. When recruited, child soldiers are cooks, guards, and even serve in combat. The United States military does not use child soldiers.

Manufacturing

The manufacturing industry, in which employers violate labor laws, is another business sector that uses forced labor not only globally but also in the United States. The importation of low-cost items puts pressure on U.S.-based manufacturers who are forced to keep costs down. The reason forced labor exists in the United States is because labor laws do not protect the worker. Manufacturers are not held responsible when subcontracted foreign firms produce goods with forced labor. This system allows manufacturers to profit from forced labor without being held responsible for violating the law (Buckley, n.d., p. 117).

The exploitation by U.S.-owned companies' takes place worldwide. Chinese workers who produce covers for one of Apple's iPhones are exposed to labor violations. They stand on their feet more than 11 hours a day and work more than 100 hours of overtime per month. The Chinese factory is owned by an American company located in St. Petersburg, Florida. Women are forced to take pregnancy examinations. Wages in Apple's supplier factories are barely enough to live on, thereby forcing workers to work overtime to meet basic needs. Chinese workers are not the only workers exploited by U.S.-owned companies (Chinese Labor Watch, 2013). Other companies that used forced labor include Victoria's Secret, Philip Morris, Toys "R" Us, Urban Outfitters, Forever 21, and Hershey. All these companies deal with suppliers who exploit workers through poor working conditions and forced labor ("5 Giant Companies," 2008).

Construction

Construction is another industry in which trafficking and forced labor occurs. Workers who are legally recruited with false information on obtaining a good paying job in another country are held in captivity. Upon arrival their travel documents are taken from them, they are provided wages, and it is not uncommon that threats and violence are used against them. One of the main reasons for forced labor, such as construction, is debt bondage, which was previously discussed (Building and Wood Workers' International, 2013).

An example of forced labor abuses has been occurring in Qatar, a small Gulf state in the Middle East. In 2010 Qatar won the bid to host the 2022 World Cup. As a result new soccer stadiums, a new airport, new roads, soccer facilities for players, new hotels, and a bridge between Bahrain and Qatar has to be built. To complete the construction migrants were recruited from other countries. Thousands of male workers were recruited from Nepal, Sri Lanka, Pakistan, and Bangladesh to work in low-paying construction jobs. Often migrant workers paid fees for the construction jobs with the hope to support families and have a stable position. The working conditions are poor along with the uninhabitable living conditions. For example, five or six people are living in one small room, sometimes without a mattress to sleep on or air conditioning. The workers also received low pay or underpayment while working 9 to 11 hours per day, often traveling up to 4 hours to the construction site. Also, workers work in dangerous situations without safety precautions. Employers frequently failed to secure work permits for workers who they employed. This restricted their freedom of movement, which could lead to deportation or arrest (Human Rights Watch, 2012).

The author did not find forced labor in the U.S. construction industry, but this does not mean that it does not exist, only that it has not been discovered.

Male Victims

It has come to the attention of authorities that men and boys are the victims of labor and sex trafficking. Generally, the sex trafficking of boys is hidden, which reflects a taboo in most countries of the world. In the countries of Afghanistan and Sri Lanka, boys are more likely to be subjected to prostitution than girls. Men have been identified as sex trafficking victims in the United States (U.S. Department of State, 2013).

Elements of Forced Labor

The Human Rights Center, University of California, Berkeley considers forced labor a serious problem in the United States for four reasons. Forced labor is hidden, inhumane, widespread, and criminal (Human Rights Center, 2004, pp. 5–6).

Hidden—Thousands of men, women, and children are trafficked each year and forced to work without pay in extremely poor conditions. They are forced to work in brothels, sweatshops, farms, and private homes. Those kept under control are not allowed freedom and their documents of identification are taken from them.

Inhumane—Victims have been tortured, raped, assaulted, and murdered. Some have been subjected to forced abortions, dangerous working conditions, poor nutrition, and humiliation.

Widespread—Forced labor exists in 90 cities in the United States. It is practiced in a wide range of industrial sectors, including domestic service, the sex industry, food service, factory production, and agriculture. Although many victims are immigrants, some are U.S. residents or citizens.

Criminal—Forced labor is universally condemned and outlawed. Its practice in the United States violates a host of laws including indentured servitude, money laundering, and tax evasion. Yet criminals find it a highly profitable and lucrative enterprise. The workers are forced to be docile, and when problems arise, "employers" know they can rein in workers with threats and physical violence. Criminals also have learned that the odds are good that they will never be held accountable in a court of law.

Trafficking Offenders

Human trafficking involves the transportation, abduction, and subjugation of people for financial profit. This crime generates big profits for the trafficker. Those involved in fighting human trafficking perceive it as a modern form of slavery. Not only are the rights of victims violated but also their health and safety may be jeopardized. The exploitation of labor has not received the attention of sex trafficking. The attention on sex trafficking may be the product of political ideology pertaining to the definition of human trafficking. Victims of trafficking are not only forced into violation of sexual activities but also to various forms of forced labor besides prostitution. In the United Kingdom over half of the human trafficking victims were involved in forced labor. Children were often forced to beg, perform domestic work, and had organs harvested (Alvarez and Alessi, 2012, p. 143).

The offenders of labor trafficking will use violence, threats, lies, and various forms of coercion to force their victims to work against their desire. Victims of trafficking may be forced to work in homes as domestic workers, on farms doing the harvesting or planting of crops, and in factories working in unhealthy and unsafe conditions. These forced laborers may receive little or no salary. There is a wide variety of forced labor work that victims are forced to do (Project America, p. 1). Although physical coercion may be used in trafficking, it is not a requirement; intimidation may be sufficient for trafficking. Offenders can withhold earnings, government documents, identification papers, and threaten undocumented workers that they will inform the authorities of their illegal status. This action can be considered bonded labor. Deception or abduction can be used by traffickers against victims. An example may be a promise to a woman by a trafficker that she will work as a server but upon arrival finds she has been forced into prostitution. As another example, a migrant worker thinks he has agreed to be paid for his work but finds he has been trafficked (Shamir, 2012, p.87).

Human trafficking can be considered manipulation and exploitation, which includes the work the victim will be forced to do along with the poor working conditions. The victim may have agreed to perform a specific job but does not agree to a number of the working conditions, such as low pay, long working hours, and restricted freedom of movement. Trafficking involves not only labor laws and rights violations but also human rights and health issues. Victims of trafficking can be found in private residences in upper-class economical neighborhoods or be in debt bondage as in South Asia. Other victims may be forced to work on pineapple farms in the state of Washington and forced to live in extremely poor conditions (Shamir, 2012, pp. 87–88).

Locating Traffic Offenders and Victims

The Trafficking in Persons Report recognizes that there are a variety of private-sector professionals, community workers, government officials, and others who often encounter trafficking victims who, with training and knowledge of human traffickers, could identify victims. These groups include the following (U.S. Department of State, 2013, p. 11):

Government officials who inspect or have access to establishments where trafficking may occur are uniquely positioned to identify trafficking victims, including labor inspectors, port inspectors, factory inspectors, food industry inspectors, consular inspectors, agricultural inspectors, housing inspectors, tax authorities, and postal workers.

Private-sector employees who may encounter trafficking victims in the place of work (e.g., employees of hotels, restaurants, bars, beauty parlors, and groceries).

Law enforcement officers who are on the frontline of crime and are often those who have primary contact with trafficking victims, for example, all police (sometimes trafficking victims are identified through investigation of nontrafficking crimes), immigration officers, and border guards.

Health care professionals who often encounter trafficking victims, for example, emergency room personnel, health clinics, doctors, nurses, dentists, OB/GYNs, and practitioners at family planning clinics and HIV/AIDS clinics.

Transportation professionals who often encounter trafficking victims either being transported or otherwise exploited (e.g., truck, taxi, and bus drivers; train attendants; and employees at truck and rest stops).

Education officials, such as principals, guidance counselors, teachers, and school nurses, who are uniquely positioned to identify children who are being exploited.

The 2013 report further indicated that trafficking victims frequently seek assistance from a variety of agencies on various issues. Individuals and agencies that are often in a position to identify victims are religious ministers; and agencies that work with immigrants, children, homeless, refugees and other vulnerable individuals. Social workers and volunteers who work with domestic violence, sexual assault, or runaways could also identify victims of trafficking.

Summary

Human trafficking has received a great deal of attention in the twenty-first century. Primarily the emphasis of human trafficking has been on sex trafficking with forced labor trafficking receiving little attention. Forced labor is hidden and not visible to the public. Not only does forced labor occur in other countries, but it also takes place in the United States.

Forced labor has been defined by the International Labor Convention as "all work or service which is exacted from any person under the menace of any penalty and which the said person has not his services voluntary." The United States Trafficking Victims Protection Act has also defined forced labor of human trafficking as recruiting, harboring, and transportation of persons through the use of force, fraud, or coercion for involuntary servitude or slavery.

There are a variety of causes for forced labor of human trafficking. These include people who are extremely poor, poorly educated, and struggling to survive. Forced labor takes place when the employment is illegal, a person is not of legal age, or working conditions are below the acceptable level. Forced labor can take place in a variety of occupations. These include agriculture, domestic work, bonded labor, manufacturing, and construction.

There are a variety of ways that victims of forced labor trafficking can be identified along with offenders. This would include government officials, health care workers, transportation workers, and educators. Training and education are important not only to the previous fields of work but also for the general public if human trafficking is to be stopped.

Key Terms

coercion
forced labor
Global Slavery Index
International Labor Organization (ILO)
manipulation
smuggling
Trafficking Victims Protection Act (TVPA)

Review Questions

1. What are the key elements that separate human trafficking from smuggling?
2. Describe the different forms of forced labor.
3. How are victims recruited into forced labor?
4. What environmentally contributes to forced labor?
5. Are there any common themes between the types of forced labor?

References

"5 Giant Companies Who Use Slave Labor" (2008) Business Pundit, www.business-pundit.com/5-giant-companies-who-use-slave-labor/?img+42008.

Alvarez, Marie Beatriz, and Edward J. Alessi (2012) "Human Trafficking Is More Than Sex Trafficking and Prostitution: Implications for Social Work." *Affilia* 27(2): 142–152.

Andres, Beate (2008) *Forced Labour and Human Trafficking.* Geneva: International Labour Office.

Aronowitz, Alexis A. (2009) *Human Trafficking, Human Misery.* Westport, CT: Praeger.

Bales, Kelvin, and Steven Lize (2005) "Trafficking in Persons in the United States." National Institute of Justice.

Bajrektarevic, A. (2000) "Trafficking in and Smuggling of Human Beings—Linkage to Organized Crime—International Legal Measures." Statement Digest, International Centre for Migration Policy Development, Vienna, Austria.

Blagbrough, Jonathan (2008) "Child Domestic Labour: A Modern Form of Slavery." *Children and Society* 22(3): 179–190.

Buckley, Chrissey (n.d.) "Forced Labor in the United States: A Contemporary Problems in Need of a Contemporary Solution." *Topical Research Digest: Human Rights and Contemporary Solution,* www/du.edu/korbel/hrhw/research/slavery.us.pdf.

Building and Wood Worker's International (2013) "Trafficking and Forced Labour in the Construction Industry." June 21, www.bwin.org.

Burke, Marcy C. (2013) *Human Trafficking: Interdisciplinary Perspective.* New York, NY: Routledge.

Chinese Labor Watch (2013) "Chinese Workers Exploited by U.S.-Owned iPhone Supplier: An Investigation of Labor Conditions at Jabil Green Point in Wuxi, China." September 5.

Eltman, Frank (2007) "Long Island Couple Found Guilty in 'Slavery' Case." Associated Press, http://www.nysun.com/new-york-couple-found-guilty-in-slavery-case/68205/.

Federal Bureau of Investigation (2008) "Girl Was Raped, Forced to Cook and Clean," News, November 13.

Federal Bureau of Investigation (2013) "Human Traffic Awareness," News Blog, January 11, http://www.fbi.gov/news/news_blog/human-trafficking-awareness.

Hager, Sovereign (2010) "Farm Workers and Forced Labor." *Syracuse Journal of International Law and Commerce* 38(173).

Human Rights Center (2004) "Hidden Slaves: Forced Labor in the United States." University of California, Berkeley.

Human Rights Watch (2008) "Facts about Child Soldiers." http://www.hrw.org/news/2008/12/03/facts-about-child-soldiers. December 3.

Human Rights Watch (2012) "Building a Better World Cup: Protecting Migrant Workers in Qatar Ahead of FIFA."

National Consumer League (2000) "Working Teens Should Be Aware of Dangerous Jobs." http://www.cdc.gov/niosh/pubs.html.

Project America. "Labor Trafficking in the US." www.project.org/human-trafficking-in-the-us??mpl=component&print=18pages.

Sellers, Sean, and Greg Asbed (2011) "The History and Evolution of Forced Labor in Florida Agriculture." *Race/Ethnicity: Multidisciplinary Global Contexts* 5(1).

Shamir, Hila (2012) "A Labor Paradigm for Human Trafficking." *UCLA Law Review* 60(1).

Stopping Forced Labour (2001) Geneva: International Labour Conference.

U.S. Department of Labor, Bureau of International Labor Affairs (n.d.) "Forced and Bonded Labor." www.dol.gov/ILAB/media/reports/iclp/sweat2/bonded.htm.

U.S. Department of State (2013) Trafficking in Persons Report.

Walk Free Foundation (2013) *The Global Slavery Index.* www.walkfree.org.

Wilson, Jeremy M., and Erin Dalton (2008) "Human Trafficking in the Heartland: Variation in Law Enforcement Awareness Response." *Journal of Contemporary Criminal Justice* 24:296.

Zhang, Sheldon X. (2012) "Looking for a Hidden Population: Trafficking of Migrant Laborers in San Diego County." U.S. Justice Department.

Zhang, Sheldon X. (2012) "Measuring Labor Traffic: A Research Note," *Criminal Law Social Change* 58: 469–482.

Federal Law Enforcement and Human Trafficking

12

JEFF BUMGARNER

Contents

Major Issues

- Constitutional limitations on federal police power
- Application of the Commerce Clause
- The development of federal law enforcement in the United States

Introduction

Human trafficking is one of the most pernicious forms of abuse that people inflict on others in the modern era. Often dubbed the modern form of slavery, it involves the treatment of human beings—often children and teenagers—as chattel to be traded or sold into exploitative and illegal servitude. Victims of human trafficking are frequently forced into prostitution, exotic dancing, and pornography production. Other victims are forced into illegal labor relationships as domestic servants, sweatshop factory workers, and agricultural workers.

There are a myriad of federal and state criminal laws in the United States that confront human trafficking in its many forms. At the federal level, there are several departments and agencies that play a role in the thwarting the illegal trafficking of people to, from, and within the United States. These federal agencies are the subject of the present chapter. Whereas other chapters in this book offer readers a detailed explanation of the history and forms of human trafficking, as well as strategies employed to confront it, this chapter will provide readers with a detailed examination of the agencies in the federal law enforcement community involved in fighting this dreadful form of oppression. In particular, this chapter will offer a brief history of nature and jurisdiction of federal law enforcement in the United States, as well as a snapshot of federal law enforcement in the modern times. The chapter will then examine with some detail the particular agencies of the federal government that play lead roles in enforcing federal laws regarding human trafficking.

History of Federal Law Enforcement in America

Today in the United States, there is a general awareness of federal law enforcement, particularly as manifested in a select few key agencies. Most Americans have heard of, and are aware of, agencies such as the Federal Bureau of Investigation (FBI) and the U.S. Secret Service. These two agencies have very high public profiles, appearing regularly in news stories as well as in popular fictional accounts on the movie screen and in crime novels. Most Americans also file documents every year with the Internal Revenue Service (IRS) and are vaguely aware of the fact that there is a law enforcement unit within the IRS to pursue tax evaders. The Bureau of Alcohol, Tobacco, Firearms and Explosives (ATF) is also fairly well known in American culture. There have been many news stories over the years (some favorable, some unfavorable) that prominently featured ATF special agents clad in their blue raid jackets with the yellow-stenciled letters "ATF" on the back.

Indeed, these federal agencies and a few others are readily identifiable to most Americans. Much less known is the fact that there are actually dozens of federal law enforcement agencies engaged in a myriad of functions. Federal law enforcement agencies exist in every federal cabinet-level department and several independent departments; they can be found in all three branches of government (i.e., the executive branch, Congress, and the judiciary).

Constitutional Authority of Federal Law Enforcement

Often misunderstood about American federal law enforcement is the fact that federal law enforcement agencies— even the well-known ones—operate with relatively narrow authority. It can be said that federal law enforcement jurisdiction is a mile wide and an inch deep. It is wide because federal agents possess law enforcement authority in all 50 states and in all U.S. territories. It is shallow, however, because the national government in the United States does not possess a general police power. Instead, federal authority is limited to those powers that are enumerated in the U.S. Constitution. Broader police power—that is, the authority to regulate the day-to-day affairs of the people—belongs to the states. Indeed, the Tenth Amendment to the U.S. Constitution states: "The powers not delegated to the United States by the Constitution, nor prohibited to the States, are reserved to the States respectively, or to the people." Under the U.S. Constitution, power is to be shared between states and the national government. What's more, states are considered sovereigns, and sovereigns can police their own people and territory as they see fit.

So if powers not delegated to the federal government belong to the states, what powers are in fact delegated to the federal government? Does the Constitution envision some federal police power? The answer is that it certainly does. For example, Article III, Section 3, speaks to the federal crime of treason. And Article I, Section 8 (commonly referred to as the "Necessary and Proper Clause"), states that Congress has power to "make all laws which shall be necessary and proper for carrying into the execution the foregoing powers, and all other powers vested by this Constitution in the government of the United States."

The foregoing powers referred to above are listed in the Constitution, and include the power to regulate taxation, interstate and international commerce, immigration and naturalization, bankruptcy, counterfeiting securities and coin, piracy, and insurrection. All of these domains of regulation imply a federal law enforcement responsibility. Indeed, several amendments contained in the Bill of Rights offer protections to citizens from the federal government engaged in criminal investigation and prosecution (i.e., the Fourth, Fifth, Sixth, and Eighth Amendments). So, the notion that the federal government possesses some appropriate law enforcement function should not be controversial. More controversial, however, is just what that function ought to be.

Proponents of a strong federal government with a robust police power argue that the Preamble of the Constitution offers something of a blank check when taken in tandem with the Necessary and Proper Clause. The Preamble states that the Constitution is "ordained and established" for the purpose of

- Establishing justice
- Ensuring domestic tranquility

- Providing for the common defense
- Promoting the general welfare
- Securing the blessings of liberty

Clearly, there are many potential criminal laws that a well-intentioned Congress might pass in pursuit of the noble aims articulated in the Preamble. However, critics of a broad federal police power note that the Preamble is not itself a "clause" of the Constitution. It merely states the purpose of it. What's more, they would point to the framers of the Constitution for clarity with regard to the scope of federal domestic power.

James Madison, the chief author of the Constitution, wrote in *Federalist 41* that the powers of the federal government to provide for the common defense and general welfare of the people are embodied in the enumerated powers. He specifically said that there are no additional powers to be inferred from the Preamble. Madison asked rhetorically: Why enumerate powers at all if they are merely a sample contained in a general power (Bumgarner Crawford, and Burns 2013)?

In *Federalist 45*, Madison wrote that the federal government's powers under the new Constitution would be "few and defined," and that they would relate principally to external objects, such as war, peace, foreign commerce, and tariffs. Of the power of the state governments, Madison said they were "numerous and indefinite," and that they would relate to the lives, liberties, and properties of the people, the internal order, and the improvement and prosperity of the state (Bumgarner et al., 2013). This thinking, which was predominant at the time the Constitution was written and adopted, was rooted in the belief that the closer people were to their government, the better. Or put another way, the more power a government had over its people, then the more imperative it was that the people be in position to hold that government accountable. And clearly, people have greater direct influence over state and local officials than national ones.

Despite Madison's understanding of the limits on federal power in the late eighteenth century, including police power, it is certainly true that the federal government has seen its jurisdiction in law enforcement matters grow exponentially over the decades. Although still limited in jurisdiction, the federal law enforcement apparatus of today is far more interwoven into the fabric of American law enforcement than it had been closer to the nation's founding.

Early Manifestations of Federal Law Enforcement

In the later part of the eighteenth century and first part of the 19th century, American federal law enforcement, pursuant to the federal government's exercise of its enumerated powers, was manifested in four areas of responsibility (Bumgarner 2006; Bumgarner et al. 2013):

1. Enforcing taxes and tariffs
2. Serving the federal judiciary
3. Securing public facilities
4. Protecting the postal system

In 1789, Congress passed the Tariff Act, which authorized the federal government to collect duties on imported goods. This same year, Congress also created the mechanism for collecting said duties. The Fifth Act of Congress, among other things, created the first federal agency: the Customs Bureau. Organizationally, Customs was placed in the Department of the Treasury. The agency employed "collectors" in each Customs district, as well as "surveyors" and naval officers to assist the collectors in garnering the revenue. In 1790, Congress appropriated funds for 10 warships, which were to be operated by Customs as the Revenue Cutter Service—the precursor to the modern-day U.S. Coast Guard (Saba 2003). The Revenue Cutter Service engaged directly in law enforcement responsibilities as it enforced tariff and trade laws, and interdicted smugglers and pirates. The Revenue Cutter Service also enforced anti-slave trade laws, including the prohibition of using American vessels for the slave trade and the ban on the introducing of new slaves from Africa into the United States (U.S. Coast Guard 2002).

Another area of federal law enforcement related to the federal judiciary. The Judiciary Act of 1789 created 13 federal judicial districts. It also created the federal district and circuit (appellate) courts. Under the law, each judicial district would have a presidentially appointed United States attorney and United States marshal. U.S. marshals and their deputies constitute the first federal law enforcement officers with exclusively law enforcement duties. Those duties resembled those of a county sheriff and included

- Serving federal court orders
- Capturing and delivering federal prisoners
- Compelling jurors to serve

U.S. marshals served as the primary federal investigative and enforcement arm through the 19th century. Among the federal criminal laws U.S. marshals enforced were the Alien Act of 1798 (requiring deportation of foreigners deemed dangerous), the Sedition Act of 1798 (criminalizing criticism of government), anti-slave trade laws, and ironically, the Fugitive Slave Act (which required that slaves who escaped to nonslave states in the north would be returned to their owners upon capture) (Calhoun 1989).

One of the federal government's enumerated and exclusive powers is the authority to establish and maintain a postal system. Ben Franklin was appointed postmaster general of the Colonial postal system in 1753. In that capacity, Franklin created the position of surveyor in 1772. Postal surveyors were responsible for regulation and audit functions pertaining to the mail. The Postal Inspection Service, which itself is a storied law enforcement agency, traces its own lineage back to the duties of postal surveyors in the Colonial postal system. In 1792, the United States Postal Service (USPS) was established as a permanent federal agency. Then, in 1801, the working title for surveyors became "special agent." In 1830, the Postal Service created within itself the Office of Instructions and Mail Depredations. This office served as the investigative and inspection branch of the Postal Service. Special agents in this office were responsible for investigating and preventing embezzlement and robberies (of mail riders, stage coaches, steamboats, trains carrying the mail). Special agents were authorized to carry firearms and make arrests as federal officers (USPS 2007).

The final manifestation of federal law enforcement in the early years after the nation's founding was that of policing federal property. From 1790 to 1800, Congress met in Philadelphia while public buildings were being constructed in Washington, DC. The new District of Columbia had been partitioned from Maryland and Virginia for the purpose of serving as the nation's capital. It was thought that the capital city should not be located in any one state but should be in exclusively federal territory. However, the District of Columbia had no infrastructure to support the United States government. So funds were appropriated and buildings were to be constructed. Congress established a commission for managing federal real property. To police the grounds during and after construction of federal buildings, the commission initially hired six night watchmen. The use of night watchmen to patrol federal property continued until 1828, when Congress formally authorized the establishment of a Capitol Police Force, whose responsibilities including patrolling and policing the Capitol grounds and other public buildings in Washington, DC (Bumgarner et al. 2013).

Despite these early incarnations of narrowly tailored federal law enforcement authority and application shortly after the nation's founding, the United States would see its federal law enforcement footprint expand dramatically throughout the latter half of the 19th and the 20th centuries as the nation itself would expand. This included, among others, the creation of the Department of Interior 1849 and its absorption of the Capitol Police; the creation of the U.S. Secret Service in the Treasury Department in 1865; the creation of the Justice Department in 1870 and its absorption of the various U.S. marshals into the department as a single U.S. Marshals Service; the creation of the Forest Service within the Department of Agriculture (in 1905) and the National Park Service within the Interior Department (in 1916)— both with federal law enforcement authority; and of course the creation of the Bureau of Investigation within the Justice Department in 1908 (whose name would change in 1935 to the Federal Bureau of Investigation). In conjunction with the creation of new federal agencies, and the overhaul of existing ones, came new federal criminal laws to be enforced.

Commerce Clause

But how could Congress significantly expand the police power of the federal government given the limited enumerated powers bestowed on it in the Constitution? In many cases, the answer is found in the enumerated power of Congress to regulate interstate commerce. Indeed, the Commerce Clause of the Constitution is the primary basis of authority behind most federal criminal statutes today.

In 1824, the U.S. Supreme Court ruled in *Gibbons v. Ogden* that the Commerce Clause of the Constitution gave Congress broad authority to regulate commercial matters. The court noted that the wisdom and discretion of Congress must be relied upon to know how far to take that authority. Over 100 years later in *Wickard v. Filburn* (1942) the Supreme Court affirmed Congress's authority under the Commerce Clause—even extending the authority to matters relating to intrastate commerce and noncommercial activity, if that activity when viewed in the aggregate would affect interstate commerce. So, for example, a federal law regulating the production of alcohol for personal consumption might be completely legitimate because, in the aggregate, if everyone makes their own gin, the commercial liquor industry's interstate transactions could be impacted.

In recent years, however, the Supreme Court has scaled back the federal government's authority under the Commerce Clause. In the 1995 case of *U.S. v. Lopez*, the court ruled that the Gun Free School Zones Act of 1990, which made it federal felony to possess a gun within a 1,000 feet of a school, was unconstitutional. The government's defense of the law was rooted in "interstate commerce" reasoning:

- Guns may result in violent crime
- Violent crime has an aggregate economic impact spread across the country
- Violent crime reduces willingness to travel across state lines to perceived unsafe areas
- Fear of guns in school distract students from learning, which also has an aggregate economic impact

However, the Supreme Court found that this logic would permit the federal government to connect virtually any criminal issue to interstate commerce and thereby bestow on the federal government broad police power.

The Supreme Court reiterated its opposition to the federal government possessing a general police power under the Commerce Clause in the case of *U.S. v. Morrison* (2000). The case concerned provisions of the Violence against Women Act of 1994—a federal law making it easier for victims of domestic violence to sue their alleged attackers in federal court. Chief Justice William Rehnquist wrote in the majority decision:

> We accordingly reject the argument that Congress may regulate noneconomic, violent criminal conduct based solely on that conduct's aggregate effect on interstate commerce.
>
> The Constitution requires a distinction between what is truly national and what is truly local. In recognizing this fact we preserve one of the few principles that has been consistent since the Clause was adopted. The regulation and punishment of intrastate violence that is not directed at the instrumentalities, channels, or goods involved in interstate commerce has always been the province of the States.
>
> Indeed, we can think of no better example of the police power, which the Founders denied the National Government and reposed in the States, than the suppression of violent crime and vindication of its victims.

The decisions in *Lopez* and *Morrison* are just two of several Supreme Court rulings in which the breadth of the federal government's police power was pared back. Many legal observers have noted that the federal government simply no longer has the nearly unfettered authority to define criminal conduct and then pursue lawbreakers that many Americans assume it has. Even so, there continues to be a range of federal criminal laws that seem squarely aligned with the constitutionally assigned responsibilities of the U.S. government. And to that end, there continues to be a robust federal law enforcement community engaged in a wide range of police, investigative, and regulatory functions.

Federal Law Enforcement Today

Overview of Federal Law Enforcement

Law enforcement in the United States is very decentralized. There are over 12,000 municipal police departments and over 3,000 county sheriff's departments. All 50 states have state police or highway patrol agencies as well as criminal investigative agencies. Finally, there are over 1,700 special jurisdiction departments (e.g., park districts, airports, college campuses). State and local law enforcement agencies employ nearly 1 million sworn officers (i.e., those with the power to carry firearms and make arrests).

Although the federal law enforcement community has grown substantially since the 9/11 terror attacks, it remains in its totality a small portion of America's total law enforcement population. In 2000, there were 88,000 sworn federal officers and agents. Approximately 41 percent of these were principally engaged in criminal investigative activities; 19 percent were engaged in police patrol activities; and 13 percent were utilized in immigration and inspection efforts (Reaves and Hart 2001).

By 2008, the number of federal law enforcement officers and agents had grown to 120,000. Of those, 37 percent were employed in criminal investigative positions; 21 percent were engaged in police patrol functions; and 15 percent were assigned to immigration and inspection duties (Reaves 2012). While the federal law enforcement community experienced a 36 percent increase in staffing from 2000 to 2008, the uniformed law enforcement agencies—especially along the border and at ports of entry—received the greatest share of these increases. Criminal investigative personnel, as a share of the total federal law enforcement pool, declined in percentage (even as real numbers went up).

U.S. Department of Justice

The U.S. Department of Justice (DOJ), which sets federal crime policy and coordinates all federal criminal justice efforts, has seen its budget remain flat in recent years. In fiscal year 2012, the total budget for DOJ was $27.2 billion. For fiscal year 2013, the budget request was for $27.1 billion. About 49 percent of the budget was set aside for law enforcement activities, which would include the investigation and prosecution of human trafficking. Prisons and detention was the second largest budget category for DOJ, slated to consume 32 percent of the budget. The remainder of the budget was dedicated to litigation, grants, administration, and other line items (DOJ n.d.).

The Department of Justice employs over 113,000 people. Approximately 6,000 of these employees are assistant United States attorneys (AUSAs), working across the country in the 94 judicial districts. Assistant U.S. attorneys are the line-level federal prosecutors in the 93 U.S. Attorney's Offices (the districts of Guam and the Northern Mariana Islands are covered by one U.S. Attorney's Office). In fiscal year 2010, AUSAs filed 68,591 criminal cases nationwide. These cases involved over 91,000 defendants. Of these cases, 44 percent were immigration related, 20 percent were narcotics related, and violent crimes accounted for 16.5 percent. The cases cumulatively experienced a 93 percent conviction rate, with 81 percent of convicted offenders receiving prison time as part of their sentences (DOJ 2010).

The U.S. Department of Justice, Offices of the United States Attorneys, has identified human trafficking as a priority area of prosecution under the umbrella of civil rights violations. Of course, federal prosecutors cannot prosecute cases of trafficking without law enforcement officers first investigating alleged human trafficking, collecting evidence, and arresting alleged violators. To foster success at the criminal investigative level, U.S. Attorney's Offices in fiscal year 2010 funded and coordinated 39 human trafficking task forces around the country made up of local, state, and federal law enforcement officers. In 2012, the DOJ Civil Rights Division and the United States Attorneys' Offices brought a total of 55 forced labor and sex trafficking prosecutions, which was a record for such prosecutions in a single year (Department of State 2013).

There are two key federal law enforcement agencies that play critical and primary roles in the investigation of human trafficking. These agencies are the Federal Bureau of Investigation (FBI) and the Bureau of Immigration and Customs Enforcement (ICE). In addition to the FBI and ICE, which are the lead agencies on this matter, other federal agencies also play significant roles. These include the Bureau of Customs and Border Protection (CBP) and the Department of Labor Office of Inspector General (DOL-OIG).

Key Federal Agencies in the Fight against Human Trafficking

Federal Bureau of Investigation

The FBI's origins are traced to 1908 after Attorney General Charles Bonaparte had advocated to President Theodore Roosevelt and Congress that the Justice Department needed to have its own detective bureau. Bonaparte noted in a letter to Roosevelt that the Departments of the Treasury, Post Office, Interior, Agriculture, and Commerce and Labor all had officers whose duties included the detection of federal criminal offenses and the collection of evidence for prosecution of offenders, while the Justice Department had none.

Although the U.S. marshals organizationally had been placed under the auspices of the DOJ in 1870, they operated largely independent of DOJ, with deputies answering to the presidentially appointed U.S. marshal in each judicial district. They did not carry out their duties at the behest of the attorney general.

In June 1908, Bonaparte administratively created a detective unit at DOJ by hiring nine Secret Service agents, as well as 25 new agents. He placed Stanley Finch at the head of the unit, giving him the title of chief examiner. He then sent a memorandum to all Justice Department employees requiring them to refer all potential criminal matters to the chief examiner, who would then decide whether one of his agents should investigate the case. In 1909, George Wickersham became attorney general of the United States after William Howard Taft was elected president. Wickersham too believed in DOJ maintaining its own investigative unit. He supported the unit and formally gave it the name "Bureau of Investigation" (Bumgarner et al. 2013).

The Bureau of Investigation saw its authority expand considerably in the two to three decades after its creation. Several federal criminal statutes were passed for which the Bureau of Investigation was designated as the primary investigative agency. These included the Espionage Act of 1917 (an antisubversive law), the National Motor Vehicle Theft Act 1919 (which barred taking stolen automobiles across state lines), the Federal Kidnapping Act of 1932 (making it a federal crime to kidnap across state lines), the Federal Bank Robbery Statute of 1934 (federally outlawing the robbery of federally insured banks), and several interstate flight laws (prohibiting the fleeing of local justice by crossing state lines).

However, one of the very first laws passed for which the Bureau of Investigation was responsible to enforce was the Mann Act of 1910, which outlawed "white slavery." In particular, the law prohibited the interstate or international transportation of any female for the purpose of prostitution or other illegal acts relating to sexuality. The law was dubbed the "White Slave Traffic Act" because most of the women and girls pulled into the sex trade at the time were from European countries.

In 1921, a young Justice Department attorney was named head of the General Intelligence Division of the Bureau of Investigation. His name was John Edgar Hoover. In 1924, Hoover was named as the director of the Bureau of Investigation. Hoover was a very savvy leader for the bureau, making use over the years of mass media and political connections and leverage to expand the authority and reach of the organization. The agency's name was changed to the "Federal Bureau of Investigation" in 1935, at a time when the bureau went to great lengths to publicize its many high-profile successes. The "FBI" moniker has become embedded in American culture as synonymous with professional, educated, and exceptional law enforcement.

Today, the FBI is the largest criminal investigative law enforcement agency in the federal government and has the broadest investigative jurisdiction among federal agencies. It remains housed in the Department of Justice where it started. In 2012, the FBI employed 35,664 people, including 13,778 special agents (criminal investigators) and 21,886 support staffers. The support staff includes professional positions such as crime and intelligence analysts, language specialists, forensic scientists, computer specialists, attorneys, and other positions (FBI 2012).

The FBI has a physical presence in all 50 states. It operates out of 56 major offices, called field offices, in America's largest cities. The bureau also has special agents working in nearly 400 medium and small cities. These offices are known as "resident offices" or "resident agencies" (RA) and can be staffed by as few as one or two special agents.

In fiscal year 2012, the FBI budget totaled $8.1 billion. This was an increase over the previous year's budget by $119 million and represents nearly a 60 percent increase over the previous 10 years. The FBI's budget in fiscal year 2002 was only $5.1 billion.

The FBI has identified several investigative priorities. One of these priorities is the investigation of civil rights and human rights violations. Included in this category is the crime of human trafficking. There are several federal criminal laws found in Title 18 of the United States Code that bar involuntary servitude, forced labor, and sexual trafficking (18 USC, sections 1581, 1584, 1589, 1590, 1591, 1592, and 1594a). The FBI reports that in recent years, the agency has stepped up its investigation of human trafficking complaints. According to the FBI, the pending number of cases against human traffickers increased from 167 in 2009 to 459 in 2012. Further, FBI investigations of human trafficking since 2009 have resulted 480 arrests, 336 indictments and informations, and 258 convictions (FBI 2012).

One of the FBI's most successful nationwide investigative initiatives in recent history has been the Innocence Lost project. The project targets the problem of children being recruited into prostitution, which is a common manifestation of human trafficking. This initiative has resulted in over 1,300 convictions and over 2,600 children recovered or identified.

Bureau of Immigration and Customs Enforcement (ICE)

The Bureau of Immigration and Customs Enforcement (ICE) is a part of the U.S. Department of Homeland Security (DHS). The DHS was created in the wake of the 9/11 terror attacks with the passage of the Homeland Security Act of 2002. The act created DHS as the newest cabinet-level department in the federal government. DHS began operating as a department in March 2003. The creation of DHS amounted to the largest reorganization of the federal government since the creation of the Department of Defense in 1947 (Bumgarner 2006).

The Homeland Security Act of 2002 combined 22 preexisting federal agencies into DHS, primarily under 4 major directorates at the time:

- Border and Transportation Security
- Emergency Preparedness and Response
- Science and Technology
- Information Analysis and Infrastructure Protection

ICE was established as the primary criminal investigative law enforcement agency of DHS; it was organizationally located within the Border and Transportation Security Directorate.

Initially, ICE law enforcement personnel consisted primarily of criminal investigators of the U.S. Customs Service (part of the Treasury Department prior to the creation of DHS), criminal investigators of the U.S. Immigration and Naturalization Service (part of the Department of Justice prior to the creation of DHS), and criminal investigators and uniformed officers of the Federal Protective Service (part of the General Services Administration prior to the creation of DHS). The Federal Protective Service has since been removed from ICE and placed in another directorate.

Today, ICE has two main law enforcement elements: Homeland Security Investigations (HSI) and Enforcement and Removal Operations (ERO). The latter element is primarily concerned with the apprehension, detention, and removal of criminal aliens who are at large in the United States. However HSI, as the criminal investigative arm of ICE, conducts criminal investigations of criminal matters formerly under the jurisdiction of U.S. Customs and the Immigration and Naturalization Service (INS). This includes the crime of human trafficking, as well as smuggling in all forms, cybercrime, trade violations, and other offenses.

Today, ICE operates on an annual budget of approximately $6 billion. The agency employs over 20,000 persons working in over 400 offices in the United States and worldwide. Within ICE, HSI employs over 10,000 persons, including 6,700 special agents (ICE 2013). Recognizing the importance and seriousness of the issue, HSI maintains a distinct unit devoted to human trafficking and human smuggling. The unit spearheads the agency's criminal investigative efforts against human trafficking and facilitates training for local law enforcement and public awareness campaigns. Indeed, in 2010 ICE launched the Blue Campaign, which is an ongoing aggressive and coordinated effort to educate law enforcement officers, victim advocates, and the public as to the warning signs and indicators of human trafficking and how to respond to them. This campaign and other efforts have resulted in ICE's recognition as the premier federal law enforcement agency for confronting domestic and international human trafficking. In 2011, ICE carried more than 1,900 human-rights-related cases (mostly human trafficking) involving suspects from 95 countries (Woods 2011).

ICE–HSI has also led the way in the federal law enforcement community in meeting the needs of trafficking victims during and after the criminal justice processes run their course. Most ICE field offices employ full-time victim specialists, and every field office is staffed with special agents who have been trained in victim assistance and have been assigned the role of victim advocate as a collateral duty (ICE 2013).

Other Agencies

While the FBI and ICE are clearly the two lead law enforcement agencies at the federal level involved in the fight against human trafficking, there are other federal agencies that are also active in the fight. The Departments of Justice and Homeland Security have both partnered with several other federal departments in an effort to confront human trafficking. Departments that have contributed resources and personnel toward training and support for criminal investigations during 2012 include the Departments of State, Health and Human Services, Education, Transportation, and the Interior (Department of State 2013).

Most significantly, however, have been the efforts of the U.S. Department of Labor (DOL). Principally, there are two different agencies within the DOL that are regularly involved with the FBI and ICE in the effort to bring human traffickers to justice: the Wage and Hour Division (WHD) and the Office of Inspector General (DOL–OIG). Both of these agencies have actively participated on federal human trafficking task forces. The WHD is the arm of the Department of Labor that enforces federal minimum wage and overtime protections for workers. This agency is more regulatory than law enforcement in nature. However, WHD works closely with the Labor Department's Office of Inspector General. The Office of Labor Racketeering and Fraud Investigations is the investigative arm of the DOL–OIG and employs special agents with full law enforcement authority relative to federal criminal laws that are triggered by abusive labor practices, including human trafficking (Bumgarner et al. 2013).

It is also worth noting that ICE is not the only agency within the Department of Homeland Security actively involved in countering the human traffickers. The Bureau of Customs and Border Protection (CBP) is also a major homeland security element for thwarting human traffickers. As noted earlier, with the creation of the Department of Homeland Security, the investigative elements of U.S. Customs and INS were combined to form ICE. The uniformed and inspection elements of U.S. Customs and INS were combined to form CBP. This includes border inspectors as well as agents of the U.S. Border Patrol. Today, the three uniformed branches of CBP are CBP Field Operations, Air and Marine Unit, and the U.S. Border Patrol.

The U.S. Border Patrol is the highest profile agency within CBP and employs 21,165 border patrol agents; 18,516 of the Border Patrol agents are on the southwestern border (87 percent of border patrol agents) and are actively engaged in the fight against human traffickers and human smugglers going to and from Mexico. In 2012, the Border Patrol arrested 365,000 illegal aliens and smugglers (73 percent were Mexican nationals). Although most of those arrested were merely undocumented individuals entering the country illegally, some who were captured were actively engaged in the machinations of human smuggling and human trafficking. Not surprisingly, the Border Patrol also seized significant amounts of illicit drugs, including 2.3 million pounds of marijuana and 12,160 pounds of cocaine (Bumgarner et al. 2013).

Summary

Although federal law enforcement is widely held in high esteem in American culture, most policing is not done at the federal level. Rather, general police power is the province of the states. Federal law enforcement agencies have wide geographic reach, but narrow authority under the U.S. Constitution's enumerated powers. Close to the nation's founding, federal law enforcement responsibilities were focused on four areas: collecting tariffs, serving the federal judiciary, securing federal real property, and protecting the postal system. Over time, the number of federal law enforcement agencies grew as the nation grew, and the authority of these agencies expanded. Traditionally, Congress has used the Commerce Clause of the U.S. Constitution as a rationale for most federal criminal statutes. The Supreme Court has generally permitted this—although in recent years, the court has attempted to rein in the use of the Commerce Clause to justify federal laws relating to criminal offenses traditionally handled by state and local law enforcement.

Today, federal law enforcement makes up a fraction of the total American law enforcement community. In 2008, sworn federal officers and agents numbered about 120,000. About a third of these officers were engaged primarily in criminal investigative duties. Two key federal investigative agencies have emerged as leaders in the fight against human trafficking: the Federal Bureau of Investigation (FBI) and the Bureau of Immigration and Customs Enforcement (ICE), which is part of the U.S. Department of Homeland Security. Federal prosecutors have also made a significant commitment nationwide to confronting human trafficking. U.S. Attorney's Offices around the country have coordinated human trafficking task forces consisting of federal, state, and local law enforcement agencies. Several other federal agencies also regularly commit resources in the fight against human trafficking. These include the Bureau of Customs and Border Protection (CBP); the U.S. Border Patrol (which is a part of CBP); the Department of Labor Office of Inspector General–Office of Labor Racketeering and Fraud Investigations; and various other law enforcement and regulatory elements of the Departments of Justice, Homeland Security, Interior, Education, Transportation, Labor, and Health and Human Services.

Key Terms

assistant United States attorney (AUSA)
Blue Campaign
Commerce Clause
Customs and Border Protection (CBP)
Department of Homeland Security (DHS)
Department of Justice (DOJ)
Department of Labor–Office of Inspector General (DOL–OIG)
enumerated powers
Federal Bureau of Investigation (FBI)
Homeland Security Act of 2002

Homeland Security Investigations (HSI)
Immigration and Customs Enforcement (ICE)
Mann Act
Necessary and Proper Clause
Tenth Amendment
U.S. Attorney's Office
U.S. Border Patrol
U.S. v. Lopez
U.S. v. Morrison

Review Questions

1. What are the federal government's enumerated powers under the U.S. Constitution?
2. What is the Necessary and Proper Clause of the Constitution?
3. What is the Commerce Clause of the Constitution?
4. In what four areas did federal law enforcement manifest itself early in America's history?
5. What did the Supreme Court say in *U.S. v. Lopez*? In *U.S. v. Morrison*?
6. How has the Department of Justice made human trafficking a priority?
7. What is the role of the FBI in investigating human trafficking?
8. What is the role of ICE in investigating human trafficking?
9. What other federal agencies play a role in confronting human trafficking?

References

Bumgarner, Jeff, Charles Crawford, and Ronald Burns. *Federal Law Enforcement: A Primer*. Durham, NC: Carolina Academic Press, 2013.

Bumgarner, Jeffrey. *Federal Agents: The Growth of Federal Law Enforcement in America*. Westport, CT: Praeger, 2006.

Calhoun, Fredrick. *The Lawmen: United States Marshals and Their Deputies, 1789–1989*. Washington DC: Smithsonian Institution Press, 1989.

Federal Bureau of Investigation. *FBI Quick Facts*. Retrieved from http://www.fbi.gov/about-us/quck-facts.2012.

Immigration and Customs Enforcement. *Homeland Security Investigations*. Retrieved from http://www.ice.gov/about/offices/homeland-security-investigations, 2013.

Saba, Anne. "U.S. Customs Service: Always There ... Ready to Serve." *U.S. Customs Today*, February 2003.

Reaves, Brian. *Federal Law Enforcement Officers 2008*. Washington, DC: Bureau of Justice Statistics, 2012.

Reaves, Brian, and Timothy Hart. *Federal Law Enforcement Officers 2000*. Washington DC: Bureau of Justice Statistics, 2001.

United States Coast Guard. *U.S. Coast Guard: An Historical Overview*. Washington DC: USCG Historian's Office. 2002.

United States Department of Justice. *United States Attorneys' Annual Statistical Report: Fiscal Year 2010.* Washington DC: Executive Office of the United States Attorneys, U.S. DOJ, 2010.

United States Department of Justice. *FY 2013 Budget Performance Summary.* Retrieved from http://www.justice.gov/jmd/2013summary. n.d.

United States Department of State. *Accomplishments Document: President's Interagency Task Force 2013.* Washington DC: Office to Monitor and Combat Trafficking in Persons, 2013.

United States Postal Service. *The United States Postal Service: An American History 1775–2006.* Washington DC: USPS, 2007.

Woods, John. *Statement of John Woods, Deputy Assistant Director, National Security Investigations Division, Homeland Security Investigations, U.S. Immigration and Customs Enforcement*, before the House Committee on Foreign Affairs, October 13, 2011.

Law Enforcement Awareness and Training in Human Trafficking

13

VLADIMIR A. SERGEVNIN

Contents

Major Issues

Human trafficking involves national and often transnational criminal activity, but it is the local law enforcement officer who is most likely to encounter such crimes that may be related to trafficking in human beings. Nationwide efforts are undertaken in the United States to confront the crime of human trafficking, including the enactment of legislation providing resources to both law enforcement and victim service agencies working to identify and assist trafficking victims and prosecute traffickers. It is important that states have passed legislation criminalizing human trafficking and are directing law enforcement agencies to adopt training programs to improve identification and interdiction efforts. The author compares the different training efforts to human trafficking and suggests how to raise awareness about human trafficking and improve the responses of law enforcement agencies. This chapter is an exploratory assessment of the nature and extent of the local law enforcement training response to trafficking in human beings within the United States.

Introduction

Law enforcement encounters with human trafficking issues are happening more frequently in recent times. When mishandled, everyone loses; family members are wounded by suffering of the loved ones, police officers are overburdened with extremely complicated cases, and police departments must address community outrage. The training, practices, and morale of law enforcement officers have a profound impact of how cases of human trafficking are handled.

There is an agreement among researchers that many victims of human trafficking are not identified and not helped because a deficit of proper preparation and training for law enforcement agencies (Bruch, 2004; Chacon, 2009; Chang and Kim, 2007; Decker et al., 2009; Farrell, McDevitt, and Fahy, 2008; McDevitt, 2010; Wilson, Walsh, and Kleuber, 2006). There is strong evidence that agencies with a special unit or task force, protocols, or training are 2 to 3 times more likely to identify cases of human trafficking than those without such remedies. However, according to one 2008 survey only 18 percent of agencies nationwide, and 38 percent of medium to large agencies have conducted any type of human trafficking training. Of those agencies with human trafficking training, the majority (47 percent) have utilized in-service training or specialized regional training for investigators (43 percent) (Farrell et al., 2008).

Also recovering from a national economic crisis does not provide budget opportunities in financing local agencies toward extended human trafficking personnel options, awareness, and training endeavors. These and many other issues can influence departmental policies, change an atmosphere for specific police responses, or the development of specialized units for human trafficking cases. Law enforcement awareness and training in dealing with human trafficking require more than the traditional responses to criminal behavior and should consider a comprehensive approach taking into account all dimensions of this phenomenon.

Challenges of Law Enforcement Training
Response to Human Trafficking

The importance of human trafficking training for law enforcement officers, along with other proactive and reactive approaches such as special task force units and enhanced policies and protocols, is emphasized in the literature on human trafficking (Clawson, Dutch, Solomon, and Grace, 2009; Clawson, Small, Go, and Myles, 2004; David, 2007; Gallagher and Holmes, 2008; Goździak, 2010; Torg, 2005; Wilson and Dalton, 2008). The scope and quality of needed training is rarely addressed. However, in the past some 10-plus years since the federal Trafficking Victims Protection Act (TVPA), which included provisions related to training, researchers have been growing increasingly concerned about the inadequacy of human trafficking training for law enforcement agencies in the United States and internationally. One of the first attempts followed by others, in 2003, of dealing with human trafficking victims focused on training as a means to change the attitudes of law enforcement officers (Hughes, 2003). This was a result of the common notion that most law enforcement officers tend to be biased against victims of human trafficking and view them rather as criminals than victims. The training approach was aimed to raise the awareness of law enforcement personnel to the needs of such individuals.

Awareness and training programs, which would apply principles of serving individuals with specific needs, were perceived as key strategies in developing special units and task forces within law enforcement agencies. Examination of the first several years of anti-human trafficking efforts suggested that for federal, state, county, and local law enforcement there is need for adequate and ongoing education, training, and commitment at all levels of these agencies (Clawson et al., 2009). Law enforcement officers needed training in human trafficking so that they could provide urgent crisis intervention when other professionals and nongovernmental organizations (NGOs) were not available. Law enforcement agencies have some additional significant internal challenges in dealing with human trafficking training mainly because of the hidden nature of this crime.

Perception

The reality is that human trafficking is far more prevalent than most law enforcement professionals and communities wish to recognize. According to the national survey conducted by the Institute on Race and Justice at Northeastern University in 2008 between 73 and 77 percent of local, county, and state law enforcement view human trafficking as rare or nonexistent in their communities; however, agencies serving larger communities (over 250,000 population) are more likely to have concerns about human trafficking, especially sex trafficking as a more serious problem. Only 7 percent of the law enforcement forces in the random sample have investigated a case of human trafficking (Farrell et al., 2008). In another national survey of municipal, county, and state agencies, three-fourths of law enforcement leaders indicated that human trafficking was rare or nonexistent in their community and only 10 percent indicated investigating a human trafficking case (Farrell, McDevitt, and Fahy, 2010). It is not necessarily that these communities actually do not have these cases, but rather they go unidentified. According to the same survey 19.8 percent of law enforcement agencies with any type of human trafficking training will identify and investigate these crimes, in comparison with only 4.4 percent of agencies without training (Farrell et al., 2008). Also law enforcement agencies are often hesitant to identify victims as human trafficking victims because of the belief that these victims were complicit in their own victimization and this approach has an impact on the volume of delivered training. Small to medium law enforcement agencies are less likely to provide specialized training to their personnel. Only 18 percent of local, county, or state law enforcement agencies have had some type of human trafficking training; while 38 percent of medium to large agencies serving populations over 75,000 and 65.6 percent serving population 250,000 and above have adopted training. In contrast a majority (91 percent) of special human trafficking task forces have some type of training (Farrell et al., 2008). Another survey of 163 municipal and county law enforcement agencies serving populations of 150,000 or more found only 7 agencies (8 percent) reported they had conducted or received training in human trafficking (between 2002 and 2005) with the average length of training around 2.5 hours. In this survey agencies that had participated in training in human trafficking were more likely (71 percent) to recognize that human trafficking is the problem within jurisdiction in comparison with those agencies that did not hold training sessions (14 percent) (Wilson, et al., 2006). Generally, those law enforcement agencies serving larger jurisdictions are more likely to establish specialized units (or assign personnel), conduct training, develop protocols that will have better probability to investigate cases of human trafficking than those agencies without such approaches in place. Small agencies are less likely to have training, protocols, specialized units, or personnel, and have fewer chances to identify and investigate any cases of human trafficking and are serving under assumption that these jurisdictions are free from this type of criminal activities.

Legal Mandates

The introduction of the federal Trafficking Victims Protection Act (TVPA) required the development of related to training. This legislation directs the Department of Justice (DOJ) and Department of State (DOS) to develop training programs to educate appropriate personnel in identifying victims of severe forms of trafficking and providing for the appropriate protection for them. According to the Polaris Project, as of 2013, 39 states passed anti-trafficking laws but only 29 states (74 percent) have mandated and encouraged training for law enforcement. There are several different ways that states legislate human trafficking laws and training: first group of 12 states (Arkansas, California, Georgia, Indiana, Kentucky, Minnesota, Nebraska, Nevada, New Jersey, New York, Ohio, and Wyoming) require human trafficking training and outline specific curricula; second group of 9 states (Connecticut, Florida, Iowa, Missouri, New Mexico, Texas, Washington, Alaska, and Mississippi) require training without establishing specific curricula by law; third group of 8 states (Idaho, Kansas, Massachusetts, North Carolina, Oregon, South Carolina, Virginia, and West Virginia) permit but do not require human trafficking training; and the fourth group of states have failed to enact any statutory provision with respect to human trafficking training. However, it does not mean that human trafficking awareness training is not available in this last group of states. In 2013, for the first time, two states successfully fulfilled all required and rated categories: Washington and New Jersey. In some statutes, states detailed the most critical topics of training. For example, according to Indiana legislation, law enforcement officers have to be trained in human and sexual trafficking laws, be able to identify cases of human and sexual trafficking, establish communications with victims, use appropriate investigative methods, establish collaboration with federal law enforcement agencies, protect rights of all victims, and to utilize community resources to help victims (Polaris Project, 2013a).

The lack of uniformity of legal responses from federal and state governments does not allow effective response to this nationwide issue. Expressing concern with this issue the National Conference on Commissioners on Uniform State Laws, also known as the Uniform Law Commission (ULC), has established a Committee on the Prevention of and Remedies for Human Trafficking. In August 2013 a new act had been approved by this group, which provides important new tools in the fight against human trafficking, including some important provisions on law enforcement training. As a result, in 2014 Nebraska, Pennsylvania, Virginia, Arizona, Alabama, and New Hampshire are planning to adopt uniform Prevention of and Remedies for Human Trafficking bills (Uniform Law Commission, 2014).

Asymmetrical Threat

The term *human trafficking* refers to a host of criminal activities that may affect police response and as a result the awareness and training design. Some of these acts, such as sex services, immigration violations, documents forgery, and forced labor, are not perceived by police officers as serious and life threatening. There is a lack of understanding by many police officers in the United States of the multidimensional nature of human trafficking and the value of this specific training to policing. Police often learn about cases of human trafficking (52 percent) during the course of other investigations, for example, drug raids and calls for domestic violence (Farrell et al., 2008). It often appears as a byproduct of traditional focuses of patrol and investigations. Human trafficking can be domestic and international in nature, and small law enforcement agencies are less likely to be trained and prepared to deal with international human trafficking cases due to language, cultural, and other complications. More than 70 percent of law enforcement agencies have less than 25 sworn officers. About half (49 percent) of all agencies employed fewer than 10 full-time officers (Reaves, 2011). These small departments comprised the majority of police departments in the United States and may have little exposure to the training opportunity as opposed to the considerable assets of large metropolitan areas such as New York or Chicago. Also law enforcement officers are working under recent cuts of personnel and urgent time constraints leading to rationalizing that they have to deal with a separate issue and not with the whole picture of human trafficking case. Ironically the crime control strategies of a majority of law enforcement agencies may preclude officers from intervening and could result in tragedy. Inadequacies of the law enforcement human trafficking training were contributing factors in underestimating the threat. There is a need for training of police (especially small law enforcement agencies) in the United States to achieve identification and understanding of human trafficking as a composite crime, the trends and threats, and the nature and extent of the law enforcement response by employing critical thinking, or what is described as intelligence-led policing.

Response Reclassification

Traffickers and victims are often involved in traditional crimes in law enforcement jurisdictions. Untrained officers too often identify them as prostitutes, pimps, kidnappers, employers hiring illegal immigrants, and so on. In many trafficking cases there is some disagreement or confusion about whether individuals are victims, offenders, or occupy multiple statuses at different times. As a result when individuals are defined early in the investigation as offenders (e.g., prostitutes, labor law violators, or illegal aliens) it is problematic for task force members to "redefine" the individuals as victims (Farrell et al., 2008). But according to the TVPA, these individuals should be classified and treated as trafficking victims or perpetrators. This needed reclassification is challenging for law enforcement agencies and requires an adequate and ongoing awareness, training, and continuous commitment at all levels of these agencies. Specific to human trafficking training for law enforcement should allow uncovering the real nature of these criminal activities. Police officers are called to intervene in a significant number of human trafficking situations. Because of the embedded law enforcement modus operandi asymmetrical response (viewing victims of human trafficking through the prism of traditional crime) much needed awareness efforts and training can contribute substantially only through changing the patrol philosophy. Law enforcement agencies should be concerned in these cases with protection of communities and, very important, with the victim(s) of human trafficking. It will require law enforcement officers to reclassify prostitution cases into cases of human trafficking or immigration violations.

Cooperative Response

The coordination of both national and local governments and organizations is a critical element of anti-trafficking law enforcement actions. This is a winning strategy advocated by the Campaign to Rescue & Restore Victims of Human Trafficking under the U.S. Department of Health and Human Services (2012). In the forefront of coordination there is the President's Interagency Task Force to Monitor and Combat Trafficking in Persons (PITF), which serves as a channel to coordinate government-wide efforts and discuss new initiatives in the struggle to end modern slavery. However, the majority of officers are traditionally reluctant to call for professional outside emergency intervention assistance: immigration officers, medical (especially mental health) personnel, interpreters, local NGOs for housing and counseling, monetary assistance, and so forth. Law enforcement departments should have in place cooperative agreements with plethora of outside agencies (see Chapters 12, 14, 15, and 16 for a detailed discussion of such agreements). The cooperative agreement should include provisions for summoning a health professional, NGO, community representative(s), and others. The cooperative agreement should also delineate procedures for temporary housing for the victim of human trafficking and not placing a victim of human trafficking into police custody, which could exacerbate victimization. Annual State Department reports on human trafficking are promoting federal partnerships with law enforcement agencies to encourage training (Bureau, 2014).

Law Enforcement Policy or Protocol

A surprisingly low percentage of law enforcement agencies have a formal policy or protocol in dealing with human trafficking. According to a nationwide survey in 2008, approximately 9 percent of local, county, or state law enforcement agencies in the random sample and 13 percent of medium to large agencies serving populations over 75,000 have a protocol or policy on human trafficking (Farrell, McDevitt, and Fahy, 2008). Because very few agencies have a policy or protocol, it has an impact on victims who in many cases refrain from seeking assistance from police due to fear of discriminatory treatment or fear of being reported to immigration officials.

Victimization of Trafficked Persons

There is considerable concern both in law enforcement and communities with regard to criminal victimization of trafficked individuals. They are vulnerable for many reasons. They may be singled out because traffickers perceive that they are young and less able to defend themselves. They may not cooperate with law enforcement officers (according to 2008 survey only 70 percent of victims of human trafficking cooperated with police) (Farrell et al., 2008). Local law enforcement officers have to be trained to recognize potential victimization and provide services to victims who may have had poor relationships with law enforcement (e.g., migrants, immigrants, runaways, minorities, etc.). Victims of transnational human trafficking are more easily persuaded than native-born citizens, and may be the victims of fraud or other schemes. This requires crime prevention techniques, awareness campaigns, and victim and community education.

Current Approaches to Training

Since the early 2000s training programs on human trafficking have been primarily designed as cultural awareness and sensitivity courses. Many police departments have been stressing the importance of educating the entire police force. From 2003 to 2005, there has been a dramatic increase in the range of the programs and courses especially developed by federal government, law enforcement entities, and public and private agencies to address issues of human trafficking awareness and training. According to one of the surveys, among those agencies who had provided training specific to human trafficking, the types of training provided included in-service training (46.8 percent), new recruit training (15.5 percent), roll-call training (11.3 percent), publications (24.9 percent), online training (10.9 percent), regional training (43.8 percent), national training (14.7 percent), and offsite training (38.9 percent) (Farrell et al., 2008). As a result of this inadequacy, there has been strong demand from federal, state, and local governments; law enforcement; and NGOs to enhance and improve interaction, through training, between law enforcement and human trafficking victims.

In the United States, the literature indicates that more states are providing some training to law enforcement officers on how to deal with human trafficking cases. However, research efforts generally do not describe the standards, quality, or effectiveness of training efforts. Further analysis is needed to determine whether modern awareness and training approaches are adequate to meet law enforcement demands. Comprehensive and multi-disciplinary training should be delivered to law enforcement personnel. Without well-designed training, police officers will continue to be placed in crisis situations without scientific knowledge or assistance they need to deal with such cases.

The initial mostly awareness approach of the 2000s in training for law enforcement officers to deal with human trafficking cases and victims changed with establishing special units and task forces and incorporation of a more specialized focus on investigations and victims assistance. There are several areas of present-day approaches that must be separately examined.

Human Trafficking Training by Federal Law Enforcement

Although the focus of the federal law enforcement agencies is on victim services, there is heavy emphasis on awareness and training activities. Actions focused on awareness and training highlight the importance of increasing general understanding among police personnel of the crime as a necessary step leading to victim identification and access to services.

The federal government has provided strong national leadership in promoting and providing human trafficking training for federal agencies, but to train local law enforcement agencies remains crucial to the successful identification and investigation of these crimes nationwide. Since passage of the TVPA, federal authorities increased funding to law enforcement, NGOs, and other service providers for training and promoting availability of protocols for identifying and responding to human trafficking victims. Following the TVPA provisions, the DOJ (through the Bureau of Justice Assistance [BJA]) has developed programs for federal, state, and local law enforcement, courts, health service providers, and crime prevention personnel. To combat human trafficking, BJA's efforts have been two-pronged: (1) to develop training for law enforcement and communities to identify trafficking in persons and rescue victims by working with federal law enforcement and victims service providers; and (2) to support and fund task forces based on a strategy of collaboration among state and local enforcement, trafficking victim services providers, federal law enforcement, and U.S. Attorneys Offices (Bureau of Justice Assistance, 2014a). Similar programs have been developed by the Department of Homeland Security and the DOS. In 2012 President Obama delivered a speech on human trafficking at the Clinton Global Initiative Annual Meeting and outlined steps his administration would take to improve the federal government's response to human trafficking. Since 2004 the federal government has funded a total of 42 anti-human trafficking task forces, which had some success in identifying 3,336 persons as potential victims of human. These task forces have also trained 85,685 law enforcement officers and others in human trafficking awareness and victims' identification (Bureau of Justice Assistance, 2014a).

In the recent years there were several important initiatives in human trafficking awareness and training by federal government. In 2008, the Department of Homeland Security (DHS) and U.S. Immigration and Customs Enforcement (ICE) developed a human trafficking billboard campaign focused on raising public awareness and prevention. Department of Health and Human Services (HHS) funded the Rescue & Restore Victims of Human Trafficking public awareness campaign. Also HHS's National Human Trafficking Resource Center (NHTRC) provided nationwide training and technical assistance, and hired a child protection specialist to provide specialized training for identification and care of child trafficking victims (Department of Homeland Security, 2014; Trafficking, 2010).

In 2009 DOJ task forces trained over 13,000 law enforcement officers and other personnel. All task forces received weeklong intensive training on human trafficking. The FBI provided training to agents attending the annual civil rights conference, including legal issues, victim services, and suggested victim interview techniques. DHS delivered comprehensive training for all officers and agents of U.S. Customs and Border Protection (CBP), and made a web-based human trafficking course available to officers and agents of ICE. Also ICE hosted training sessions for more than 6,000 federal, state, and local law enforcement officers nationwide. Fulfilling the Immigration and Nationality Act (INA) Section 287(g)—which authorizes the federal government to enter into agreements with state and local law enforcement agencies, permitting designated officers to perform immigration law enforcement functions—provided that the local law enforcement officers receive appropriate training and function under the supervision of sworn ICE officers concerning the investigation, apprehension, and detention of unauthorized immigrants, on victim and witness protections, including victim-based immigration relief. ICE provides a 4-week training program at the Federal Law Enforcement Training Center (FLETC) ICE Academy (ICEA) in Charleston, South Carolina, conducted by certified instructors (ICE, 2014). The Department of Defense (DOD) developed mandatory law enforcement training on identification, investigation, and information sharing with civilian law enforcement agencies. The Department of Education hosted a national conference at which it informed school personnel and law enforcement about the problem of human trafficking, and their role in identifying and preventing trafficking (U.S. Department of State, 2010).

In 2010 the federal government made considerable efforts in enhancing law enforcement training. In collaboration with several civil organizations, DOJ developed an online task force resource guide, and conducted national training for 700 task force members and law enforcement, governmental, and nongovernmental partners, which included advanced training to identify, investigate, and prosecute human trafficking cases and assist human trafficking victims. In turn task forces trained over 24,278 law enforcement officers and other individuals likely to come into contact with human trafficking victims. The FBI provided training to over 1,000 new agents and support personnel as well as training 960 state and local law enforcement officers. DHS has updated mandatory training for more than 40,000 CBP officers and agents. Also web-based training and continued in-person trainings that reached more than 14,000 federal, state, and local law enforcement officials has been launched. DOD continued already developed mandatory training to its law enforcement personnel (on identification, investigation, and information sharing) and updated its mandatory general human trafficking awareness training, with the potential to reach 3.5 million military members and civilian employees. HHS conducted online trainings on human trafficking. The Department of Education enhanced efforts in training chiefs of school police forces (U.S. Department of State, 2011).

In 2011, DOJ provided three regional training forums across the nation and through existing task forces delivered over 570 trainings and reached more than 27,000 individuals. The FBI trained more than 760 new agents and support personnel. The DHS Federal Law Enforcement Training Center trained over 2,000 state, local, and federal officers in human trafficking indicators and DHS Customs and Border Protection offered basic human trafficking training. ICE trained or provided anti-trafficking materials to more than 47,000 individuals. DOD provided mandatory online training to all its personnel (U.S. Department of State, 2012). In 2011, U.S. Attorney General personnel conducted over 75 training programs for federal and local law enforcement agencies, DOJ-funded task forces, nongovernmental and health care organizations, business leaders, academia, and legal practitioners across the nation. The FBI conducted over 250 training courses to audiences that included federal, state, and local law enforcement officers and civilian agencies. Under the Strategic Action Plan on Services for Victims of Human Trafficking (SAP) several agencies and DHS were expanding training efforts to federal, state, tribal, and local law enforcement (Polaris Project, 2013b).

The ICE Homeland Security Investigations (HSI) directorate is a critical asset in the ICE mission, responsible for investigating a wide range of domestic and international activities arising from the illegal movement of people and goods into, within, and out of the United States. Since 2007 alone, the HSI has given more than 140,000 human trafficking presentations to federal, state, and local law enforcement entities, NGOs, and governments of host countries where HSI has a presence (Dinkins, 2014).

Between 2012 and 2014 all federal law enforcement agencies have developed online options of human trafficking training. For example, DHS launched a web-based training course to law enforcement officials to train officers on human trafficking identification and response. It is an interactive

30- to 40-minute course based on four videos depicting human trafficking scenarios law enforcement officers may encounter during routine duties. The training is law enforcement sensitive and available on the FLETC Electronic Learning Portal (www.fletc.gov/elpsplash/) for law enforcement officials through the Regional Information Sharing Systems (RISS), a secure intranet that facilitates law enforcement communications and information sharing nationwide (Human Trafficking Awareness Training, 2014). U.S. Department of Health and Human Services, Division of Anti-Trafficking in Persons (ATIP), is providing periodic webinar trainings on a variety of anti-human trafficking topics including identifying and assisting trafficking victims and conducting outreach. Upper Midwest Community Policing Institute (UMCPI) and the National Judicial College (NJC) delivers a 1.25-hour webcast for state trial judges who will confront human trafficking cases as task forces and law enforcement attack the crime of human trafficking. Most recently FLETC developed a web-based human trafficking training course that teaches law enforcement officers how to recognize human trafficking encountered during routine duties, how to provide safety to victims, and how to start human trafficking investigations (Polaris Project, 2014). According to the *Federal Strategic Action Plan on Services for Victims of Human Trafficking* (2014), in the United States 2013–2017 the DHS's Blue Campaign, DOJ, DOS's Office to Monitor and Combat Trafficking in Persons, and HHS will expand human trafficking awareness efforts on social media, Twitter, and Facebook.

Human Trafficking in Basic Law Enforcement Recruit Training

Basic training about the nature and elements of human trafficking is critical to promoting successful identification and enforcement. While awareness and training concerning trafficking in human beings is moderately well developed on the federal law enforcement level, it is the local police officer, rather than the federal agent, who is most likely to encounter such crimes.

Recognizing significant importance of this type of training in 2006 the International Association of Chiefs of Police took initiative and delivered a short guide on human trafficking identification and investigation which provides law enforcement officials basic information about the problem of human trafficking and suggests a number of national resources for assistance (Farrell, 2008).

As mentioned earlier there are only 12 states (Arkansas, California, Georgia, Indiana, Kentucky, Minnesota, Nebraska, Nevada, New Jersey, New York, Ohio, and Wyoming) that require human trafficking training and outline specific curricula. Generally this curricula will be developed through the Police Officer Standards and Training (POST) Commissions, a primary responsibility of which is to provide for the establishment and delivery of a state-certified basic law enforcement officers training course which carries with it the need to establish adequate training sites, to approve and certify the training curriculum, to approve instructional content and performance objectives, to assure instructor credentials and qualifications, and to evaluate training outcomes (Jurkanin, 2013).

In the majority of states, human trafficking training is not a standard part of the state basic training curriculum. However, the problem of human trafficking has been seeing some improvement via violence against women content (Sexual Assault, Stalking and Interpersonal Violence).

There is strong evidence that human trafficking basic training needs significant improvement. Basic police training is very limited in the duration and curriculum and has to cover myriad important issues. On average, academy training programs included 761 hours of classroom training (about 19 weeks). A third of academies had an additional mandatory field-training component with an average length of 453 hours. However, special topics covered by basic training programs included a median 14 hours (Bureau of Justice Statistics, 2009). Although federal law enforcement agencies are delivering many courses, a significant number of instructors have limited experience in this area of expertise. The use of problem-based learning methods and scenarios is rather rare. In addition, field training officers have limited knowledge and practical skills in human trafficking cases. But it is crucial that police officers to be aware of such crimes and be able to identify the most important signs of human trafficking.

It is an urgent goal to enhance basic recruit training. Police officer standard boards have not only to introduce human trafficking curriculum but to review and update it frequently accordingly to suit encounters with human trafficking victims. To design a learning module that would focus on practical skills through scenario-based approach, a review of protocols and analysis of case studies would be beneficial. All field training officers should go through annual mandatory training in how to deal with human trafficking cases. In order to improve basic recruit training, the state's POST agencies should review the diversity of training curriculum and include mandatory segments. The basic training module should focus on human trafficking identification, problem-based scenarios, simulations, role-plays, discussions, review of the protocols and analysis of case studies. All field training officers should go through special training for dealing with human trafficking issues.

In-Service Training

In-service training is required by almost all law enforcement agencies nationwide. In a selected number of police departments, a significant number of police officers are attending in-service training sessions. In North Carolina a survey of 121 law enforcement organizations revealed that 40 police agencies, or 65.6 percent, received human trafficking training during their in-service training. Only five agencies receive training through ICE. Over one-third (39.3 percent) indicated that training was obtained through extracurricular sources (Jayson, 2013). However, according to one 2008 survey only 18 percent of agencies nationwide, 38 percent of medium to large agencies, have conducted any type of human trafficking training. Of those agencies with human trafficking training, the majority (47 percent) have utilized in-service training or specialized regional training for investigators (43 percent) (Farrell et al., 2008).

In-service training is significantly different in curriculum and time frame from department to department. The duration of training is determined by the agency and the instructor. Among the benefits of in-service training is that the agency can select some specific topic for the gravity of the issue in their jurisdiction. However, the approach dealing with awareness issues is addressed at most of the in-service training sessions. If the officers are not aware of signs or indications of trafficking then most of these crimes will not even be investigated. In-service training sessions also focus on the differences of indicators of sex and labor trafficking, knowing how to approach the victim, interviewing victims and providing assistance to them, understanding the impact of trafficking on the victim, and providing them an environment to begin to live in safety.

Some law enforcement agencies also provide in-service training on how to handle victims with different culture and language. The victim-centered approach is emphasized in in-service training modules for police officers. In-service training also focuses in related crimes, such as prostitution, immigration violations, drugs and guns trafficking, money laundering, and organized crimes.

The International Association of Chiefs of Police (IACP) has developed and distributed video training for roll-call sessions titled "The Crime of Human Trafficking: A Law Enforcement Guide." It is a three-part training package for law enforcement officers on the crime of human trafficking and also includes a discussion guide and an accompanying guidebook. The aim of the IACP's training package is to give direction for effective officer response and community collaboration, and provide guidance and resources for assisting victims. The training package includes the following: information about the definition of the crime of human trafficking, methods by which traffickers operate and reasons why victims may be reluctant to report, means for detecting and investigating these crimes, ways to address the safety and other needs of victims, and information on federal laws and resources (IACP, 2014).

Federal agencies' assistance is instrumental in directing in-service training for state and local law enforcement. BJA is working with police organizations to provide technical assistance and training to improve the abilities of agencies to (1) identify and rescue victims, (2) proactively investigate trafficking and successfully prosecute traffickers, and (3) raise the awareness of communities to the menace of trafficking and the plight of its victims.

In-service training sessions are limited by ability of the agencies to expose a majority of the officers to this training, budget constraints, and time devoted. According to recent statistics, the average number of in-service training hours required by American police agencies each year is 35 hours. As part of in-service training curriculum implementation, law enforcement agencies have a tendency to invite instructors from outside who might not have in-depth knowledge of local issues and environment.

Specialized Human Trafficking Task Force Training

For the federal level of law enforcement agencies, the President's Interagency Task Force to Monitor and Combat Trafficking in Persons, established by the Trafficking Victims Protection Act of 2000, serves an important role in coordinating the anti-trafficking training efforts. Recent Federal Strategic Action Plan on Services for Victims of Human Trafficking in the United States 2013–2017 indicated that federal agencies are committed to collaboratively supporting law enforcement and criminal justice systems with improved and expanded training and technical assistance. DHS and DOJ, supported by The Department of Labor (DOL) and other federal partners, are developing common teaching points that are components of a victim-centered approach to human trafficking investigations. DHS, DOJ, and DOL are continuing to provide advanced human trafficking training for each Anti-Trafficking Coordination Team as funding allows. DOJ's Office for Victims of Crime will update and enhance the Anti-Human Trafficking Task Force Strategy and Operations e-Guide (https://www.ovcttac.gov/TaskForceGuide/EGuide/Default.aspx), providing updated guidance on collaboration, identification, prosecution, and service provision that is informed by federal partners and stakeholder feedback (*Coordination, Collaboration, Capacity*, 2014).

A new training approach was launched in July 2011 by the U.S. Attorney General and U.S. Secretary of Homeland Security with establishment of anti-trafficking coordination teams (ACTeams) in six districts around the United States. In 2012, with funding support from ICE HSI, FLETC held a curriculum development conference to create an advanced human trafficking training course for these ACTeams. This 4½-day course includes interactive lecture, laboratories, and a final assignment where the teams share how they will begin a proactive investigation upon their return utilizing skills taught in the course. This course is co-owned by FLETC and ICE in cooperation between FLETC's Behavioral Science Division, role players, and the ICE Academy. FLETC partnered with U.S. ICE–HSI, the FBI, the

Human Trafficking Prosecution Unit of the U.S. Department of Justice, and the Department of Labor to deliver training to all six specialized ACTeams (Patrick, 2013).

On the state-level, task forces are more likely to have comprehensive training than other agencies. There are currently more than 20 states that have statutorily mandated state task forces. The BJA, in cooperation with the Office for Victims of Crime (OVC), funds anti-human trafficking training for task forces organized at the local or state level as part of the overall budgeting of these organizations. Developed in partnership by OVC and BJA, the Anti-Human Trafficking Task Force Strategy and Operations e-Guide is a new e-learning tool suggesting not only direction for task forces but also links to valued tools, trainings, and other resources.

It is important to note that anti-trafficking training for task forces is organized in partnership with other law enforcement agencies. Task force trainings are continuously focused on the specific characteristics of human trafficking and how these cases are different from smuggling. Task forces training plays a crucial role in developing universal understanding among its members of the nature and features of human trafficking. Trainings provide task force officers with analytical skills to identify and respond with precision to potential human trafficking incidents in their jurisdictions. Departments with human trafficking task forces usually are instrumental in spreading training to the rest of law enforcement personnel in particular department.

There are other models that differ from the federal approach to human trafficking training.

Since 2004, federal grants allowed for the creation of nine regional task forces in California to combat human trafficking. Between 2010 and 2012, California's task forces provided training to 25,591 law enforcement personnel, prosecutors, victim service providers, and other first responders. There have been developed many Peace Officer Standards and Training (POST)-certified courses that address various aspects of the crime, including how to identify victims, collaborate with victims, and develop human trafficking cases. The Human Trafficking of Minors: Statewide Law Enforcement Training Program, which is POST-certified and administered by the Westminster Police Department, is an 8-hour training course that includes segments on how to identify the signs of trafficking in minors and how to investigate these cases, including techniques to preserve data from cell phones, computers, and other devices (Harris, 2012).

A Massachusetts Interagency Human Trafficking Policy Task Force recent report indicated that there are no human trafficking requirements for law enforcement, first responders, or medical providers, and there is no systematic training plan for these entities. The Boston Police Human Trafficking Unit and the Massachusetts State Police have performed the vast majority of law enforcement training in Massachusetts. The Massachusetts training model is using the "train-the-trainer" format where law enforcement leads trainings. Identified trainers throughout the state participated in train-the-trainer sessions to develop curriculum and certify new trainers, and these certified trainers went on to teach for the Massachusetts Police Training Committee and the State Police using the identified curriculum. This train-the-trainer format has been very effective at reaching the entire state, while simultaneously standardizing the information being taught (Massachusetts Interagency Human Trafficking Policy Task Force, 2013). A similar approach has been used by the Cook County, Illinois, task force. The Training Subcommittee aims to strengthen task force capacity for human trafficking training across Cook County and the Northern District. Current activities include planning a train-the-trainer event and drafting a train-the-trainer manual (Cook County Human Trafficking Task Force, 2014).

In Arizona, the Phoenix Police Department (PPD) task force has worked with this agency's representatives to design a human trafficking training module that is now a part of department's regular in-service training at the Phoenix Regional Police Training Academy (Farrell, 2008).

In all the aforementioned programs, officers are selected based on their level of interest, tactical experiences, communication skills, and problem-solving abilities.

The integration of best practices and experience from the task force training into the basic and in-service training is one of the most effective ways of enhancing the awareness and training approaches today. The most visual benefits of such integration are better understanding of the human trafficking problem in particular jurisdictions, economical use of resources, building partnerships, and accumulation of best practices and experiences.

Executive Training

Law enforcement executives today face a plethora of challenging issues related to the new emerging criminal activities and threats to communities. In most of the states law enforcement leaders are required to go through annual training. There are many options that the police chief or sheriff can do. On the national level the International Association of Chiefs of Police (IACP) program Police Response to Violence against Women Project, with funding from the Department of Justice's Office on Violence against Women (OVW), focuses on the development of tools and policies to assist law enforcement in responding effectively to human trafficking and sexual assault stresses the importance of executive training.

Some states are using well-established training institutions. Illustrative to this trend is the Illinois Law Enforcement Training and Standards Board, which established the Law Enforcement Executive Institute, located at Western Illinois University. The Executive Institute offers a broad array of advanced and specialized courses addressing management and leadership issues. The Executive Institute was created in 1992 by the board, for the purpose of providing advanced study, research, instruction, and administrative technical assistance for the benefit of law enforcement executives throughout Illinois. Illinois Law Enforcement Training and Standards Board and Executive Institute have been responsible for developing a human trafficking training utilizing the Online Learning Network. This project was a collaboration between the Executive Institute, International Association of Chiefs of Police, Polaris Project (http://www.polarisproject.org/), End Demand Illinois (Chicago Alliance against Sexual Exploitation) (https://www.facebook.com/thecaase), and the International Organization for Adolescence (http://www.iofa.org/). The online training focused on defining, identifying, and investigation human trafficking. In 2013 the Executive Institute was invited to present for the Illinois Truck Enforcement Officers Association at Harper College. Additionally they partnered with Polaris Project, NoVo foundation (Peter and Jennifer Buffet), Federal Bureau of Investigation Uniform Crime Report (UCR) Division, Illinois State Police UCR Division, Chicago Alliance Against Sexual Exploitation, and Illinois Attorney General Lisa Madigan on a two-day training for law enforcement and UCR reporters on the topic of human trafficking. This project was funded by the NoVo Foundation and covered human trafficking and the new UCR reporting requirement for this crime. In 2012 the Executive Institute conducted an executive summit in the Oak Brook, Illinois, with Chief Nickolas Sensley, retired chief of Police for Truckee, California, and Anti-Human Trafficking Strategist for Humanity United. Approximately 100 law enforcement executives from around the state attended this summit.

University-Based Training

Higher educational programs will provide law enforcement personnel with better understanding of human trafficking and the ability to recognize and identify it victims. Many universities and colleges around the nation provide training for police officers through a variety of programs. These programs include recognizing signs of human trafficking, interacting with the trafficking victims, types of programs and services available, and the possible complications when immigrations status comes into play. Also, the research component is an important foundation for education and training. For example, Northeastern University, in conjunction with the National Institute of Justice, conducted a study to address how law enforcement defines human trafficking, the number of investigations conducted, the extent of reporting, the nature of coordination with other agencies, and the best practices in responding to human trafficking (Clawson et al., 2009). Arizona State University, for example, has partnered with the Phoenix Police Department to battle recent trends in sex trafficking through its Office of Sex Trafficking Intervention Research (STIR). ASU has made a commitment to share existing knowledge with the community in an effort to fight trafficking.

Universities throughout the country reacted to the new issue of human trafficking by creating specialized or new segments of existing criminal justice programs; however, there was a problem in finding a cadre of experienced faculty to fill the new demand.

The traditional approach in university training is holding conferences designed to educate students, law enforcement professionals, educators, social workers, healthcare professionals, and other community members about topics ranging from human trafficking to cyberexploitation. There are several centers under the umbrella of national universities specializing in human trafficking issues. As a rule they provide regular conferences, research and training resources, and databases.

Many universities have an obvious deficit of faculty who had previous experience as human trafficking practitioners. Due to the fact that the majority of the faculty came from careers in the field but lacked experience in human trafficking, universities are cooperating with practitioners in delivering these programs.

Training Supported by Nongovernmental Organizations

An NGO is an entity or organization, commonly nonprofit in nature and fully independent from the government, that is organized to focus on addressing a particular human trafficking issue. NGOs have the unique ability to promote awareness and training to law enforcement, prosecutors, and judges on the impact on victims and their needs. Human trafficking is viewed by NGOs as complex issue that often requires a change of focus on the part of law enforcement to a victim-centered approach. Teaching law enforcement how to interview and ask the appropriate questions of potential victims, and teaching prosecutors how to handle trauma in a courtroom setting: assist in the successful prosecution of traffickers. Anti-trafficking NGOs are promoting new and creative approaches to human trafficking through training and outreach to law enforcement and nongovernmental partners (Nieuwenhuys and Antoine, 2007).

In the United States the Polaris Project is a leading organization in the anti-human trafficking training among NGOs. This organization operates the National Human Trafficking Resource Center, which conducts trainings for law enforcement agencies titled "Working with Law Enforcement: Part I"; "Building a Local Crisis Response to Human Trafficking"; "Coalition Building"; "Creating a Community Response to Trafficking"; and "NGOs: Key Partners for Law Enforcement" to name a few (Polaris project, 2014).

The Freedom Network (USA), which was established in 2001, is a coalition of 35 NGOs and individual experts that provide services to, and advocate for the rights of, trafficking survivors in the United States.

Another influential nonprofit organization is the International Association of Human Trafficking Investigators (IAHTI), which provides law enforcement officers and prosecutors with the training and resources they need to reach more victims and prosecute their traffickers. Since its inception in 2009, IAHTI has grown to over 350 members, which include law enforcement officers, prosecutors, community organizations, and individuals. IAHTI has provided training for more than 1,000 investigators in 10 countries and 2 U.S. territories, with those numbers growing every year. Rather than sharing theoretical approaches based on a handbook, IAHTI's trainers bring real-world experience gained in the field (International Association of Human Trafficking Investigators, 2014).

The focus of training efforts from NGOs include the areas of awareness-raising presentations, organizing regular conferences, consultations, trainings, and materials review.

Possible Perspectives

Training is key for successful identification, investigation, and prosecution. Law enforcement and other criminal justice responders must therefore be better trained. Because human trafficking is strongly related to geographic and demographic dimensions of specific jurisdictions and only a few small agencies have undergone any type of human trafficking training, an approach of increased awareness and training to law enforcement agencies of all sizes should be developed to enhance the ability of agencies to identify and investigate human trafficking cases.

Training should defuse the denial sentiment held by many law enforcement officers that human trafficking is not a serious threat to the community and should not be a priority for police personnel.

Currently the human trafficking training curriculum that is used is based on fragmented data, limited research on the impact of training toward effectiveness of law enforcement activities, and some major cases that may not reflect the real trends in local jurisdictions.

A number of specific training strategies could be developed that more accurately reflect the needs of local law enforcement throughout the country. For example, those agencies that utilize problem-oriented methods, intelligence-led policing remedies, and scenario and role-playing trainings are more likely to identify specific characteristics of the victims.

In general, local agencies affiliated with multiagency human trafficking task forces have demonstrated enhanced awareness and better skills. Anti-human trafficking task forces should serve as integrated repositories for training best practices. There should be an important research component addition to anti-human trafficking task force training modules with the help of local colleges and universities. This will help to drift from anecdotal ideological foundation of present-day training and will allow development of a new curriculum based on research results.

Faced with weighty considerations regarding anti-human trafficking training, law enforcement agencies should agree that collective actions increase their individual abilities to address problems and help transform their training services. Officers' professional learning would be enhanced and accelerated through sharing knowledge, and their agencies and personnel will benefit from the lessons learned by their colleagues at other collaborative institutions.

And finally cultural awareness training would ease often problematic interaction between law enforcement and victims of human trafficking.

Summary

Human trafficking training plays a crucial role in ensuring that there is an effective response to the phenomena. Training should be multilevel, comprehensive and widespread across the nation's agencies and nonprofit organizations. Human trafficking training and educational programs are critical in producing new generations of highly skilled and knowledgeable law enforcement personnel, who are well prepared to serve the critical public safety mission. Nationwide training and educational programs are diverse and easily accessible for individuals seeking new skills and approaches, and for those who are currently employed in the field and seek to enhance their abilities. The federal government has provided strong national leadership in promoting and providing the human trafficking training, but to train local law enforcement agencies remains crucial to the successful identification and investigation of these crimes nationwide.

Key Terms

awareness	law enforcement
education	nonprofit organizations
human trafficking	training

Review Questions

1. Why do training, practices, and morale of law enforcement officers have a profound impact of how cases of human trafficking are handled?
2. Do majority of national law enforcement agencies view human trafficking as a serious problem for their respective jurisdictions?
3. Which size law enforcement agencies are likely to receive anti-human trafficking training?
4. Have all states passed anti-trafficking laws that mandate and encourage training for law enforcement?
5. How has the lack of uniformity of legal mandates from federal and state governments affected the response to human trafficking?
6. Do U.S. law enforcement agencies have minimum training standards on anti-human trafficking actions?
7. What is the most prevalent type of training provided to law enforcement officers in the United States today: in-service training, new recruit training, roll-call training, or online training?
8. What level of government has provided strong national leadership in promoting and providing the human trafficking training?
9. Do the majority of the states have anti-human trafficking training as a standard part of their basic training curriculum?
10. How likely is it that anti-human trafficking special task forces will receive specialized training?

References

Bruch, Elizabeth M. (2004). Models Wanted: The Search for an Effective Response to Human Trafficking. Retrieved February 2, 2014, from, http://heinonline.org/HOL/LandingPage?handle=hein.journals/stanit40&div=7&id=&page=.

Bureau of Justice Statistics. (2009). Special Report: State and Local Law Enforcement Training Academies, 2006. http://www.bjs.gov/content/pub/pdf/slleta06.pdf.

Bureau of Justice Assistance. (2014). Anti-Human Trafficking Task Force Initiative. Retrieved March 5, 2014, from https://www.bja.gov/ProgramDetails.aspx?Program_ID=51.

Bureau of Justice Assistance. (2014). Department of Justice Trafficking in Persons and Worker Exploitation Task Force. https://www.bja.gov/ProgramDetails.aspx?Program_ID=51

Chacon, Jennifer M. (2009). Misery and Myopia: Understanding the Failures of U.S. Efforts to Stop Human Trafficking. Retrieved February 2, 2014, from http://heinonline.org/HOL/LandingPage?handle=hein.journals/flr74&div=96&id=&page=.

Chang, Grace, and Kim, Kathleen. (2007). Reconceptualizing Approaches to Human Trafficking: New Directions and Perspectives from the Field(s). *Stanford Journal of Civil Rights and Civil Liberties*, vol. 3, no. 2. Loyola-LA Legal Studies Paper No. 2007-47. Available at SSRN: http://ssrn.com/abstract=1051601.

Clawson, H., Dutch, Nicole, Solomon, Amy, and Grace, Lisa Goldblatt. (2009, August). Human Trafficking into and within the United States: A Review of the Literature. U.S. Department of Health and Human Services. Retrieved February 21, 2014, from http://aspe.hhs.gov/hsp/07/humantrafficking/litrev/#barriers.

Clawson, H., Small, K., Go, E., and Myles, B. (2004). *Needs Assessment for Service Providers and Trafficking Victims.* Washington, DC: Government Printing Office.

Cook County Human Trafficking Task Force. (2014). http://www.cookcountytaskforce.org/subcommittees.html.

Coordination, Collaboration, Capacity: Federal Strategic Action Plan on Services for Victims of Human Trafficking in the United States 2013–2017 (2014).

David, Fiona. (2007). Law Enforcement Responses to Trafficking in Persons: Challenges and Emerging Good Practice. *Trends and Issues in Crime and Criminal Justice*, no. 347. Retrieved February 2, 2014, from http://works.bepress.com/fiona_david/3.

Decker, Scott H., Lewis, Paul G., Provine, Doris M., and Varsanyi, Monica W. (2009). On the Frontier of Local Law Enforcement: Local Police and Federal Immigration Law. In William F. McDonald (ed.), *Immigration, Crime and Justice* (Sociology of Crime Law and Deviance, Vol. 13), Emerald Group Publishing Limited, pp. 261–276. Retrieved February 2, 2014, from http://www.emeraldinsight.com/journals.htm?articleid=1791239&show=abstract.

Department of Homeland Security. (2014). Human Trafficking Awareness Training. https://www.dhs.gov/awareness-training.

DeStefano, A. (2007). *The War on Human Trafficking: U.S. Policy Assessed.* Piscataway, NJ: Rutgers University Press.

Dinkins, J. (2014, March). Homeland Security Investigations: Fight Human Trafficking with a Full Arsenal. *The Police Chief.* http://www.policechiefmagazine.org/magazine/index.cfm?fuseaction=display_arch&article_id=2872&issue_id=22013.

Farrell, Amy. (2011). Improving Law Enforcement Identification and Response to Human Trafficking. In John Winterdyk, Philip Reichel and B. Perrin (eds.), *Human Trafficking International Issues and Perspectives.* New York, NY: Taylor & Francis.

Farrell, Amy, McDevitt, Jack, and Fahy, Stephanie. (2008). Understanding and Improving Law Enforcement Responses to Human Trafficking: Final Report. Paper 1. Retrieved February 2, 2014, from http://hdl.handle.net/2047/d10015802.

Farrell, Amy, McDevitt, Jack, and Fahy, Stephanie. (2010). Where Are All the Victims? Understanding the Determinants of Official Identification of Human Trafficking Incidents. *Criminology and Public Policy*, vol. 9, no. 2, pp. 201–233.

Gallagher, A., and Holmes, Paul. (2008). Developing an Effective Criminal Justice Response to Human Trafficking: Lessons from the Front Line. In *International Criminal Justice Review*, vol. 18, no. 3, pp. 318–343.

Goździak, E. (2010). Identifying Child Victims of Trafficking: Toward Solutions and Resolutions. *Criminology & Public Policy*, vol. 9, no. 2, pp. 245–255.

Harris, Kamala D. (2012). The State of Human Trafficking in California. https://oag.ca.gov/sites/all/files/agweb/pdfs/ht/human-trafficking-2012.pdf?

Hughes, D. (2003). *Hiding in Plain Sight: A Practical Guide to Identifying Victims of Trafficking in the U.S.: With Particular Emphasis on Victims of Sexual Trafficking as Defined by the Trafficking Victims Protection Act 2000*. Providence, RI: University of Rhode Island, Women's Studies Program.

IACP News. (2007) Law Enforcement Video Association Awards IACP Top Prize for Video Combating Human Trafficking. *The Police Chief*, vol. 74, no. 12, December 2007. Retrieved February 2, 2014, from http://www.policechiefmagazine.org/magazine/index.cfm?fuseaction=print_display&article_id=1349&issue_id=122007.

International Association of Human Trafficking Investigators. (2014). About. http://www.iahti.org/about/.

Jayson, K. (2013) Human Trafficking in North Carolina: Human Beings as a Commodity. N.C. Governor's Crime Commission Criminal Justice Analysis Center. https://www.ncdps.gov/div/GCC/pubs/Human_Trafficking_North_Carolina_2013.pdf.

Jurkanin, T. (2013) Police Officer Standards and Training (POST) Commissions: A Report on Their Growth, Development, and Current Status. *Law Enforcement Executive Forum*, vol. 13, no. 3, pp. 1–18.

Massachusetts Interagency Human Trafficking Policy Task Force. (2013). Findings and Recommendations. http://www.mass.gov/ago/docs/ihttf/ihttf-findings.pdf.

McDevitt, J. (2010). Human Trafficking: The Stats, the Trends and the Law Enforcement Response. Retrieved February 8, 2014, from http://www.ncja.org/sites/default/files/documents/Human_Trafficking.pdf.

Nieuwenhuys, Céline, and Pécoud, Antoine. (2007). Human Trafficking, Information Campaigns, and Strategies of Migration Control. *American Behavioral Scientist*, vol. 50, no. 12 , pp. 1674–1695.

Patrick, C. (2013). Combating Human Trafficking: A Look at the Federal Law Enforcement Training Center's Efforts. http://www.dhs.gov/blog/2013/01/25/combating-human-trafficking.

Polaris Project. (2013a). 2013 State Ratings on Human Trafficking Laws. Retrieved February 17, 2014, from http://www.polarisproject.org/what-we-do/policy-advocacy/national-policy/state-ratings-on-human-trafficking-laws.

Polaris Project. (2013b). Training for Law Enforcement. Polaris Project Report. Retrieved February 17, 2014, from http://www.polarisproject.org/storage/documents/2013_Analysis_Category_4a_-_Training.pdf.

Polaris Project (2014). Online Training. Retrieved February 8, 2014, from http://www.polarisproject.org/what-we-do/national-human-trafficking-hotline/access-training/online-training.

Reaves, B. (2011, July). Census of State and Local Law Enforcement Agencies, 2008. Bulletin. Washington, D.C.: U.S. Department of Justice, Office of Justice Programs, Bureau of Justice Statistics.

Torg, Cynthia Shepherd. (2005). Human Trafficking Enforcement in the United States. Retrieved February 2, 2014, from http://heinonline.org/HOL/LandingPage?handle=hein.journals/tulicl14&div=24&id=&page=.

Trafficking in Person Report 2010. (June 2010). U.S. Department of State. Washington, D.C. Retrieved February 15, 2014, from http://www.state.gov/j/tip/rls/tiprpt/2010/142761.htm.

U.S. Department of Health and Human Services, Office of Refugee Resettlement (ORR). (2012). About Rescue & Restore Coalitions. Retrieved February 5, 2014, from http://www.acf.hhs.gov/programs/orr/resource/about-rescue-restore-coalitions.

U.S. Department of State. (2010). Trafficking in Person Report 2010. Retrieved February 15, 2014, from http://www.state.gov/j/tip/rls/tiprpt/2010/142761.htm.

U.S. Department of State. (2011). Trafficking in Person Report 2011. Retrieved February 15, 2014, from http://www.state.gov/j/tip/rls/tiprpt/2011/index.htm.

U.S. Department of State. (2012). Trafficking in Person Report 2012. Retrieved February 10, 2014, from http://www.state.gov/j/tip/rls/tiprpt/2012/index.htm.

U.S. Department of State. (2013). Trafficking in Person Report 2013. Retrieved February 10, 2014, http://www.state.gov/j/tip/rls/tiprpt/2013/.

U.S. Immigration and Customs Enforcement. (2014). Fact Sheet: Delegation of Immigration Authority Section 287(g) Immigration and Nationality Act. Retrieved February 15, 2014, from http://www.ice.gov/news/library/factsheets/287g.htm.

Uniform Law Commission. (2014). Legislation: Prevention of and Remedies for Human Trafficking. Retrieved February 21, 2014, from http://www.uniformlaws.org/Legislation.aspx?title=Prevention%20of%20and%20Remedies%20for%20Human%20Trafficking.

United Nations Office on Drugs and Crime. (2009). *Anti-Human Trafficking Manual for Criminal Justice Practitioners*. New York: UNODC.

Wilson, Deborah, Walsh, William F., and Kleuber, Sherilyn. (2006). Trafficking in Human Beings: Training and Services among US Law Enforcement Agencies. In *Police Practice and Research: An International Journal*, vol. 7, no. 2, pp. 149–160.

Wilson, Jeremy M., and Dalton, Erin. (2008). Human Trafficking in the Heartland: Variation in Law Enforcement Awareness and Response. *Journal of Contemporary Criminal Justice*, vol. 24, no. 3, pp. 296–313.

Not in Our City

14

STACIE DONALDSON

Contents

Major Issues

- The need for a shift in the community's *perception* of the issue of human trafficking; the importance of viewing those who have been sexually exploited as victims and survivors, not criminals
- The need for *partnership* between community volunteers and the professionals who provide direct services to trafficking victims and survivors, and understanding the important roles each can have
- An encouragement for community members to focus on *prevention* efforts

I'd heard of brothels and red light districts, but in my mind, they were far-away places, and the people in them were adults making their own choices. The young women in movies like *Pretty Woman* or in stories I'd heard were alluring and almost glamorous. If I'd ever given it much thought (and I hadn't), it never would have occurred to me that behind their seductive smiles lay broken hearts, pain, and fear.

But on February 23, 2010, I read a blog post that would challenge my preconceived notions and ultimately change the focus of my life. It described young women in Thai villages whose desperately impoverished families were being cruelly deceived. Wealthy strangers would arrive, offering to take village girls to the city, promising unsuspecting parents their daughters would receive an education or find a job, and would be able to send money home to support the family. The dream of a better life for their daughters—and themselves—clouded any doubts or suspicions as to the sincerity or motives of those making the promises.

But, I learned, when the young women arrived in the city, instead of jobs or classes waiting they would find only brothels. They would be beaten, drugged, threatened, and repeatedly sexually assaulted until they were emotionally broken to the point of doing whatever their captors demanded, simply hoping to survive. They might be taken far from home, often removed from anyone who even spoke their language. They were told (or would soon discover on their own) that law enforcement often looked the other way, or even participated in their abuse.

I had no idea.

But there was more. Not only were they being deceived and forced, but the young girls and boys involved were just that: young. I read of girls who were 15. Or only 12. Or 6. Their alluring smiles were an act—something they'd been taught to do to please those who would use them—and they learned, because they truly had no other choice.

I wept. I couldn't sleep. I wondered how I hadn't known this was happening, and now that I knew, I wondered how to respond. I began reading all I could find on the subject. I wrote an article for a local paper about education and job programs I'd learned about for trafficking survivors overseas. I read about forced labor trafficking, of both children and adults, and encouraged those around me to shop carefully, supporting companies that have good track records of caring for their workers. Eventually, my husband and I would become stateside volunteers for the Thailand organization I'd first read about.

But as I talked with my new friends in Thailand, another question kept popping up. "Stacie, don't you know this is happening in the United States as well?" Here? I couldn't wrap my mind around it. How could something like this go on in our country without it making the news on a regular basis? Maybe on the West Coast or in Washington, DC (where the Thai organization was based)—maybe. But Wichita, Kansas?

Just a few months after that initial conversation, I had my answer.

In late 2010, local media broke the story of a massage parlor, shut down by Wichita police after they discovered evidence of human trafficking there. Cathy Cooper, a local pastor's wife, recalls hearing the story on the news:

My husband and I had just attended a conference in Atlanta, Georgia, where a woman told her story of being trafficked as a young child in another country. I was repulsed to think of this happening to anyone. As I tried to sleep at night, I was haunted by dreams and thoughts of what was happening to precious children around the world. At that time, I could see how it would happen in poor countries like hers, but not in the United States. Maybe even in large cities like Atlanta, but not in Wichita.

Within days of our return to Wichita, the police raided an Asian massage parlor less than 50 yards from my backyard. I knew the massage parlor was there but had no idea the girls were being trafficked. I realized trafficking *did* happen in Wichita.

Before that story broke, I'd been attempting to make connections with friends, family members, and colleagues, looking for any opportunities to share what I was learning. I worked to encourage those around me to get involved in the international projects I was aware of—helping to provide safety, education, and job training for survivors of trafficking around the world. The police raid at the massage parlor opened my eyes in the same way it opened Cathy's: I realized for the first time that human trafficking could happen—and does happen—everywhere.

I contacted members of law enforcement and tried to find out more about the massage parlor case. I wondered if something could be done to help the young women discovered there. Officers I spoke with were sympathetic to the plight of the victims and appreciated my concern, but couldn't share information about an ongoing case—and I didn't really know what questions to ask.

But that story was just the beginning. A few months later, Wichita citizens would wake up to a Sunday morning headline about another local victim.

Jennifer White, who would eventually become the founder of ICT SOS, echoes Cathy Cooper's disbelief, as she recalls the story: "In the spring of 2011, I read an article in the *Wichita Eagle* about the trial of a pimp and a john who were accused of selling a 13-year-old girl at a Quik Trip convenience store in Wichita. Thirteen. My oldest daughter was 12 at the time."

Jennifer tried to put the story out of her mind, but couldn't, and eventually contacted Ron Sylvester, the *Eagle* reporter who wrote the article, and asked if he knew some way she could help. "I'm not a social worker," Jennifer told him. "I'm not a police officer. I'm a mom."

Ron's suggestion was to connect with Street Outreach Services (SOS) at the Wichita Children's Home. The Street Outreach program provides rescue and support services to lost, runaway, and homeless children and teens, as well as those involved in sexual exploitation and human trafficking. They are also the local representatives for the national Safe Place program, so if a young person goes to a Quik Trip, a fire station, local library, or any other establishment displaying a "Safe Place" sign in Wichita, and asks for help, it's the local Street Outreach team who answers the call.

Jennifer met with their staff, and together they planned a donation drive to help provide supplies for the teens Street Outreach serves. In Wichita, the airport code ICT is sort of local shorthand for anything Wichita related, and since Street Outreach Services (SOS) was part of the donation—and also a call for help—the reporter spread the word about it via Twitter: #ictsos. It never occurred to anyone that what they were planning would go much further than this one event or that the name would stick. Hoping to collect a few bags of needed items, Jennifer was overwhelmed by the response: donations filled the back of her SUV, along with another van. Clearly, members of the community wanted to help; they just needed to know where to start.

I hadn't heard about the donation drive yet, but I'd read that same newspaper article and was convinced again that I needed to find a way to get involved. A few days later, a friend who knew I was concerned sent me a Facebook invitation about a group of citizens who were meeting regularly to talk about what else could be done, following the donation drive. "Have you ever heard of Jennifer White?" he asked. I hadn't, but I was about to—and I had no idea at the time what that would mean.

Over lunch at a crowded Jason's Deli, Jennifer and I told each other our stories, and shared our desire to make a difference. She invited me to their next meeting, where law enforcement and social service providers would be on hand to give us accurate information about trafficking in our community and where we could help next.

That summer, Jennifer and I were invited to join a multidisciplinary group called the Anti-Sexual Exploitation Round Table for Community Action (ASERCA), of which Wichita State University's Dr. Karen Countryman-Roswurm is founder and coordinator. Dr. Roswurm is also the executive director for the Center for Combating Human Trafficking (CCHT) at Wichita State and is a leading expert in the field. Being part of ASERCA has enabled us to build direct relationships with leaders in a variety of local agencies (law enforcement, social services, medical providers, legal representatives, and others) and to learn more about the needs in our community.

Jennifer was already well connected in social media circles, and continued to use both Facebook and Twitter to share general information (articles, websites, etc.) about trafficking, as well as spreading the word each time we'd hear about another agency in need of volunteers or items. She set up a web page where people could keep up with the needs, and ICT SOS began collecting donated items on a regular basis—most of which began filling Jennifer's living room until they could be dropped off at the designated organization.

We found that while the professionals do want to spread the word about needs in our community, they are also genuinely busy meeting those needs themselves, and don't always have time to go and speak to every small group that simply needs a short presentation on the basics. As we continued to build relationships with the agencies, sharing that introductory information has slowly become another role in which a few trained volunteers have been able to serve. Armed with local statistics and accurate information received from those on the frontlines, we began sharing information about trafficking with church groups, book clubs, neighborhood associations, and other community members just like us, who had read the same articles we'd read and who just wanted to know what they could do. Our relationships with members of law enforcement and direct service providers have proved invaluable to us in this. From them we have learned not only information about trafficking but also gained a better understanding of what to share and what not to. For instance, we learned that it's not appropriate to share details of a survivor's story, even if he or she gives permission. It's exploitive—and unsafe for a variety of reasons—to post names or photos of young people who have been victims, or even those who may be at risk of becoming victims. And, sometimes, even those who want to help can do more harm than good by offering a place to stay or other "incentives" to someone who has been exploited, if the young person feels that the offer is in exchange for telling his or her "story" or providing some sort of volunteer service. All of a sudden, a well-intentioned offer can feel just as manipulative as that of someone seeking to control a victim. These were not things we'd have known without the relationships we have with the professionals. We continue to read and attend conferences as we can, but we learn the most—and are most grateful for—the professionals who continually invest in our understanding and empower us to take their knowledge and share it with others. It's vital for community members who want to join this movement to listen to those on the frontlines and follow their instructions.

When we talk to groups, we begin by sharing our personal experiences with those who invite us. We share how we (like most of them) were initially shocked by the realization that human trafficking happens in our community, and that in addition to trafficking and sexual exploitation, there are a number of other, often preventable, abuses happening right in our own neighborhoods that most of us don't even see. We explain that although the term "human trafficking" is relatively new, and awareness efforts and continued training make instances more easily identifiable today, the issue has been in our communities far longer than most of us had imagined. "I've been working with sexually exploited teens on the streets of Wichita for over 30 years," one Street Outreach worker told us. "This is not new."

A Shift in Perception

As I began to read more, and listened to the officers and service providers I met, I realized I'd been living in a rather insulated world, and—like many people—had made inaccurate and unfair assumptions about who these young people were and how they'd found themselves in these situations. As we continued to talk to friends and family, and shared with the church and civic groups who invited us, we realized that most of them were in the same place we'd been: insulated ignorance. So, when we share with groups, one of the first things we address is the need for a shift in perception.

It's usually not difficult for most people to recognize that trafficked young people in Thailand or Cambodia are forced or deceived, and are obviously victims in need of help. In the United States, however, the lines are a little more blurred, and due to a lack of understanding of the issue, victims are sometimes viewed as the criminals or as though they are "choosing" to participate. Sometimes people don't understand that these young people have often run away from a background of violence and abuse or neglect, and may not have ever had one single, healthy relationship with an adult who can guide him or her in making wise choices. They may naively be lured in by a "friend" on Facebook or deceived by other false promises, and are just as surely innocent victims as a child forcibly taken from her village in Thailand.

Young victims of sex trafficking in the United States—the average age of entry is 12 to 14 years of age—have most likely been tricked into believing that the person wielding the power truly cares about them, despite how they are treated. The pimp is an expert in exploiting vulnerabilities, so victims may be "groomed" by someone who leads them to believe he is a boyfriend or a father figure—someone the young person believes will take care of them, only to have the relationship become physically and emotionally abusive. Whatever the methods, it's important to help our community see that whether the captivity is physical (actually being held against their will) or emotional (deception that causes them to stay), victims of sex trafficking truly believe they have no other option.

Partnerships

In addition to shifting perceptions, the second focus we try to help community members see is the importance of joining forces. "We are not the experts," Jennifer often tells people, "but we know who the experts are, and we work with them." The volunteer base at ICT SOS understands we are not law enforcement or social service providers, we are not professionals, and we are not able to offer the ongoing care trafficking survivors need—nor do we try. Instead, we focus on supporting the agencies and individuals who do have that expertise.

Again, I discovered I'd been living in an insulated world. Not only had I no concept of the scope of the issue, but (I'm ashamed to admit) I'd never even heard of most of the resources and organizations we have already serving this population in our community. Sedgwick County is blessed to have a number of agencies that understand that those being manipulated and caught up in trafficking (or those who are at risk) are truly the innocent parties. The dedicated professionals who work at these agencies work hard to meet needs, and can always use volunteers and donated items, but don't often have the time or resources to organize projects for the community to carry out.

This is where community members asking the right questions can make a difference. We recommend people find out what is already being done well in the community, and join those who are doing it. Multiply efforts instead of duplicating them. Rather than deciding ahead of time what to do for them, community members need to ask those who are already on the frontlines what they truly need most and find ways to meet those needs. Sometimes it's the simple solution—donating hoodies, snacks, or bottles of shampoo—that can make a difference, and these are often things service providers don't have time to hunt for.

Prevention

"I wish someone cared the *first* time they ran away," Anne Ellis told me once. Anne is a social worker embedded with the Wichita Police Department's Exploited and Missing Child Unit (EMCU), and works daily with young women who have been trafficked or who are at greater risk of becoming victims. She sees young people who drop out of school, run away from home (or a foster home), or simply don't have any real guidance. They are the kids most people label as "trouble," and few look beneath the surface to see what situations (abuse, neglect, poverty) they might be running away from.

Often, people who have not heard much about domestic trafficking before hear our brief presentation and immediately want to know how they can help. We point them toward volunteer opportunities within local agencies that focus on prevention—mentoring, tutoring, foster parenting, and other ways to invest in the lives of young people before they become victims. We also encourage volunteers to participate in our awareness events: staffing a booth and handing out information at events, participating in our annual 5k run, or donating (and encouraging their friends to donate) some of the hygiene items, sweatshirts, duffel bags, prepackaged snacks, and other items our partner agencies need on a regular basis. We have volunteers who sort donations, make deliveries, write thank-you notes, pass out posters, make phone calls, provide weekly snacks for a local survivor support group, and more. Some of the best volunteers are ones like Cathy Cooper, the pastor's wife mentioned earlier, who started out attending meetings and volunteering with ICT SOS but has since gone on to find her own niche as a dedicated volunteer with a local agency. As a result, we don't see Cathy at our meetings as often as we used to, because she's busy serving young people—and that's really how it's supposed to work.

Cathy describes it this way:

> For me, this has been God's leading in my life. As my youngest left for college, I prayed about how I should use my extra time as an empty nester. As I began to be exposed to this repulsive crime of trafficking, I was overwhelmed with my inadequacies and the massive job of stopping this. God kept opening doors for me to volunteer. [During monthly ICT SOS meetings], we were exposed to many organizations that were helping to prevent children at risk from fall-

ing prey to this crime. There were so many ways we could help, but I knew I couldn't volunteer for all of them.

One major project that ICT SOS championed was remodeling a church basement for SOS [Street Outreach]. Here the youths (14–21 years old) in crisis situations could come for showers, food, laundry services, Internet connections, help with finding shelter, school or work opportunities, mentoring and a safe place to enjoy friendships. The youths named it Opportunity Zone (OZ). Volunteers were trained to help the staff and assist the youths. This is where I really wanted to concentrate my time. Over the last two years, I have been stretched, amazed, humbled, encouraged, and impressed with the staff of SOS and the young people I've met and grown to love. It is exciting to watch as many youths begin to take positive steps in changing the trajectory of their lives.

All of these are simple ways community members can join the fight against human trafficking—simple, but not insignificant. They are definitely making a difference.

Since 2011, we have certainly made mistakes, but we've done our best to support the agencies we work with, and we are constantly learning. Here are a few things we've learned that might help other communities who want to join the movement.

Get to know how and why things are done the way they are before suggesting a change. No one likes to hear, "Why don't you just ..." from someone who is new to any issue, as though the answer is simple to anyone who is looking. Chances are good that if the problem could be solved as simply as that, it would already be done. That isn't to say new ideas aren't welcome, but the professionals who are handling these cases know how things work and (I learned quickly) aren't eager to hear quick "solutions" from folks who have seen a documentary and read a couple of books. Everyone benefits from volunteers who, at least initially, listen more than they speak.

Recognize the complexity of the problem. Understand that one part is affected by another, and that there's no cookie-cutter response to this issue. What works to serve victims in Dallas may not work exactly the same way in Wichita. John Vanek, a retired police officer and trafficking consultant in San Jose, California, tells the story of a group of some well-meaning women in Northern California who created a shelter for trafficking survivors outside a large city. Part of their intention was to remove the women and girls who stayed there from the environment where they'd become victims. Not a bad idea, but in the process they created a place that was over an hour's drive from medical appointments, court, job training, and other vital services their clients needed. They never had a single person move in. A few months later, these same women moved to an area in Southern California—a different setting, with different logistics (and its own set of problems, of course) but were far more successful there. "When organizations enter the anti-trafficking field," Vanek told me, "they need to take time to learn all the needs of the victims and the other organizations who serve victims."

Community organizations can be advocates for the good guys. Once, while wearing an ICT SOS T-shirt, I was approached by a woman whose opening remark was simply, "Wichita police aren't doing *anything* about escort services in this city." Thanks to a conversation I'd recently had with a local officer, I was able to assure her—without giving away confidential details, since I didn't have any—that there was more strategy and undercover work going on than she realized.

Often, citizens don't realize all that's involved in decisions that are made. For instance, despite increased awareness and undercover work, we still have massage parlors in Wichita, which causes some in our community to mistakenly believe law enforcement isn't making much progress in fighting human trafficking. However, through our conversations with officers directly involved, we are able to gain insight into their focus and help the community better understand when the subject comes up. In the case of massage parlors, Wichita Police Department Captain Brent Allred explains: "I don't want to downplay the massage parlors because we need to continue our efforts to close those places that are fronts for human trafficking ... but the online ads [where young victims are often posted] have grown over the years and continue to grow. So much of it is out there that we can't keep up. We need to focus our efforts to get those ads removed and shut down those sites because the number of victims it impacts on a daily basis is so much greater." ICT SOS works diligently to communicate to our community the work that is being done, helping people understand that much of the real work happens behind the scenes.

Serving looks like work. Sometimes community members who want to join the fight against human trafficking believe the work will be exciting and that the rewards will be significant—and immediate. They expect to be on the streets "rescuing" victims and to always have their efforts appreciated by those they seek to help. But that's not often the case. Most victims have been so manipulated and deceived that they aren't even able to recognize or acknowledge they've been victimized, and aren't looking to be "rescued." As Sedgwick County District Attorney Marc Bennett says often, "Success doesn't come in big moments." Yes, there are occasional arrests and convictions. Lives are changed and seeing progress can be emotionally rewarding. But, for the most part, those who seek to help (both volunteers and professionals) settle for gradual progress and small victories. Further, community members must leave direct services to those with the training to provide it, and work in a support role to those professionals. Helping community members who want to "get involved" understand this is important, if we want to engage and equip volunteers who are willing to stay committed over time and meet actual needs.

Events and Education

In addition to collecting supplies and connecting volunteers with other local agencies, ICT SOS also wanted to create an impact through a larger-scale project that would benefit the fight against trafficking in our city. In late 2011, Liz Perry—already a volunteer at the Wichita Area Sexual Assault Center (WASAC)—approached Jennifer with the idea of hosting a 5k race to raise funds, as well as awareness about trafficking in Wichita. Neither Jennifer nor Liz had ever organized a race event but had both competed in the past. They jumped in with both feet and began planning our inaugural Race for Freedom 5k.

The recipient of funds raised by the first race would be the independent living program at Carpenter Place, a local home for girls. The program gives young women a safe place to live, opportunities to continue their education, job and life skills, and transportation to and from school and work. Many of the young women who choose to complete the program have aged out of the foster care system or have even been homeless. The program allows them to get a firm foundation under their feet as they transition into adulthood so that they are in a position to be self-sufficient. A young woman with an education, a job, transportation, emotional support, and other tools to be successful is a much harder target for anyone who may intend to exploit her. Proceeds from the race would provide a security system in the building to give the staff and residents an even safer environment in which to flourish.

Liz and Jennifer sought out a team of people with skills in marketing, race logistics, decorating, hospitality, and some who were just willing to do whatever it took. Liz laid out the plan and donated her graphic design skills. Local celebrities were engaged to emcee the event. We enlisted the help of Clark Ensz, a longtime race director and legend in our local running community. He was excited about the plans, but cautioned the team that a good first-year event in our city usually drew somewhere around 200 to 300 runners. On September 8, 2012, when the starting gun (actually an air horn) went off, 911 registered runners were lined up at the starting line.

The race also kicked off a month-long lineup of community awareness events including documentary screenings, a conference, and a concert in Wichita's Farm and Art Market Square. The concert, a joint event put on by a local church, drew around 1,000 people and has since become an annual event.

In 2013, the race continued to grow. This time, our recipient would be the Child Advocacy Center of Sedgwick County (CACSC) to help it further its mission of providing collaborative care for child victims of human trafficking, abuse, neglect, sexual exploitation, and other crimes against children. The CACSC works closely with the police department's Exploited and

Missing Child Unit (EMCU), the District Attorney's office, and medical providers to coordinate medical, therapy, legal, and investigative services to help those in need. In 2013, the Race for Freedom raised $27,000 toward the CACSC goal to create a "one-stop shop" for families and children in crisis, in which all of these services will be colocated.

Our hope is to use the event to support a specific project in our community each year by donating the proceeds to one of our partner agencies to help in the work they are doing. A race may not be the best way to do this in every community, but ICT SOS has found a niche in ours and has been able to grow the number of participants and the sponsorships as the event matures.

Our most recent venture has been in the area of *prevention education*. Because the average age of entry into sex trafficking among young people in the United States is 12 to 14 years old, we feel it's important to be reaching the students who might be directly impacted. We researched a number of curriculum options and eventually forged a partnership with FAIR Girls, an organization in the Washington, DC, area, using a curriculum called *Tell Your Friends*. *TYF* is a four-session program designed for middle school and high school students. Through the use of video, music, group discussion, and other interactive exercises, kids learn definitions and indicators of possible trafficking or exploitation instances, and are encouraged to think through how media might influence and shape the way society views those involved. They also consider the power of words, how the language we use to describe people affects the way we think of them. Another exercise covers healthy versus unhealthy relationships, helping them see behaviors that might be warning signs of someone who is attempting to control a relationship. It has been powerful to see a "light bulb" moment for some kids—kids who start out resisting, but who eventually realize the truth behind some of what they're hearing.

As with the other projects we've taken on, we first went to our partners to find out from them how best to approach this. We shared information about the curriculum as we researched, and members of several local agencies attended the training to hear details, ask questions, and weigh in on the content. They helped us tailor it to meet state and local needs, making sure we had accurate information and connections to resources and service providers who can follow up with individual students, if needed.

Our teaching team now takes *TYF* into middle and high school church groups, after-school organizations, residential facilities, and classrooms, and we look forward to seeing the program grow.

Not in Our City

When we began, we couldn't believe what was happening here—surely not in *our* city! Today, we view that statement a little differently. Our eyes have been opened, and we understand that these things happen everywhere. But, through education and awareness, partnerships, and meeting needs, ICT SOS stands with our community as we say that exploitation will not win here. *Not in our city.*

Summary

The chapter begins with a common misconception about human trafficking: that it only happens in countries outside the United States rather than right in our own hometowns.

We briefly looked at two Wichita cases reported in the news that brought domestic trafficking to the city's attention, and the response of a community volunteer named Jennifer White, whose simple donation drive idea eventually became a grassroots nonprofit organization called ICT SOS.

We discussed three major needs ICT SOS encourages community members to address: perception, partnership, and prevention.

Finally, we described several community awareness programs ICT SOS has led or participated in since 2011. These are offered as examples other communities might implement in their areas, and focus on ways community members and professionals in the anti-trafficking field can collaborate in the fight.

Review Questions

1. How are international trafficking and domestic trafficking different from one another? In what ways are they similar?
2. Why is it so important that victims of trafficking and exploitation are not viewed as the perpetrators or criminals? How does understanding this distinction make a difference in the way they are treated or in the kinds of services they receive?
3. What can be done to help a community understand that young people involved in trafficking are victims not criminals?
4. What are some things volunteers need to learn from the professionals who provide services to exploited young people? What might the professionals learn from the volunteers?
5. Beyond simply reducing the number of victims, what other positive differences do prevention efforts make? (Consider far-reaching effects of prevention and positive investments in the lives of young people versus the possible long-term effects once someone has been exploited.)

Providing Effective Services to Victims of Human Trafficking

15

Theoretical, Practical, and Ethical Considerations

DORTHY STUCKY HALLEY, SHARON L. SULLIVAN, AND JENNIFER RAPP

Contents

Major Issues

- There are numerous misconceptions about human trafficking that impact the development and implementation of effective services.
- In order to provide adequate assistance to human trafficking victims, it is critical to understand the victim's psychological perspective.

- Law enforcements' treatment of victims can significantly influence victim cooperation.
- An effective response to human trafficking requires a cooperative and collaborative approach.

Human trafficking is a devastating human rights violation that remains largely invisible to the public eye. Until very recently, it has remained largely invisible to professionals, as well. The single leading cause of lack of access to services is lack of identification.* As we become more aware of the problem, more victims will be identified. Once identified, specialized short-term (emergency) and long-term services are needed to aid victims. There are many challenges first responders and other service providers must overcome to be effective in their work with human trafficking victims. The gravity of this problem has led the President's Interagency Task Force to Monitor and Combat Trafficking in Persons to develop the *Federal Strategic Action Plan on Services for Victims of Human Trafficking in the United States 2013–2017*. States are now grappling with ways to effectively serve this population. This chapter provides an overview of the theoretical, practical, and ethical considerations.

Common Misperceptions

Although human trafficking is an age-old problem, the modern-day response is an emerging field fraught with misperceptions that impact the development and implementation of effective services.

1. *Human trafficking is an international problem. If we focus on identification at our border crossings we can resolve human trafficking here.* Many people think human trafficking refers to human smuggling. Although smuggling may be a part of the situation, it is a separate crime related to someone paying to be transported over an international border. Human trafficking is modern-day slavery and does not require crossing an international boundary. Most victims trafficked in the United States are from the United States. Most United States citizens believe slavery ended with the Thirteenth Amendment to the U.S. Constitution in 1865. In fact, human trafficking is the fastest growing illegal activity and the second most lucrative criminal enterprise in the world at an estimated $32 billion annually (Haken 2011; Harris n.d.) This misperception leads to developing services focused on the needs of international victims, with little capacity for serving victims that are United States citizens.

---

* Eliza Reock, Shared Hope, presentation at Topeka, Kansas, January 31, 2014.

In 2009, 12 people including 8 Uzbekistan nationals were charged with 45 counts of labor racketeering, forced labor trafficking, immigration violations, among others, in 14 states. Through Giant Labor Solutions LLC, headquartered in Kansas City, Missouri, Crystal Management Inc, headquartered in Mission, Kansas, and Five Star Cleaning LLC, headquartered in Overland Park, Kansas, Abrorkhodja Askarkhodjaev and his associates secured fraudulent leasing contracts from clients in the hotel, resort, casino, and construction industries in Missouri, Kansas, Alabama, and 11 other states. The company used foreign nationals to fulfill the contracts for housekeeping, cleaning services, and other duties.

Askarkhodjaev and his associates required the foreign nationals to work where the enterprise assigned them. They would threaten to cancel the immigration status of those who refused to work as directed. They also charged the foreign nationals multiple fees and forced them to live in apartments controlled by Labor Solutions and charged them exorbitant rent.

According to the Department of Justice, "these fees and expenses, combined with the lack of payment for hours worked, underpayment for hours worked and lack of work assignments, often resulted in the foreign national workers receiving a paycheck with negative earnings. The enterprise allegedly ensured that the workers did not make enough to repay their debt, to purchase a plane ticket home, or pay for their own living expenses while in the United States. It further controlled the foreign national workers in the Kansas City area by not allowing them to receive mail." (http://www.justice.gov/opa/pr/2009/May/09-crt-517.html)

2. *Prostitution is a victimless crime.* Our culture frames prostitution as a "choice" or a consensual act between two adults. Most people do not realize that the average age of entry into prostitution is 12 to 14 years old. Adults exploited in the commercial sex industry (prostitution, pornography, strip clubs, brothels, some massage parlors, etc.) regularly report their abuse began in childhood. They have few resources or skills to escape "the life." Not only are these individuals victimized, they are blamed for their victimization and stigmatized by society. This results in very few services available to address their needs. In the past, the focus of these limited services has largely been getting victims to "change their ways," rather than assisting them with recovery from their victimization.

3. *Most commercial sexual exploitation happens on seedy street corners.* Due to the Internet, sexual exploitation has dramatically

changed. Victims of commercial sexual exploitation are commonly sold through the Internet and can remain completely hidden from public view. Reputable hotels in any community can be sites for arranged sexual exploitation. Since the Internet is virtually unregulated, it can be difficult to identify victims. The nature of the Internet makes it difficult for law enforcement to geographically locate victims. Additionally, it makes it effortless for traffickers to move from location to location to avoid law enforcement. As noted earlier, the biggest challenge in service delivery is identification. The use of the Internet has exacerbated this problem.

4. *Labor trafficking only happens in other countries.* Americans like cheap food and goods, and often do not question supply chain practices. This encourages traffickers to exploit people for their labor and pocket the profits. Traffickers also sell contract labor and the purchaser may not know the laborers are being trafficked. This is common in housekeeping services such as hotel maid services and janitorial services. Although factories, restaurants and agriculture are high-risk industries for labor trafficking, there are also documented cases of sales crews made up of trafficked people—particularly exploited youth in door-to-door sales strategies. With labor trafficking victims so inconspicuous, again it is their identification that creates the major obstacle. Additionally, if the labor trafficking victim is from the United States there are virtually no services available. Although sex trafficking victims may receive services from a domestic violence or sexual assault program, there are no similar existing service structures that link as closely with labor trafficking. Labor trafficking victims are not always viewed as eligible for services from these organizations.

5. *Victims will immediately appreciate assistance.* Although appreciation may occur in some instances, it is not the common response. Victims often do not self-identify as trafficking victims for many reasons and may deny needing help. For good reason, many victims are terrified of receiving help. Victims may have been threatened with violence or violence to their families and friends if they report to law enforcement. Victims frequently report witnessing violence against other people who displeased or disobeyed the trafficker. This is used by the trafficker as a form of manipulation. International victims, minor victims, and many adults may not know or understand the laws and are often told by their traffickers they will be arrested if discovered by law enforcement. For many, this has already occurred in the past. Victims may not realize they are victims. This is especially common in commercial sexual exploitation where victims may have a significant traumatic bond with their traffickers.

6. *Help is available. We just need to get concerned citizens to help us get these victims off the streets.* There are not enough resources currently available to meet the needs of trafficking victims, and the resources that are available are often unspecialized and woefully inadequate. Experts estimate that 18 to 24 months of services are required for most victims to adequately recover from the trauma of being trafficked (Clawson, Dutch, and Williamson 2008; Shigekane 2007; Williamson and Prior 2009). In a 2012 report, Polaris Project documented 1,644 shelter beds, with only 529 of those designated specifically for trafficking victims, available in the United States for trafficking victims. Some states have no available beds; others have beds only for a specific type of victim. Domestic victims are eligible to apply for social services, but in many states those resources are already strained. International victims may be certified for a T-Visa, but those are limited as well. Trafficking victims need significant and specialized services. Immediate needs include housing, food, medical treatment, safety, and security. Long-term needs include mental and physical healthcare, education and life skills training, alcohol and drug treatment, income assistance, and legal assistance. Failure to provide appropriate short- and long-term services will likely result in a victim being trafficked again.

7. *We have been providing services to troubled kids and runaways for a long time, and can plug trafficked kids into existing services.* Although there are similarities with other children, there are also some critical differences: Safety is a crucial issue for staff, other residents in shelter and the trafficked person. Traffickers are invested in keeping control of their victims. They will utilize any means necessary to retrieve their victims including waiting outside of a shelter or residential treatment center, threatening or enticing victims through communication tools including social media, and kidnapping the victim from court or treatment facilities. With the influx of gang involvement in trafficking, many victims and facility staff have more than one pimp to fear. In addition, there are many reports of girls recruiting other minors from a facility and running back to their trafficker. Minors who have been trafficked for commercial sexual exploitation often believe they are in love with their pimps or they are fearful of retribution if they do not return to the pimp.

Understanding the Victim: The Victim Experience

Before we can develop effective services, it is important to understand the challenges victims face. People who have been trafficked are often psychologically traumatized by their victimization. A traumatic event is defined as "actual or threatened death or serious injury or a threat to the physical integrity of self or others" where the response of the victim is one of "intense fear, helplessness, or horror" (American Psychiatric Association 2013). The impact and effects of human trafficking often mirror those of other criminal activities such as domestic violence, sexual assault, and torture. Similarly to domestic violence, traffickers often use psychological coercion to control their victims. The forms of psychological coercion used on victims of trafficking are numerous and often vary depending on the type of trafficking and the individual circumstances of each case. In many cases trafficking victims are exploited by people known to them—neighbors, relatives, boyfriends, lovers, or fiancés—who build on trusting relationships in order to gain control. Trafficking victims are often told that if they try to escape, their families will be harmed. The traffickers instill fear in victims with threats of deportation, tales of law enforcement collaborating with the traffickers or harming the victims if caught, personal exposure, and other punishments. This is one of the most effective tools traffickers use to manipulate victims; as such, this and other forms of coercion allow traffickers to control victims often without needing to rely on physical force (U.S. Department of State 2011).

The traumatic bond is an extreme form of PTSD (posttraumatic stress disorder), a kind of Stockholm syndrome, and is a common occurrence in trafficking. Traumatic bonding is described as "strong emotional ties that develop between two persons where one person intermittently harasses, beats, threatens, abuses, or intimidates the other" (Dutton and Painter 1981). The trafficker will often intersperse violence or threats of violence with kindness and praise. In trauma bonds, the imbalance of power creates a cycle where the victim feels helpless and seeks approval to avoid additional abuse. This creates a cycle where the victim feels helpless and seeks approval to avoid additional abuse. The victim often engages in denial of the abuse, or its severity, as a form of emotional self-protection. One self-protection strategy is dissociation, where the victim experiences the abuse as if it is happening outside their body or to another person. This allows the victim to separate the abusive aspects of the relationship from the desirable aspects. This cognitive dissonance allows the victim to cope with contradicting behaviors and survive the abuse by changing how they perceive reality. "Studies also show a person is more loyal and committed to a person or situation that is difficult, uncomfortable, or even humiliating; and the more the victim has invested in the relationship, the more they need to justify their position. Cognitive dissonance is a powerful 'self-preservation' mechanism that can completely distort and override the truth, with the victim developing a tolerance for the abuse and 'normalizing' the abuser's behavior, despite evidence to the contrary" (Victims and Survivors of Psychopaths n.d.). When there is a trauma bond, the victim identifies positively with the trafficker and believes that the relationship, despite the abuse, is a loving one (American Psychiatric Association 2013). The victim masks the abusive behavior, perhaps not admitting it even to themselves. This belief system may make it nearly impossible for the victim to disclose the abuse to law enforcement and other service providers.

Trafficking victims may also suffer from other mental disorders including anxiety, mood, dissociative, and substance abuse disorders (Williamson, Dutch, and Clawson 2010). Multiple studies indicate a high rate of PTSD in trafficking victims. High rates of extreme anxiety and fear, self-destructive behaviors, profound shame and guilt, despair, loneliness, and hopelessness are also reported. Trauma victims frequently display symptoms of hypervigilance, irritability, and an exaggerated startle response. They may also have difficulty concentrating and falling or staying asleep (American Psychiatric Association 2013). Some victims reexperience traumatic events through recurrent, intrusive, distressing recollections and dreams. They may experience intense psychological distress or physical reactivity when exposed to things that resemble or symbolize an aspect of the trauma. Often, trauma victims avoid stimuli associated with their traumatic events. As a result they may not be able to recall important aspects of traumatic events. The victim may appear uninterested in participating in investigations or exhibit feelings of detachment from others (American Psychiatric Association 2013). It is important that law enforcement understand these symptoms are a result of trauma rather than deliberate noncompliance or defiance.

Trafficking victims also experience significant bodily abuse. Investigators regularly document bruises, broken bones, burns, branding and scarring; chronic back, visual, or hearing problems from work in agriculture, construction, or manufacturing settings; and skin or respiratory problems caused by exposure to agricultural or other chemicals. Additionally, victims may suffer from infectious diseases, such as tuberculosis and hepatitis, which are spread in overcrowded, unsanitary environments with limited ventilation, and untreated chronic illnesses, such as diabetes or cardiovascular disease. Victims who have been sexually assaulted or used in the commercial sex industry often have reproductive health problems, such as sexually transmitted diseases (including HIV/AIDS), urinary tract infections, pelvic pain, injuries from sexual assaults, and forced abortions (Administration for Children and Families 2012).

Although many of the physical damages can be healed in a comparatively short period of time, the mental and emotional damages usually require long-term, consistent, specialized care. The betrayal by family or friends is a lingering factor that can be one of the most challenging for the victim to come to terms with. It is difficult for many to recognize their inherent value. The empowerment model is highly valued when working with trafficked people because it "means that program services are delivered with the belief that survivors possess the strength, resilience, and skills needed to identify and reach their goals and become leaders. Service providers offer non-judgmental support and begin their work with the survivors based on their existing strengths. An empowerment model does not seek to question a survivor's judgment, behaviors, or choices, but rather sees their resilience as a source of strength" (Wright, Johnson, and Sterling 2012, 11). Law enforcement can immediately help victims reframe their self-image by treating them well, acknowledging the skills that allowed the victim to survive horrible experiences, and empowering them to act on their own behalf. Working with trafficked people is often difficult. They have many reasons to distrust people, especially law enforcement. It takes skill, patience, and tenacity to be successful. An effective officer will be able to see through the tough exterior and recognize the survivor within the victim.

Pimp Control

Pimps are traffickers. They force adults and minors to provide commercial sexual services through physical abuse, lies, threats, manipulation, and false promises. Pimps are opportunistic, dangerous, and greedy. Victims are often given quotas ranging from $500 to $1,000 or more per night. The pimp confiscates all the money. Victims are severely punished for failing to make quotas or attempting to keep any of the money. Victims in the United States are most commonly U.S. citizens. Females are most commonly used in commercial sexual exploitation, but men, boys, and transgender youth are also prostituted. Immigrants to the United States may be victimized, but it is less common. When immigrants are prostituted, it is often by someone of their own nationality. According to the U.S. Department of Justice the average age of entry into prostitution in the United States is 13 to 14 years old. A pimp can make $150,000 to $200,000 per child victim and the average pimp has 4 to 6 girls. Gangs are increasingly becoming more involved in commercial sexual exploitation. A prostituted person will be owned by the whole gang rather than a single pimp, making it even more difficult to escape.

The finesse or Romeo pimp poses as a boyfriend. They are con artists who most often target victims with low self-esteem or unhappy home lives. These pimps will romance a child, make her feel special, entice her away from her environment and then convince her to be prostituted to prove her love for him or to get money to help them attain "their dreams." Often, the victim feels she "owes" the pimp, since he has been caring for her. If the child resists, she may be physically abused or gang raped, but he is usually able to pressure her into agreeing to be prostituted. A runaway child is often picked up by a trafficker (or john) within the first 48 hours of running away. A pimp might pick up a boy off the streets, take him into his home, convince the child that he loves him, and then sell the child to his friends. The "boyfriend" pimp deceives the child into believing he/she cares about the child, making escape much more complex. Indeed, for many children, the situation is better than the circumstances they ran away from. Multiple studies show 70 percent to 90 percent of people who are exploited in the sex industry were abused as children before being trafficked.

The gorilla (guerrilla) pimp uses violence, abuse, and intimidation to recruit and keep victims. They often "break" a girl's resistance through physical and sexual abuse, isolation, coercion, threats, and drug abuse. Their victims may be kidnapped, someone they know, or purchased from another pimp.

Family members also traffic their relatives. These traffickers may use the tactics of both the gorilla and the Romeo pimp, but they always exploit the power dynamics inherent in families. The victims are often minors, although adults are also trafficked. Society finds family trafficking especially abhorrent due to our cultural expectation that families nurture and care for each other.

In order to traffic another person, the pimp must convince the victim of two things. First, the victim does not own anything—not their body or their mind. The pimp owns the victim and is entitled to sell the victim's body and keep all the money. Second, the pimp is omniscient. The victim cannot do anything without the express permission of the trafficker. Pimps work to break the will of a victim in order to have total control over them. The trafficker will always exploit the victims' vulnerabilities and use them to keep the victim off balance. This process contributes to the development of the traumatic bond.

Scenario

Julia, a 14-year-old who was kicked out of her mother's home after she disclosed to her that her stepfather was molesting her, was relieved when her best friend's boyfriend mentioned he knew of a safe place where she could stay: his brother Josh's house. Unfortunately, after she stayed there a week, Josh started expecting sexual favors in return for her meals and stay. A few weeks later, he expected her to have sex with a working buddy of his, for money. Although Julia resisted the idea, she knew she didn't want to be out on the streets in January and reasoned it was better than her life at home. From that point on, life became more difficult, with more and more expectations for her to have sex with whoever Josh arranged her to meet. No longer working at a job, Josh had become reliant on his newfound business venture: pimping Julia. Julia was tired of this arrangement and reasoned that she could rent a place of her own if she could only come up with the money. The trouble was Josh always got the money, not her. One morning, while Josh still slept, Julia found his stash of cash hidden in a pill bottle in the bathroom. She slipped $700 into her bra, took his class ring and gold chain off the sink counter, and slipped out of the house. Julia attempted to pawn the jewelry at a local pawnshop at the same time that plainclothes Officer Tyrone happened to be next in line, investigating another reported theft. It was obvious to both the pawnshop owner and Officer Tyrone that she had stolen goods. Officer Tyrone checked with dispatch, and sure enough, they had received a call from a Josh Brown, who reported that a girl who fits the description of the young girl at the counter had stolen an identifiable gold chain and initialed class ring, along with about $1,000 cash. After interviewing Julia, Officer Tyrone realizes there is more to the story than a simple theft. Yet, Julia is not telling him anything about the sex trafficking, so he doesn't have enough evidence to charge Josh, but plenty of evidence of her theft of his items.

If you were Officer Tyrone, what would you do?

Effective Response and Services for Victims

As noted in the Federal Strategic Action Plan, coordination, collaboration, and capacity must be accomplished. The international and intranational components require federal, regional, state, territorial, tribal, and local collaboration and coordination to deliver services successfully. Through this effort, the weak links in capacity can be determined and addressed through technical training, targeted training, and focused funding. Building effectiveness in services requires particular attention to identification, assessment, and short and long-term services.

Identification and Response

An improved awareness and understanding of the dynamics relevant to human trafficking has changed perspectives, policies, and procedures regarding identification and response to both labor and sex trafficking. In the past, labor trafficking was largely left to federal response, as it was viewed as an international problem. International labor trafficking victims were commonly viewed as immigrants who were simply choosing to work in the United States for low wages, with little recognition that labor trafficking of nationals existed. Some state labor departments and local law enforcement agencies viewed labor trafficking as beyond their purview. Currently, collaborative models are emerging that utilize state and local law enforcement along with federal agencies. State and federal labor departments have a role to play as well.

A paradigm shift regarding the *purpose* of law enforcement's identification of victims of sex trafficking is emerging. As the criminal justice system recognizes the buyer's role in perpetuating a violent and exploitive industry, law enforcement increasingly investigates and charges the purchasers with crimes. As a result, the identification of those selling sexual relations can be focused on meeting their needs as victims rather than treating them as criminals. After all, if no one was buying, the traffickers would not have a market for their commodity: human beings.

Since victims of human trafficking, whether sex trafficking or labor trafficking, often do not self-report, law enforcement is responsible for making a good assessment at the time of contact. It is critical that law enforcement and other first responders are equipped with good assessment tools. Polaris Project (www.polarisproject.org) offers extensive assessment tools in their resource section. The National Human Trafficking Resource Center Hotline (1-888-373-7888), run by Polaris Project, also offers translation services in 170 languages. At first contact, law enforcement should attempt to establish the following:

Is the victim in control of his/her identification documents? If not, who is?
Does the victim have someone speaking or interpreting for him/her?
Is the victim's movement or communications restricted or monitored?
Is the victim afraid to speak about him/herself in the presence of others?
Is the victim aware of his/her location (city/state)?
Is the victim under 18 and engaging in commercial sex?
Were there incidences or evidence of physical or sexual assault?
Is the victim doing a job he/she was recruited for or something different?
Is the victim's salary being confiscated to pay off a debt to an employer?
Is the victim being held against his/her will?
Has the victim or his/her family been threatened with harm if the victim attempts to escape or report the abuse? (Polaris Project n.d.)*

Additionally, the Federal Bureau of Investigation notes that many law enforcement officers may encounter sex trafficking without realizing it when they are called about problems with gangs; runaway and homeless children; domestic violence calls; and complaints at truck stops, motels and strip clubs,

---

* Additional resources for law enforcement include Department of Homeland Security, http://www.dhs.gov/topic/human-trafficking, http://www.ice.gov/human-trafficking/; U.S. Department of Health and Human Services: Campaign to Rescue and Restore Victims of Human Trafficking, http://www.acf.hhs.gov/trafficking/index.html; U.S. Department of Justice: Trafficking in Persons, http://www.justice.gov/actioncenter/crime.html#trafficking; U.S. Department of Labor: Office of Child Labor, Forced Labor, and Human Trafficking (OCFT), http://www.dol.gov/ilab/programs/ocft/; U.S. Department of State: Human Smuggling and Trafficking Center, http://www.state.gov/m/ds/hstcenter/; U.S. Department of State: Office to Monitor and Combat Trafficking in Persons, http://www.state.gov/g/tip/. Each resource offers wallet cards that can be printed or ordered.

among others (Walker-Rodriguez and Hill 2011). In fact, 79 percent of trafficking victims are used in commercial sexual exploitation (United Nations Office on Drugs and Crime 2009).

To counter the messages of the traffickers, it is imperative that law enforcement and other service providers treat trafficked people as victims, not criminals. While human trafficking victims may have committed crimes, it is usually an aspect of their victimization and a way for the trafficker to maintain control. To be successful law enforcement should convey an attitude of concern for the victim's welfare and safety. It takes time to establish trust with a traumatized person. Condemnatory statements and judgmental attitudes reinforce the negative predictions of the trafficker. Many victims are already shamed by their circumstances and negative treatment will only reinforce their sense of shame. A compassionate attitude reassures the victim that the law enforcement officer is interested in his/her safety and well-being.

In step with this approach, the emerging best practice for law enforcement is to identify and target buyers rather than victims. Buyers acknowledge that the following measures are significant deterrents for them (Demand Abolition n.d., "How to Eliminate Demand"):

- Being arrested
- Paying increased fines
- Spending significant time in jail
- Facing public recognition of their crime
- Being placed on the sex offender registry
- Receiving education on how prostitution harms women and children

There are many benefits to holding buyers accountable for their behavior. Recent studies have illustrated that buyers of sex are involved in other criminal behavior. Dr. Melissa Farley's research also indicates that when compared to nonbuyers, buyers are

- More likely to rape
- More likely to coerce for sex
- Far more likely to commit substance abuse, assaults, crimes against authority, and illegally own and carry weapons
- Much less likely to report being taught to respect women through sex education class

Some law enforcement agencies are organizing buyer sweeps, such as the five "National Day of John Arrests" organized under the leadership of Sherriff Dart, Cook County, Illinois. "The most recent sweep coincided with the 2013 Super Bowl. More than 20 law enforcement agencies, including the

FBI, worked together in 13 different states, simultaneously conducting sting activities on the streets, in hotels, in brothels, via the internet, and elsewhere" (Demand Abolition n.d., "National Day of John Arrests"). Effective response includes identifying victims, getting them necessary services, and holding the trafficker and buyers accountable for their criminal behavior. Unfortunately, prostituted women continue to be arrested much more often than their buyers (Demand Abolition, n.d., "How to Eliminate Demand").

Importance of Language

Although many agencies still use the word "prostitute," it is preferable to use terminology like prostituted person, person in prostitution, trafficked person, or commercially sexually exploited person. Some states, such as Kansas, have updated statutory language to eliminate the moniker "prostitute." Language is important. It shapes our understanding of the world. The term "prostitute" carries a cultural history and stigma that blames the victim and fails to recognize their victimization. Terms like "prostitute," "ho," "whore," "hooker," and "lot lizard" should never be used to refer to someone who is trafficked. "Sex worker" also implies the person has chosen to be commercially sexually exploited.

Assessment of Needs

In addition to identifying if someone is a victim, both immediate and long-term needs must be assessed. If the victim is in immediate danger, emergency safety precautions may be necessary prior to a thorough needs assessment. Structures need to be in place and staff adequately trained for effective assessment, no matter what time, day, or night, a victim is identified. It is beneficial to have a protocol that determines who will do this assessment, with law enforcement, child protective services, and victim advocates' roles being defined.

Placement Considerations for Youth

When considering placement for a domestic minor sex trafficking (DMST) victim, we must consider safety first and foremost. Each placement must provide safety and security for the DMST youth that enter the facility. This includes being equipped to handle internal risks such as potential self-harm or harm to others, and internal recruitment. It also includes external risks, such as traffickers' attempts to gain access to their victims.

Each identified DMST victim has different needs; uniform placement or treatment is not appropriate. Each child must be assessed and placed in the most suitable environment initially, with a plan developed to assist them to achieve independence and restoration. As they heal, moving them to a less restrictive environment while maintaining connection with support is vital.

Placement considerations for youth are largely determined by the individual or agency that has custody of the youth. Sixty-nine percent of providers surveyed for the National Colloquium require guardian consent or assignment by the state to provide services to DMST victims (*National Colloquium 2012 Final Report* 2013). Placement is challenging because many things need to be considered in addition to who has custody:

- Home situation—Thirty-five percent are first trafficked by a family member or foster parent.
- Location and relationship with exploiter—If the trafficker is not arrested, and if the victim is trauma bonded with the trafficker, the victim is likely to be a flight risk. The level of danger for that victim upon flight will need consideration.
- Victim's preference—Each victim should have as much voice in the selection of placement as possible and appropriate, given the circumstances. This can enhance their healing.
- Age, gender, and sexual orientation—Certain agencies are better equipped to provide services to victims with specific needs.
- Special needs—As noted, certain agencies are better equipped than others to provide services to victims with specific characteristics. Reasons agencies have given for denying a child services include having special needs, suicidal symptoms, drug addiction, severe mental health diagnosis, pregnancy, low IQ level, history of violence, history of recruitment, sexual offender, or arson history.
- Criminal charges or material witness holds—Many victims of human trafficking have been charged with a crime or are held as material witnesses. This could require transportation to the county/state where the crime is being prosecuted.

Service Considerations for Youth

Each DMST victim must have a tailored treatment plan and a setting that meets their specific needs. This requires flexibility in programming. The assessor needs to be confident that any placement considered has capacity to serve the needs of the victim. Services must be victim centered, culturally sensitive, strengths based, and trauma informed.

- Victim centered—Helping the victim must be the primary focus of programs serving victims: not helping the criminal justice system. Confusion occurs and interagency battles erupt when there is a lack of understanding of the different roles and purposes. Ultimately, the criminal justice system benefits from service programs providing high quality, victim-centered services to victims.

- Culturally sensitive—It is best if the service provider already has the cultural and ethnic knowledge base to serve the individual. Absent that option, it is critical that the provider understands the need and immediately takes action to become educated about the victim's various cultural practices. It is inappropriate for the victim to be responsible for teaching the staff those practices and considerations. Service providers must be familiar with gang cultural practices prior to the placement of a gang-affiliated youth.

- Strengths based—Domestic minor sex trafficking victims are more than victims and should not be wholly defined by their trauma. Programming needs to be unique to the individual, identify the individual's strengths, and use those strengths to build success.

- Trauma informed—Service providers need to understand the role trauma plays in the behaviors and emotional responses of each youth, and take care to not retraumatize the youth, or replicate the power hierarchy of the trafficking circumstances. Services need to empower the victims as much as possible, helping them regain agency in a safe environment. Trauma-informed care must be implemented in daily living and educational aspects of programming, as well as counseling services. Trauma-informed work is artful, as it must be tailored to each victim's experience.

- Type of facility/program—If a community has a full range of options, there are many different types of facilities and programs for human trafficking victims ranging from short to long term, and from a secure facility when the victim has criminal charges to supportive programming during home placement. Between these two extremes are staff-secure facilities specific to this population, community-based group homes, and foster homes. All too often, staff-secure facilities are unavailable, group homes are not specific to this population, and the foster homes that are available are not specialized and poorly equipped to respond to the needs of these youths. As a result, law enforcement has sometimes resorted to placing many of these youth in a detention facility on unrelated charges as a means to protect them. If a detention facility must be used, the detention facility needs to be victim centered, culturally sensitive, strengths based, and trauma informed.

- Type of staff—One of the most important criteria for working with these youth is having properly trained staff who are very familiar with the behaviors and challenges specific to the complex trauma experienced by these victims. Professionals with years of experience working with other traumatized victims report they were not prepared to work with DMST survivors. It is widely believed to be beneficial to have some staff or volunteers who are survivors of DMST to mentor these youth. Another important criterion is that staff is willing and able to develop a genuine connection with those they serve. It is this genuine connection that is instrumental in helping human trafficking victims thrive.

- Type of therapeutic services—To be effective, most service programs utilize a variety of therapeutic approaches. Approaches commonly used include cognitive therapy, eye movement desensitization and reprocessing (EMDR), transcendental meditation, trauma-informed therapy, trauma-focused therapy, recreational therapy, problem-solving activities, anger management techniques, release therapy, group therapy, individual therapy, survivor-led group therapy, gender-specific group therapy, trust-based relational interventions (TBRI), motivational interviewing, family therapy, art therapy, psychophysiological trauma treatment, safety- and empathy-based therapy, culturally sensitive therapy, yoga, and equine therapy (*National Colloquium 2012 Final Report* 2013).

Theoretical Considerations: Impact on Policy and Services

Providing services to victims of human trafficking never happens in a vacuum: federal, state, and local policy decisions heavily influence the scope of services. In fact, it is public opinion and policy that drive whether trafficking is viewed as a problem deserving services. Public policy is based on theoretical perspectives that greatly impact both the prevalence of the problem and services available for trafficking victims. Two examples of this are provided: legalizing prostitution and safe harbor laws.

Legalizing Prostitution and Impact on Services for Victims

Advocates of legalized prostitution argue that "it would reduce crime, improve public health, increase tax revenue, help people out of poverty, get prostitutes off the streets, and allow consenting adults to make their own choices. They contend that prostitution is a victimless crime" (ProCon.org 2014). Clearly, there is no need for services for victims, if it is a victimless crime.

Opponents believe that legalizing prostitution increases sexually transmitted diseases such as AIDS, global human trafficking, and violent crime including rape and homicide. They purport that prostitution is inherently immoral, commercially exploitative, empowers the criminal underworld, and promotes the repression of women by men (ProCon.org 2014). The arguments are complex. Although this is a challenging area to research due to its criminal nature, it is clear that many people who are used in the commercial sex industry are not adults and are at great risk of violence, and when they do "choose" the sex industry, it is from economic necessity rather than free choice. This perspective opens the door to understanding the need for adequate services.

The direct impact of these divergent theoretical perspectives playing out through public policy can be recognized through a comparison of the public policies of the Netherlands and Sweden.

The Dutch Approach

In 2000, the Netherlands legalized prostitution with the hope that regulation of the sex trade would result in fewer people being prostituted (involuntary prostitution, minors, trafficked immigrants) and improve the health, well-being, independence, and social status of those who choose prostitution for themselves. The concept was that women would be independent workers, registered with the Chamber of Commerce and pay income tax in order to legally work in brothels (windows) and sex clubs. The law requires the women in prostitution to get regular health checks and use condoms during sex acts (Brants 1998, Dutch Ministry of Foreign Affairs 2012). Buyers are not required to get health checks. By most accounts, the legalization of prostitution has had the opposite and unintended results. The Netherlands has seen an increase in underage and adult sex trafficking, criminal activity, and trafficking of undocumented immigrants (Raymond 2003, Carrigg n.d.).

Additionally, many people in prostitution could not register with the government because they were in the country illegally, often because they were trafficked. The unintended consequence is that these people were driven even further underground with even less access to resources and help (Otieno 2012). It was believed that if prostitution was legal, people involved in prostitution would be able to circumvent pimps. Under legalization, pimps became managers and businessmen rather than criminals. Violence became an "occupational hazard" rather than a crime. Amsterdam became a sex tourism destination, motivating traffickers to illegally bring women from Africa, Eastern Europe, and Asia to meet demand (Bindel 2013).

The Swedish Approach

Many anti-trafficking organizations argue that to eliminate sex trafficking, societies must reduce the demand for commercial sex. Trafficking is a crime of greed. As long as there is a high demand for commercial sex, criminals will exploit vulnerable people. Sweden enacted legislation in 1999, referred to as the Swedish or Nordic model, which makes it legal to sell sexual services, but illegal to purchase sexual services or sell someone else for sex acts. Under this model pimping, procuring, and operating a brothel are illegal. Those who purchase sexual services are sentenced to pay fines or serve a prison term.

The Swedish government states that the reason behind this legislation is the importance to society of fighting prostitution. "Prostitution is considered to cause serious harm both to individuals and to society as a whole. Large-scale crime, including human trafficking for sexual purposes, assault, procuring and drug-dealing, is also commonly associated with prostitution.... The vast majority of those in prostitution also have very difficult social circumstances" (Government of Sweden, Ministry of Gender Equality 2009). Sweden actively pursues gender equality in its legislation and cultural values. Although the laws are gender neutral, demand for sexual services is constructed as a form of violence against women. The goals of the legislation are to act as a deterrent to those who purchase sex, thus reducing the demand for commercial sex. Consequently, it is believed that the number of people recruited and involved in commercial sex will be reduced.

The 2010 Swedish government report *SOU 2010:49: The Ban against the Purchase of Sexual Services* indicates some effectiveness of the Nordic model. Before the ban on the purchase of sexual services, incidences of street prostitution were similar in the three capital cities of Norway, Denmark, and Sweden. The 2010 report shows that street prostitution in Sweden was reduced by 50 percent. Meanwhile, "the number of women in street prostitution in both Norway and Denmark subsequently increased dramatically. In 2008, the number of people in street prostitution in both Norway and Denmark was estimated to be three times higher than in Sweden" (Swedish Institute 2010, 7). The report goes on to note that Internet prostitution has increased in all three countries, but the rate of increase appears to be lower in Sweden. People working in the field indicate no increase in the rate of indoor prostitution (such as sex clubs, hotels, massage parlors, etc.) so there is no indication that street prostitution has moved indoors. Overall, the legislation is credited with decreasing commercial sex even while comparable countries have seen an increase.

Significant to the success of the legislation is the arrest and prosecution of buyers of commercial sex. Swedish police have conducted numerous operations against prostitution-related crimes. The majority of the prosecutions have been against purchasers of sexual services. In 8 out of 10 cases the buyer admitted the offense. When the suspect admitted the offense, the prosecutor generally did not bring legal proceedings and the buyer was fined (Swedish Institute 2010, 10). In 85 percent of the prosecutions, purchasers have been assessed "a penalty of 50 days of fines proportional to the offender's income" (Swedish Institute 2010, 11). A new penal provision, human trafficking for sexual purposes, implemented in July of 2002, resulted in "a dramatic increase in the number of prosecutions for infringements of the ban on the purchase of sexual services that originate from procuring and human trafficking cases" (Swedish Institute 2010, 10). Additionally, based on the 2010 report, Sweden raised the maximum penalty for purchasing sexual services to imprisonment for one year. The purpose of this was to "create scope for a more nuanced assessment of penalties in serious cases of purchases of sexual services" (Government of Sweden, Ministry of Gender Equality 2009).

Safe Harbor Laws and Impact on Service Provision

Another example of theoretical perspectives influencing public policy and impacting services is the influx of safe harbor laws in the United States. Federal law now provides that "victims of trafficking should not be inappropriately incarcerated, fined, or otherwise penalized solely for unlawful acts committed as a direct result of being trafficked" (TVPA 2008, Sec. 102(a)(19)). Safe harbor laws are state laws that provide legal protections for minor victims of commercial sexual exploitation. In states without safe harbor laws, prostituted minors are often treated as criminals or delinquents rather than victims. Safe harbor laws prevent minor victims of commercial sexual exploitation from being prosecuted for prostitution. Instead, the laws recognize these children as victims of abuse and neglect, triggering a child protective response. This means minors are exempt from prosecution for prostitution and they cannot be held as juvenile delinquents.

There are conflicting views regarding the effectiveness of the safe harbor laws, with the most prevalent concern being that such laws make it difficult to prosecute traffickers (pimps) and buyers (johns). If the victim is not cooperative with the criminal justice process, and there is no criminal charge option regarding the victim, prosecutors fear they will not have the ability to prosecute the case against the pimp or the john. Proponents argue there is nothing about safe harbor laws that destroys the right of the state to exercise a material hold on a witness, even when the witness is a victim.

New York and other state safe harbor laws require specialized services for trafficked children. Other states, such as Kansas, have adopted a modified version with a theoretical perspective that does not include total absolution from being charged with a crime related to selling sexual relations. Nonetheless, it includes specialized services and recognition that children involved in trafficking are victims and should be considered children in need of care rather than juvenile delinquents (Committee on Judiciary 2013).

The Polaris Project notes that experienced practitioners have found that mainstream programs of the child abuse and neglect system routinely fail these children. The law should require protection and recovery programs for child victims such as

- Placement in programs that treat such children with respect and dignity and do not stigmatize these victims because of their involvement in commercial sex
- Mentorship by survivors of the same crime or, when that is not possible, by other caring professionals who are familiar with the special trauma associated with commercial and noncommercial sexual abuse
- Protocols that ensure immediate placement of these victims in appropriate, preidentified locations, without undue questioning from untrained law enforcement officers or other officials (Polaris Project 2013)

Child victims have experienced significant physical and mental trauma, and need specialized care. Placing minor victims in jail creates additional trauma and harm. Appropriate, specialized services are critical for the health and well-being of the child.

Safe harbor laws presume that a prostituted child is a victim of exploitation and therefore subject to the care and protection of the state. These laws may also require mandatory reporting from first responders, teachers, medical staff, social workers, child protective services, and other people that might come in contact with the child. Under the William Wilberforce Trafficking Victims Protection Reauthorization Act of 2008, federal, state, or local officials who suspect a minor may be a victim of human trafficking are required to notify the U.S. Department of Health and Human Services within 24 hours to facilitate the provision of interim assistance. In some states, mandatory reporters are only required to report suspicions of child sexual exploitation if the youth is being exploited by a parent or caregiver. Because many children are exploited by a third party, safe harbor laws must redefine sexual exploitation as a form of child abuse regardless of who is exploiting the child. Safe harbor laws may also provide an exception to confidentiality requirements for doctors, nurses, and other mandatory reporters in the health fields. Finally, safe harbor laws may require aggressive prosecution of pimps and johns in order to deter the commercial exploitation of children.

Only a few states have strong and effective safe harbor laws at this time, but these laws can be a powerful tool to protect the most vulnerable members of society and ensure they are not punished for their victimization. It is important that children who have been commercially sexually exploited receive the services they desperately need. Too often, the system has repeatedly failed them. Safe harbor laws can offer them an escape from a life of exploitation, a safe place to heal, and a chance to create a healthy life.

Ethical Considerations

Human trafficking is often identified as modern-day slavery, with an emphasis being placed on the victim's inability to leave, inability to keep their earnings, and inability to be their own agent. As with most things, there is a "gray area":

1. Human trafficking or prostitution?

   Those who are underage and involved in the sale of sexual relations can be recognized as victims much more readily than those over the age of 18.

   Point: Adults who want to be involved in the sale of sexual relations should not be automatically assumed to be "victims." They might be choosing this as their career. For some it is a very lucrative business. Perceiving them as victims is an injustice to them, as they simply want to be viewed as a sex worker. It is also an injustice to those who truly are enslaved to be merged with this group.

   Counterpoint: Since most involved in "the life" were first trafficked between the age of 12 and 14, many adults involved in the sale of sexual relations know no other way to make a living. They don't wake up on their 18th birthday knowing how to take charge of their life, and have their pimp bid them farewell. They remain oppressed, are often brainwashed, and simply trying to survive. As one who was previously involved in the life retorted, "No one would choose to have sexual relations with up to 20 different people every night, never knowing who is going to pull a gun on you, stab you, have an STD, stink, or expect kinky sex and possibly even kill you! That is not something anyone chooses to do—it is something people do to survive. They are victims."*

2. Victim or criminal?

   There is a wide range of variance in victims' experiences and behaviors. Where is the line between classifying someone as a victim or a criminal? If they are a child, they need protection, but if they are an adult and participating in selling sexual relations, should they be charged? If they are a child or adult and recruit other girls for the pimp, should they be charged? If they assault another victim when instructed by the pimp to do so, should they be charged?

   Point: This is clearly criminal behavior, and they should be held accountable. It is counterproductive to excuse the behavior due to their own victimization. Most of the pimps were victimized

* Kristy Childs, Demand Conference, Kansas City, Missouri, 2013.

sometime in the past, should we not arrest them, either? Letting people off just perpetuates the problem.

Counterpoint: Law enforcement uses discretion every day in charging people with crimes; this is no different. We know human beings have limits to the amount of torture they can experience before breaking. Traffickers are highly skilled at pushing people past their limits, and do so on a regular basis, using tactics similar to the tactics used in prisoner of war camps. There are numerous reports of prisoners who violated laws while in these torturous camps, as a matter of survival, and we would not consider charging them with those crimes. We need to afford victims of trafficking with this same consideration. They are often merely trying to survive their circumstances.

3. Lock up or let go?

Placing a status offender or victim in a locked facility is considered to be ineffective at best, and often harmful to the healing process for victims of human trafficking. On the other hand, victims of human trafficking frequently run away, putting themselves in harms way.

Point: The National Standards for the Care of Youth Charged with Status Offenses notes that "research and evidence-based approaches have proven that secure detention of status offenders is ineffective and frequently dangerous" (Coalition for Juvenile Justice 2013, p. 12). This document further states it jeopardizes their safety and well-being, and may increase the likelihood of delinquent or criminal behavior. Placing a victim of human trafficking in a locked environment also replicates the control the pimp had over them, making it difficult for them to view the criminal justice response as different or helpful. This approach violates their rights to self-determination and to be treated like a victim rather than a perpetrator.

Counterpoint: Some victims are at great risk if their pimp or gang regains access to them. For whatever reason—be it brainwashing, unfamiliarity with our country, or "love" for their pimp—some victims are unlikely to keep out of harms way and will be in grave danger if they are not in a locked facility. As one judge noted, "I'd rather have an angry victim in a locked facility, than a dead one in a ditch." Although self-determination is a valuable ethical consideration, it does not rank as high as protection of life. When we know a child is in grave danger, it is the system's responsibility to protect them.

Conclusion

As we begin to acknowledge and understand human trafficking in the United States, we recognize the need for additional services that address the unique victimization of trafficked people. When we look for victims, we find them. When we prosecute the buyers of human beings, we begin to impact the demand. Law enforcement is often the first responder that victims encounter. The officer's willingness to focus on accessing necessary services for the victim is critical. An educated, compassionate criminal justice response can be the first step in the victim's healing journey.

Key Terms

cognitive dissonance
commercial sexual exploitation
domestic minor sex trafficking (DMST)
eye movement desensitization and reprocessing (EMDR)
Federal Strategic Action Plan
National Human Trafficking Resource Center Hotline
Polaris Project
President's Interagency Task Force to Monitor and Combat Trafficking in Persons
safe harbor laws
traumatic bonding
William Wilberforce Trafficking Victims Protection Reauthorization Act (2008)

Review Questions

1. Discuss the common misconceptions with human trafficking, and how these misconceptions impact the development and implementation of effective services.
2. What are the ethical considerations in dealing with human trafficking?
3. Discuss the impact legalizing prostitution would have on services for victims.
4. What role does identification and response play in effective services for victims?

References

Administration for Children and Families. (2012). "Fact sheet: Identifying victims of human trafficking." http://www.acf.hhs.gov/programs/orr/resource/fact-sheet-identifying-victims-of-human-trafficking#Psychological (accessed January 12, 2014).
American Psychiatric Association. (2013). *Diagnostic and Statistical Manual of Mental Disorders* (5th ed.). Arlington, VA: American Psychiatric Publishing.
Bindel, Julie. (2013). "Why even Amsterdam doesn't want legal brothels." *The Spectator*, February 2. http://www.spectator.co.uk/features/8835071/flesh-for-sale/ (accessed January 20, 2014).

Brants, Chrisje. (1998). The fine art of regulated tolerance: Prostitution in Amsterdam. *Journal of Law and Society*, 25.4, 621–635.

Carrigg, Hannah. (2008). Prostitution regimes in the Netherlands and Sweden: Their impact on the trafficking of women and children in illicit sex industries. *The Monitor*. http://web.wm.edu/so/monitor/issues/14-1/1-carrigg.pdf (accessed July 20, 2014).

Clawson, H. J., Dutch, N. M., and Williamson, E. (2008). *National Symposium on the Health Needs of Human Trafficking Victims: Background Brief*. Washington, DC: U.S. Department of Health and Human Services, Office of the Assistant Secretary for Planning and Evaluation.

Coalition for Juvenile Justice. (2013). *National Standards for the Care of Youth Charged with Status Offenses*.

Committee on Judiciary. (2013). "Senate Bill 61." http://www.kslegislature.org/li/b2013_14/measures/documents/sb61_00_0000.pdf.

Demand Abolition. (n.d.). http://www.demandabolition.org.

Demand Abolition. (n.d.). "How to eliminate demand." http://www.demandabolition.org/how-to-eliminate-demand/.

Demand Abolition. (n.d.). "National Day of Johns Arrest." http://www.demandabolition.org/national-day-of-johns-arrests/.

Dutch Ministry of Foreign Affairs. (2012). Dutch Policy on Prostitution Questions and Answers 2012. http://www.minbuza.nl/binaries/content/assets/minbuza/en/import/en/you_and_the_netherlands/about_the_netherlands/ethical_issues/faq-prostitutie-pdf--engels.pdf-2012.pdf (accessed July 20, 2014).

Dutton, D. G., and Painter, S. L. (1981). Traumatic bonding: The development of emotional attachments in battered women and other relationships of intermittent abuse. *Victimology: An International Journal*, 1(4), 139–155.

Federal Strategic Action Plan on Services for Victims of Human Trafficking in the United States 2013–2017. http://www.ovc.gov/pubs/FederalHumanTraffickingStrategicPlan.pdf (accessed January 25, 2014).

Government of Sweden, Ministry of Gender Equality. (2009). "Legislation on the purchase of sexual services." http://www.government.se/sb/d/4096/a/119861 (accessed January 20, 2014).

Haken, Jeremy. (2011). *Transnational Crime in the Developing World*. http://www.gfintegrity.org/storage/gfip/documents/reports/transcrime/gfi_transnational_crime_web.pdf (accessed March 1, 2014).

Harris, Kamala D. (n.d.) "Human trafficking." Office of the Attorney General, State of California Department of Justice, https://oag.ca.gov/human-trafficking.

National Colloquium 2012 Final Report: An Inventory and Evaluation of the Current Shelter and Services Response to Domestic Minor Sex Trafficking. (2013).

Otieno, Caroline Achieng. (2012). "The pitfalls of legalizing prostitution in Amsterdam." http://thewip.net/contributors/2012/07/the_pitfalls_of_legalizing_pro.html (accessed January 20, 2014).

Polaris Project. (2012). "Shelter beds for human trafficking survivors in the United States." https://na4.salesforce.com/sfc/p/300000006E4S9liF7eeqnpIT97HRFH4FvCSI5v4= (accessed January 10, 2014).

Polaris Project. (2013). "Sex trafficking of minors and "Safe Harbor."" http://www.polarisproject.org/what-we-do/policy-advocacy/assisting-victims/safe-harbor (accessed January 25, 2014).

Polaris Project. (n.d.). "Assessment questions." https://na4.salesforce.com/sfc/p/ 300000006E4S/a/600000004TAN/YVn95BGD80..Hl9g.6evxwnNHC7N6lfZAiikPt48ljc= (accessed January 10, 2014).

ProCon.org. (2014). "Prostitution." http://prostitution.procon.org/ (accessed January 20, 2014).

Raymond, Janice. (2003). Ten reasons for not criminalizing prostitution and a legal response to the demand for prostitution. *Journal of Trauma Practice*, 2, 315–332.

Shigekane, R. (2007). "Rehabilitation and community integration of trafficking survivors in the United States." *Human Rights Quarterly*, 29, 112–136.

Swedish Institute. (2010). "Selected extracts of the Swedish government report SOU 2010:49: 'The ban against the Purchase of Sexual Services. An evaluation 1999-2008),'" p. 7. http://www.government.se/content/1/c6/11/98/61/2ac7d62b.pdf (accessed January 20, 2014).

U.S. Department of State. (2011, June 27). "Remarks on the release of the 2011 Trafficking in Persons Report." www.state.gov/secretary/rm/2011/06/167156. htm (accessed June 13, 2012).

United Nations Office on Drugs and Crime. (2009). *Global Report on Trafficking in Persons* (accessed January 10, 2014).

Victims and Survivors of Psychopaths. (n.d.). "Traumatic bonding." http:// victimsofpsychopaths.wordpress.com/traumatic-bonding/ (accessed January 12, 2014).

Walker-Rodriguez, Amanda, and Hill, Rodney. (2011). "Human sex trafficking." http://www.fbi.gov/stats-services/publications/law-enforcement-bulletin/ march_2011/human_sex_trafficking (accessed January 10, 2014).

Williamson, C., and Prior, M. (2009). Domestic minor sex trafficking: A network of underground players in the Midwest. *Journal of Child and Adolescent Trauma*, 2(1), 46–61.

Williamson, Erin, Dutch, Nicole, and Clawson, Heather. (2010). "Evidence-based mental health treatment for victims of human trafficking." http://aspe.hhs. gov/hsp/07/humantrafficking/mentalhealth/index.shtml#_ftn3 (accessed January 12, 2014).

Wright, Joy, Johnson, Lynne, and Sterling, Blair. (2012). "Proposal: A statewide system of specialized services for survivors of prostitution and sex trafficking." http:// www.enddemandillinois.org/sites/default/files/FINAL%20Proposal%20for%20 Specialized%20Services%20May%202012.pdf (accessed January 13, 2014).

Human Trafficking Laws and Legal Trends

16

ALISON MCKENNEY BROWN

Contents

Major Issues

- Federal law has had to develop innovative legal approaches to prevent human trafficking.
- State common law crimes have been ineffective at combating human trafficking offenses.
- State and federal prosecutors have struggled to provide evidence of legal intent to traffic human beings.
- Effectively defining coercion has been a critical element in writing human trafficking laws.

Human trafficking has become a "hot topic" in the general media, yet the perception that victims of human trafficking crimes bear a responsibility for their victimization has long hampered the criminal justice system from increasing the priority associated with preventing and ending these types of offenses. Individuals who are vulnerable to victimization tend to either have an illegal status or a status that denies them full independence under the law. Children who run away from home, immigrants entering the country illegally, the mentally impaired, and individuals who are not able to prove their lawful status as a resident or citizen are the easiest targets of trafficking victimization.

Unfortunately, the very fear used to dominate an individual into submitting to victimization is a valid fear, and the victim will continue to suffer until they perceive that the harms associated with their fear are less frightening than the harms they are suffering as trafficking victims. The three 10-year-olds missing from the foster care system will sit quietly in the back seat of the car while the driver receives a traffic citation, never screaming to the police officer to rescue them from their abuser, the only person they believe can ever love them. The 15-year-old runaway will continue to knock on the doors of semitrucks to sell herself to avoid being returned to an unhappy home life. The 20-year-old whose legal residency has expired will continue to serve as a prostitute to maintain the hope that she might someday find a way to join regular society. The mentally ill 40-year-old will continue to participate in sexually deviant behavior because he has nowhere else to go. The 60-year-old will continue to clean someone else's house, care for someone else's children, cook meals eaten by others, earn no income, hide from strangers, and never complain, to avoid being prosecuted for being in the country illegally. The trafficking victim can be any age, any race, any ethnicity, used for any purpose, and belong to either gender; the only elements they tend to have in common are helplessness and fear that existed both before the victimization began and continued throughout the victimization.

At the same time, criminals and criminal organizations have learned that the best way to avoid detection of a criminal act is for the evidence of the crime to not look like evidence of a crime. When a police officer searches a car and finds several automatic weapons, the officer is going to take steps to determine the lawful status of those weapons and the individual transporting them. When a police officer searches a car and finds several 10-year-olds, she is unlikely to be concerned as long as they are lawfully seatbelted into the backseat. The human trafficker is less likely to be interfered with by law enforcement and able to sell his product multiple times a day for several years. The gun trafficker has greater risk of detection and can only sell his product once.

The inability to clearly identify the victim or the situation has allowed society to ignore the phenomenon of human trafficking for a very long time, and prevented governments from developing effective legal tools to discourage and end human trafficking. The laws in many states have only recently begun to allow the criminal justice system to effectively address the associated crimes in a manner that both recognizes and protects the victims while actually prosecuting the perpetrators. This chapter will provide an overview of federal human trafficking laws as well as a review of the legal trends within the states associated with recognizing human trafficking crimes and effectively preventing and prosecuting those crimes, while attempting to assist the victim in both recovering from the trauma of victimization and addressing the issues that allowed them to be victimized in the first place.

Federal Anti-Trafficking Laws

All schoolchildren are taught in the United States that slavery is illegal. The Thirteenth Amendment to the United States Constitution states: "Neither slavery nor involuntary servitude, except as a punishment for crime whereof the party shall have been duly convicted, shall exist within the United States, or any place subject to their jurisdiction."

Despite this clear prohibition, and various criminal laws against kidnapping and criminal restraint, in 2000 Congress found that "trafficking in persons continues to victimize countless men, women, and children in the United States and abroad." Congress passed the Victims of Trafficking and Violence Protection Act of 2000 (VTVPA). The VTVPA also recognized that existing laws were piecemeal and often served to protect the trafficker while further victimizing the trafficking victim. "No comprehensive law exists in the United States that penalizes the range of offenses involved in the trafficking scheme. Instead, even the most brutal instances of trafficking in the sex industry are often punished under laws that also apply to lesser offenses, so that traffickers typically escape deserved punishment" (VTVPA, para. 14). The VTVPA defines human trafficking in multiple ways, but found that generally victims of human trafficking "are often forced through physical violence to engage in sex acts or perform slavery-like labor. Such force includes rape and other forms of sexual abuse, torture, starvation, imprisonment, threats, psychological abuse, and coercion" (22 U.S.C.S § 7101 (b)(6) (2014)). The VTVPA recognized that the element of coercion differentiates an individual who is a willing participant in either a criminal act or a lawful act by an adult, from an individual who participates in an act against his or her will.

This first comprehensive federal response to the ever-growing phenomenon of trafficking in human beings, sought to impose measures to prevent trafficking (22 U.S.C.S § 7104), prosecute traffickers (22 U.S.C.S § 7109), and protect the victims of trafficking (22 U.S.C.S § 7105). Subsequently, the VTVPA was reauthorized through the Trafficking Victims Protection Reauthorization Acts (TVPRA) of 2003, 2005, 2008, and 2013. Other federal laws were developed and expanded to carry out the goals of the VTVPA. For example, the Peonage, Slavery, and Trafficking in Persons Act, found at 18 U.S.C.S § 1589, et seq., defines and makes unlawful forced labor, peonage, slavery, and involuntary servitude. Similarly, the Violent Crime Control and Law Enforcement Act, Violence against Women and Combating Domestic Trafficking in Persons, creates and funds studies and investigations into the causes of trafficking, developing effective means to aid individuals victimized by trafficking, and methods to prevent trafficking and prosecute traffickers (42 U.S.C.S §§ 14044).

The old term to describe debt servitude or indentured servitude is "peonage." The federal law makes forcing an individual to work or provide services to pay off debts unlawful (18 U.S.C. § 1581, 22 U.S.C. § 7102). The term "services" usually incorporates any type of service one human being may provide, including sexual services. In addition, the concept of human trafficking incorporates involuntary servitude, which is defined to be a form of slavery (18 U.S.C. § 1584). The VTVPA, and later the TVPRA, included provisions specifically defining sex trafficking as a type of service.

Adults, as well as children, are victims of human trafficking, but the methods and means of obtaining control over victims tend to be age specific. Coercion used against adults tends to involve a fear: fear of violence, fear of deportation, or fear of prosecution. Playing on a victim's fear is effective whether the goal of the trafficker is slave labor or commercial sex services, but has been difficult to prove in a court of law. This proved true in a federal attempt to prosecute a farm family in 1988 for using psychological means to bring about the involuntary servitude of two mentally challenged men. This issue of psychological harm was eventually reviewed by the United States Supreme Court. The court specifically looked at the concept of coercion as understood within the framework of the Thirteenth Amendment. Because of the understanding of involuntary servitude arising out of the historical perception of human slavery, the court interpreted the phrase "involuntary servitude" to exclude the concept of psychological coercion (*U.S. v. Kozminski*, 487 U.S. 931, 108 S. Ct. 2751, 101 L. Ed. 2d 788, 1988 U.S. LEXIS 3032 (1988)). Public opinion surrounding that case and the suffering endured by the victims caused Congress to take action to broaden the legal concept of coercion. Under federal law, coercion now includes force, threats of force, physical restraint, threats of physical restraint to that person or another person, serious harm or threats of serious harm to that person or another person, abuse or threatened abuse of law or legal process; or any scheme, plan, or pattern intended to cause the person to believe that, if that person did not perform such labor or services, that person or another person would suffer serious harm or physical restraint (18 U.S.C. § 1584). Creating a climate of fear that causes another to act against their will is also prohibited (18 U.S.C. § 1584).

Because of the differences in motivation based on differences in age or status, additional laws were developed to both study and combat the problem of trafficking of children. Research has shown that coercion used against children is more likely to involve withholding basic essentials: food, clothing, shelter, and affection. These types of threats are effective against children because children have no legal right to function independently of adults to obtain basic essentials and have learned that they have no right to refuse to be disciplined by the adults in their lives. The VTVPA/TVPRA has modified the definition of coercion to include mere *threats* of serious harm made to the child (18 U.S.C. § 1591(e)(2)(A)). The term "serious harm" includes "any harm, whether physical or nonphysical, including psychological, financial, or reputational harm that is sufficiently serious, under all the surrounding circumstances, to compel a reasonable person of the same background and in the same circumstances to perform or to continue performing commercial sexual activity in order to avoid incurring that harm" (18 U.S.C. § 1591(e)(4)). This definition allows prosecutors to ask jurors to consider the situation as a 15-year-old runaway would perceive the situation, rather than as a middle-class adult, when seeking to determine if the child was subjected to coercion.

Provisions of the VTVPA/TVPRA target the horrors of sex trafficking and the coercion associated with that crime. The federal laws defined sex trafficking as "the recruitment, harboring, transportation, provision, or obtaining of a person for the purposes of a commercial sex act, in which the commercial sex act is induced by force, fraud, or coercion, or in which the person induced to perform such an act has not attained 18 years of age" (22 U.S.C. § 7102; 8 CFR § 214.11(a)). This definition recognized that the types of coercion used against sex trafficking victims differed based upon their age, as the fears that the traffickers were preying upon changed based upon age. The Peonage, Slavery, and Trafficking in Persons Act specifically makes sex trafficking of children by force, fraud or coercion unlawful, but defines coercion in a child specific manner (18 U.S.C. § 1591).

The punishments imposed upon offenders who traffic in children are also increased (18 U.S.C. § 1591(b)). Victimizing children under the age of 14 increases the minimum mandatory sentence of incarceration to 15 years to life, while victimizing children 14 through 17 results in a minimum mandatory sentence of 10 years to life. Sex traffickers and sex offenders have long tried to avoid these types of increased penalties by claiming to have been unaware of the child's age. This federal law addresses that tactic by merely requiring that the individual accused of child sex trafficking had "a reasonable opportunity to observe the person so recruited, enticed, harbored, transported, provided, obtained or maintained" (18 U.S.C. § 1591(c)). It should be noted, that if the accused individual was trafficking in children he/she had never seen, the government is still required to prove that the trafficker knew the people he was acquiring to traffic were children.

Transporting individuals across state lines or across national borders with the intent to use the person in the commercial sex trade is criminalized by the Mann Act (18 U.S.C. § 2421–2424). Congress originally passed the Mann Act to prevent the transport of adult women across state lines for immoral purposes but expanded its scope through several amendments. A more recent amendment criminalized transportation, both between states and outside the United States, of any person under 18 years old with the intent that the child participate in sexual activity. The 1994 amendment also made sex tourism unlawful: travel to foreign countries for the purpose of engaging in sexual activity with a minor. Under the Mann Act, U.S. citizens who take part in sexual activity with minors outside the United States may be federally prosecuted irrespective of whether the act was considered in the jurisdiction where it actually occurred.

Efforts to reduce the pool of potential victims have also taken place through various anti-trafficking legislation. The TVPA authorizes the creation of a public awareness and information program targeted to potential victims of trafficking, both domestically and internationally (22 U.S.C. § 7104(b)). The TVPA also attempts to address some of the social and economic factors that cause women and girls to become trafficking victims, by authorizing programs to create microcredit lending programs and educational opportunities (22 U.S.C. § 7104(a)). Additionally, the TVPA recognizes the role of child marriage in victimizing children and provides for the development of a multisector strategy to empower girls at risk for child marriage by recognizing the unique vulnerabilities of girls in developing countries (22 U.S.C. § 7104(j)).

The reality is that trafficking is rarely carried out by a single person. Trafficking usually involves a network of participants who each provide some necessary element of the entire process that results in an individual being trafficked. Thus, in an effort to avoid participants' claims of reduced responsibility for the harms incurred by victims, the varying roles of all participants in the trafficking schemes are specifically enumerated by several federal laws. Federal trafficking related laws make unlawful the recruitment, harboring, transportation, provision, brokering, or obtaining of a person for labor or services, for subjection to involuntary servitude, peonage, debt bondage, or slavery (18 U.S.C. § 1590; 22 U.S.C. § 7102). In this way, claims that an individual "just made a few phone calls" or "just let him stay in a room for a few days" do not excuse participation that made the victimization possible.

Other acts that support human trafficking have been addressed through federal law to prevent unknowing participation in human trafficking. For example, the Tariff Act of 1930 prohibits importing goods made with forced or indentured labor. More recently, in 2009, the Customs and Facilitations and Trade Enforcement Reauthorization Act was amended to prohibit importing goods made with slave or indentured labor to include goods that were made through the use of coercion or goods made by victims of human trafficking (§ 308). These specific laws, and others, are intended to protect the American public from unwilling support of and participation in human trafficking.

Other federal laws have been adopted to make prosecution of acts associated with human trafficking more effective. The Prosecutorial Remedies and Other Tools to End the Exploitation of Children Today Act of 2003, established enhanced penalties for engaging in sex tourism with children, both within the United States and in other countries (18 U.S.C. § 2423). Additionally, this law requires that Americans who travel to areas with significant sex tourism outside the United States be provided with materials warning them that illegal sex acts associated with human trafficking will be prosecuted. It is hoped that making sex tourism a federal crime will reduce American support of trafficking outside the United States. Additionally, this act removed the statute of limitations for crimes involving the sexual or physical abuse of a child during the child's lifetime (18 U.S.C. § 3283). Finally, to address those child victims who do not survive the horrors of sex trafficking, this act also redefined first-degree murder to include child death arising out of child abuse or child torture. Changing this definition of murder has allowed the government to win murder cases by proving the intent to abuse or torture the child without needing to prove the intent to kill the child (18 U.S.C. § 1111).

A well-known federal law has also been utilized to more effectively combat organized efforts to traffic in human beings since 2003. Congress passed the Racketeering Influenced Corrupt Organizations Act (RICO) as part of the Organized Crime Control Act of 1970 (18 U.S.C.S. §§ 1961). RICO defines racketeering activity to include numerous acts made illegal by federal law. The Trafficking Victims Protection Reauthorization Act of 2003 added human trafficking to the list of crimes that can be charged under RICO. Basically, when a person or group of people commits more than one criminal act included within the definition of racketeering, the government defines the series of acts as a pattern of racketeering activity. Any racketeering activity that is part of a scheme to generate or derive income is a violation of the RICO law. The criminal penalties for violation of the RICO law include imprisonment for up to 20 years, fines, and forfeiture of anything directly or indirectly associated with benefits derived from the racketeering activity, including any legal interest in property (18 U.S.C.S. § 1963). While this law is widely applicable, using it to deny offenders any benefit derived from trafficking in persons is one more tool to discourage this crime.

Finally, federal legislation has encouraged state governments to update legislation to more effectively address human trafficking at the state and local level. The Trafficking Victims Protection Act defines the term "state" to include all of the 50 states as well as all territories and possessions of the United States (22 U.S.C.S. §7102 (11) (21014)). The TVPA also identifies the need for federal agencies to train state, tribal, and local government and law enforcement officials to better identify victims of human trafficking, and requires an annual report documenting such training to be submitted to Congress by the Attorney General (22 U.S.C.S. § 7103 (d)(7)(P) (2014). A similar provision of that law also requires an annual report on the cooperative interaction between federal, state, local, and tribal law enforcement agencies to identify, investigate, and prosecute the criminal offenses included within the Peonage, Slavery, and Trafficking in Persons Act (22 U.S.C.S § 7103 (d)(7)(Q) (2014). Finally, this federal law provides that grant monies may be made available to states, Indian tribes, local governments, nonprofit agencies, and nongovernmental victims' service organization to provide for victims' services in any year in which Congress makes such monies available for that purpose.

State Anti-Trafficking Legal Trends

Whereas federal laws prohibiting human trafficking arise out of issues associated with foreign relations, commerce, immigration, and human rights, states have historically addressed these issues through their criminal codes. The basic crimes arising out of acts of human trafficking have typically included kidnapping, rape, prostitution, assault, battery, murder, torture, and abuse. The language of these laws, however, is often not broad enough to address the acts associated with human trafficking or have penalties that are inappropriately lenient for human trafficking offenses. As social and political forces have begun to recognize the necessity for preventing human trafficking, states have begun to act. States have had to recognize the weaknesses in their existing criminal laws and have acted to dramatically increase laws specifically targeting human trafficking. With the encouragement of organizations such as the Polaris Project and the American Bar Association, states have been able to draft and adopt effective state-level human trafficking legislation aimed at prevention, prosecution, and victim protection.

General Trafficking Prohibition Laws

As of 2013, all states have adopted language recognizing and prohibiting human trafficking (see Table 16.1). The form of these laws, however, differs from state to state. For example, West Virginia utilizes a definition for human trafficking that requires an individual to have victimized more than one person within a year for the crime to be prosecuted as human trafficking. Generally, the laws adopted by states generally prohibiting human trafficking tend to take one of two primary forms. The first form defines human trafficking as one person knowingly subjecting another person to servitude of some type through use of coercion or deception. The second form identifies specific acts used to subject another to involuntary servitude. Arkansas and Wyoming are just two states that list a wide variety of prohibited acts done with the specific intent to subject another to involuntary servitude.

The difference between these types of state law prohibitions is the differing standards of legal intent required to prove the criminal act. The first

Table 16.1 State Legal Provisions

State	State Code Abbreviations	Human Trafficking Prohibition General	Labor Trafficking Prohibition	Sex Related Trafficking Prohibition	Juvenile-Specific Trafficking Prohibition	Asset Forfeiture
Alabama	Ala. Code	§ 13A-6-152	§ 13A-6-152	§ 13A-6-152	§ 13A-6-152	§ 13A-6-156
Alaska	Alaska Stat.	§ 11.41.360	§ 11.41.360	§ 11.66.110	§ 11.66.110 (a)(2)	§ 11.66.145
Arizona	Ariz. Rev. Stat. Ann.	§ 13-1308	§ 13-1306	§ 13-1307	§ 13-1307	*
Arkansas	Ark. Code Ann.	§ 5-18-102	§ 5-18-102	§ 5-18-102	§ 12-18-1201	§ 5-5-202
California	Cal. [Penal] Code	§ 236.1	§ 236.1	§ 236.1	§ 236.1	§ 236.3
Colorado	Colo. Rev. Stat. Ann.	§ 18-3-503	§ 18-3-503	§ 18-3-503	*	§ 16-13-303
Connecticut	Conn. Gen. Stat.	§ 53a-192a	§ 53a-192a	§ 53a-192a	*	§ 54-36p
Delaware	11 Del. Code Ann.	§ 787	§ 787(b)	§ 787(b)	§ 787 (b)(2)	*
District of Columbia	D.C. Code Ann.	§ 22-1831	§ 22-1832	§ 22-1833	§ 22-1834	§ 22-1838
Florida	Fla. Stat.	§ 787.06	§ 787.06	§ 787.06	§ 787.06	§ 787.06
Georgia	Ga. Code Ann.	§ 16-5-46	§ 16-5-46(b)	§ 16-5-46(c)	§ 16-5-46, § 16-6-13.3	§ 16-5-46(g)
Hawaii	Haw. Rev. Stat.	*	§ 707-781	§ 712-1202	§ 712-1202(1)(b)	§ 712A-4
Idaho	Idaho Code	§ 18-8602	§ 18-8602 (2)	§ 18-8602(1)	§ 18-8602	§ 18-5612
Illinois	Ill. Comp. Stat.	§ 720 ILCS 5/10-9.	§ 720 ILCS 5/10-9.	§ 720 ILCS 5/10-9.	§ 740 ILCS 128/10; § 11-14 (d); § 720 ILCS 5/10-9(c)	§ 720 ILCS 5/10-9(j)
Indiana	Ind. Code	§ 35-42-3.5-1	§ 35-42-3.5-1(a)(1)	§ 35-42-3.5-1(a)(2)	§ 35-42-3.5-1(b)	§ 34-24-1-1
Iowa	Iowa Code	§ 710A.2	§ 710A.2	§ 710A.2	§ 710A.2	§ 809A.3
Kansas	Kan. Stat. Ann.	§ 21-5426	§ 21-5426	§ 21-5426	§ 21-5426(b)	§ 60-4104(q)

continued

Table 16.1 (continued)   State Legal Provisions

State	State Code Abbreviations	Human Trafficking Prohibition General	Labor Trafficking Prohibition	Sex Related Trafficking Prohibition	Juvenile-Specific Trafficking Prohibition	Asset Forfeiture
Kentucky	Ky. Rev. Stat. Ann.	§ 529.100		§ 529.010	HB 3 (2013)	HB 3 (2013)
Louisiana	La. Rev. Stat. Ann.	§ 14:46.2 (A)	§ 14:46.2 (A)	§ 14:46.2 (A)	§14:46.2(B)(3); 14:46.3; updates SB88 (Act No. 429) (2013)	§ 14:46.2 (B)(4); 539.1
Maine	Me. Rev. Stat. Ann.	*	17-A.M.R.S.§ 301(2) (E)	17-A.M.R.S. § 852	17-A.M.R.S.§ 852(1) (b)	§ 5821(9)
Maryland	Md. Crim. Law. Code Ann.	*	§ 3-701(b)	§ 11-303	§ 11-303 (b)	HB 713 (3013)
Massachusetts	Mass. Gen. Laws	ALM GL ch. 265, § 49	ALM GL ch. 265, § 51	ALM GL ch. 265, § 50	ALM GL ch. 272, § 4A, ALM GL ch. 265, § 26D	ALM GL ch. 265, § 56
Michigan	Mich. Comp. Laws	§750.462a	§750.462b	§750.462h	§750.462g	§ 600.4701
Minnesota	Minn. Stat.	§ 609.281	§ 609.282	609.322	§ 609.322; 260C.007 Subd. 31	§ 609.5315
Mississippi	Miss. Code Ann.	§ 97-3-54.1	§ 97-3-54.1	§ 97-3-54.1	§ 97-3-54.1	§ 97-3-54.7
Missouri	Mo. Rev. Stat.	§ 566.200	§ 566.206	§ 566.209	§ 566.212 and 566.213	§ 513.607
Montana	Mont. Code Ann.	§ 45-5-305	§ 45-5-306	§ 45-5-305 (3)(g)	HB 478 (2013)	*
Nebraska	Neb. Rev. Stat.	§ 28-830	§ 28-831	§ 28-831	§ 28-831	*
Nevada	Nev. Rev. Stat.	AB 67 (2013) NRS § 201.300	NRS § 200.463.(2)	AB 67 (2013) NRS § 201.300.(2)	§ 201.300.(2)(a)(1)	NRS 179.121

continued

New Hampshire	N.H. Rev. Stat. Ann.	§ 633:7	§ 633:5	§ 633:6 and 633:7	§ 633:7	§ 633:8
New Jersey	N.J. Stat. Ann.	§ 2C:13-8	§ 2C:13-8	§ 2C:13-8	§ 2C:13-8	§ 2C:64-1
New Mexico	N.M. Stat. Ann.	§ 30-52-1	§ 30-52-1	§ 30-52-1	§ 30-52-1A(2)	*
New York	NY CLS Soc. Serv.	§ 621	§ 135.35	§ 230.34	§ 447-b Services for exploited children	*
North Carolina	N.C. Gen. Stat.	§ 14-43.11	§ 14-43.12	§ 14-43.13	§ 14-43.11 Increased penalties	§ 14-2.3
North Dakota	N.D. Cent. Code	§ 12.1-40-01	§ 12.1-40-01	§ 12.1-40-01	§ 12.1-40-01 increased penalty	*
Ohio	Ohio Rev. Code Ann.	§ 2905.31,	§ 2905.32	§ 2905.32		§ 2981.02
Oklahoma	Okla. Stat.	§ 21 Okl. St. 748(B)	§ 21 Okl. St. 748	§ 21 Okl. St.748	§ 21 Okl. St. 865	§ 21 Okl. St. 1738
Oregon	Or. Rev. Stat.	§ 163.261	§ 163.266	§ 167.017	§ 167.017	§ 131.558
Pennsylvania	Pa. Cons. Stat.	18 Pa.C.S. § 3001	18 Pa.C.S. § 3001	18 Pa.C.S. § 3001	18 Pa.C.S. § 3002 increased penalty	18 Pa.C.S. § 3004
Rhode Island	R.I. Gen. Laws	§ 11-67-1	§ 11-67-1	§ 11-67-1	§ 11-67-6	§ 11-67-5
South Carolina	S.C. Code Ann.	§ 16-3-2010	§ 16-3-2020	§ 16-3-2020	§ 16-3-2020(F) increased penalty	§ 16-3-2090
South Dakota	S.D. Codified Laws	§ 22-49-1	§ 22-49-1 ?	§ 22-49-2	§ 22-49-2, age 16 and younger	*
Tennessee	Tenn. Code Ann.	§ 39-13-307	§ 39-13-308	§ 39-13-309	§ 39-13-309, age 15 and younger	§ 39-11-703

Table 16.1 (continued)   State Legal Provisions

State	State Code Abbreviations	Human Trafficking Prohibition General	Labor Trafficking Prohibition	Sex Related Trafficking Prohibition	Juvenile-Specific Trafficking Prohibition	Asset Forfeiture
Texas	Tex. [subject] Code Ann.	Tex. Penal Code § 20A.01	Tex. Penal Code § 20A.02(a)(1)	Tex. Penal Code § 20A.02(a)(3)	Tex. Penal Code § 20A.02(a)(5), (6), (7)	Tex. Code Crim. Proc. Art. 59.01
Utah	Utah Code Ann.	§ 76-5-308	§ 76-5-308	§ 76-5-308	§ 76-5-310(2) increased penalty	*
Vermont	Vt. Stat. Ann.	13 V.S.A. § 2652	13 V.S.A. § 2652	13 V.S.A. § 2652	13 V.S.A. § 2652(c)1 (B) minor not prosecuted; § 2653 increased penalty	*
Virginia	Va. Code Ann.	*	§ 18.2-48, abduction for labor	§ 18.2-48, abduction for sex	§ 18.2-356	*
Washington	Wash. Rev. code	RCW § 9A.40.100	RCW § 9A.40.100.	RCW § 9A.40.100	RCW § 9A.40.100 lower standard to convict offender	RCW § 9A.88.0001
West Virginia	W.Va. code	§ 61-2-17(b)	§ 61-2-17(a)(4)	§ 61-2-17(a)(6)	§ 61-2-17(a)(5) differing definition?	*
Wisconsin	Wis. Stat.	§ 940.302	§ 940.302(2)(a)(1) (a.)	§ 940.302(2)(a)(1) (b)	§ 948.051	*
Wyoming	Wyo. Stat. Ann.	§ 6-2-702	§ 6-2-702(a)(i)	§ 6-2-702(a)(ii)	§ 6-2-702 9a)(iii)	*

* At the time of this statutory review no specific statute was found to be applicable to the column topic. As these laws are being regularly reviewed and updated, states may have enacted applicable laws subsequent to this publication.

group of states have incorporated the customary definitions of actual intent or knowing intent, although a few such as Washington have also included the lesser standard of reckless intent. Some states avoid the use of an intent and instead include a requirement of a specific affirmative act, such as "compelling" or "inducing" another. Understanding the difference between these standards provides insight into the various approaches to prosecution of these crimes between the states. States that use the customary intent standards require prosecutors to present evidence showing that the alleged offender had some level of knowledge of the involuntary servitude that the victim suffered. States that prohibit specific acts that result in involuntary servitude require the prosecutor to present evidence that the alleged offender did one of the named acts. Those states that incorporate both standards require evidence of both the underlying knowledge of the involuntary servitude of the victim and evidence that the alleged offender participated in one of the identified acts.

Standards of Coercion

Coercion is a critical element of state-level human trafficking laws, because it is often the element of coercion that changes a consensual act into a criminal act. Adults are allowed to work for no compensation if they choose to do so. Adults are allowed to provide sex to another adult without compensation if they choose to do so. For acts that have always been understood to be unlawful, such as kidnapping, rape, and battery, criminal laws have typically required the elements of either force or fear being present in order to meet the definition of the criminal act. At common law, coercion of the victim was rarely an element of the offense. It was typically assumed that an individual submitted to be victimized through force or fear. The varying definitions of coercion identified in general human trafficking prohibitions set these types of laws apart from their common law predecessors.

Human trafficking laws acknowledge that coercion may involve force or fear but may also take other forms based upon the vulnerabilities of the trafficked population. For example, Colorado, uses the following language, which is very similar to the laws of both Delaware and Georgia:

(1) A person commits coercion of involuntary servitude if he or she coerces another person to perform labor or services by:
   (a) Withholding or threatening to destroy documents relating to a person's immigration status;
   (b) Threatening to notify law enforcement officials that a person is present in the United States in violation of federal immigration laws;
   (c) Threatening serious harm or physical restraint against that person or another person;

(d) Means of a scheme, plan, or pattern intended to cause the person to believe that, if the person does not perform the labor or services, he or she or another person would suffer serious harm or physical restraint; or

(e) Abusing or threatening abuse of law or the legal process.

(2) A person may commit coercion of involuntary servitude regardless of whether the person provides compensation to the person who is coerced.

The language of laws like Colorado's dramatically expand the concept of coercion beyond mere threat of force or actual force to include psychological pressures. Withholding immigration documents or threatening to use the law against the victim will play on the victim's fears of deportation or imprisonment but do not, in and of themselves, involve physical harm. Defining coercion to include psychological schemes that cause an individual to submit to physically harmful or criminal conditions is a significant step beyond the traditional elements of crime.

Several states include the provision or denial of an addictive substance to be a form of coercion. The Washington, D.C., trafficking law goes a step further by including a provision that provides "[f]acilitating or controlling a person's access to an addictive or controlled substance or restricting a person's access to prescription medication" as a coercive act. New York law includes an addiction provision specific to sex crimes.

A person is guilty of sex trafficking if he or she intentionally advances or profits from prostitution by:

1. unlawfully providing to a person who is patronized, with intent to impair said person's judgment:
   (a) a narcotic drug or a narcotic preparation;
   (b) concentrated cannabis as defined in paragraph (a) of subdivision four of section thirty-three hundred two of the public health law;
   (c) methadone; or
   (d) gamma-hydroxybutyrate (GHB) or flunitrazepan, also known as Rohypnol.

The only state that specifically mentions alcohol as an addictive substance in association with coercion is Maine.

Most states have followed the lead of the federal government and eliminated the element of coercion for sex trafficking of children in their human trafficking laws. Almost all states define a child for sex trafficking purposes as a person under the age of 18, again in conformance with federal law. A few states still define a child as less than the age at 16. These states seem to be correlating their sexual trafficking laws with their laws concerning the legal age of consent for sexual purposes. Most states that allow legal consent for sexual purposes to begin at age 16, however, have followed the norm in setting the age of a child for human trafficking purposes as less than age 18. Basically, these states recognize that consent to be trafficked correlates more to the legal age to enter into a binding contract rather than the age at which a child begins to explore their sexuality. Alaska differs from the norm in that its human trafficking laws define a child as a person under the age of 20, which appears to recognize the vulnerabilities of all teenagers.

The rationale for this disparate treatment is twofold. First, these laws recognize the special vulnerability of children to adults. Part of the social definition of an adult is the right of self-determination: the right to tell another adult no. The definition of a child includes the requirement to obey adults, even when the child disagrees with the adult. Second, most states limit or prohibit the right of minors to consent to sexual acts occurring on/with their bodies. This means that whether a child agrees to the act or not, sexually related conduct with a child is a crime, while those same acts between consenting adults are lawful.

The New Mexico law illustrates the differences for prosecution purposes for treating the element of coercion differently for adults and children within human trafficking laws. In that state, whether the victim is an adult or child, for a conviction the prosecutor must prove the offender recruited, solicited, enticed, transported, or obtained a person with "knowing" intent, and had "knowing" or "actual" intent that the person would be used in commercial sexual activity. In addition, to win a conviction when the victim was an adult aged 18 or older, the prosecutor must provide proof that the adult was coerced, defrauded, or forced to participate in the commercial sexual activity. If the adult agreed to participate without force, fraud, or coercion, the adult is guilty of prostituting themselves. Conversely, the reason that a child submitted to the trafficking act need not be proven. A child need not be shown to have been coerced in any way to have been made a victim of sex trafficking This determination has led to the further determination in most states that a child may not be prosecuted for prostitution: the mere fact that a child was involved in commercial sexual activity is by definition human trafficking.

New Mexico like most other states, however, treats adult and child victims the same for labor trafficking purposes. In those states whether the victim is a child or an adult the prosecution must prove that the victim was forced, coerced, or defrauded. A few states, such as Indiana, Kansas, and Minnesota, have eliminated any showing of coercion for labor trafficking of a person under the age of 18. These very recently enacted laws seem to be in response to the fact that an obedient child will submit to an adult for any purpose merely because the child is a child.

It should be noted that not every state has removed the element of coercion from the crime of child sex trafficking. New York, Utah, Ohio, and

Pennsylvania do not have laws treating the coercion of children separately from the coercion of adults. New York has recognized that children who are trafficked for sexual purposes are "sexually exploited," but the elements of the specific crime of sex trafficking are the same whether the victim is an adult or a child. New Hampshire doesn't specifically provide for any age for purposes of recognizing differing legal standards for coercion between adults and child victims of trafficking, but one of the definitions of coercion encompasses any threat of any consequence sufficient to coerce a reasonable person in the same situation to provide the service. Although this language imposes a burden upon prosecutors to identify a reason for a child's participation, it seems to recognize that the coercion standard should be based upon the individual victim.

Finally, it should be noted that several states have attempted to address the unique coercive concerns associated with individuals who have a mental defect or disorder. Several states have incorporated language into their coercion provisions that seems aimed at persons with diminished capacity. Oregon, for example, defines as coercive, "[i]nstilling in the other person a fear that the actor will withhold from the other person the necessities of life, including but not limited to lodging, food and clothing." Maine may be the only state to specifically address mental impairment within its human trafficking coercion terminology. That state includes within aggravated sex trafficking one who "[p]romotes prostitution of a person who suffers from a mental disability that is reasonably apparent or known to the actor and that in fact renders the other person substantially incapable of appraising the nature of the conduct involved." Alaska may have been considering all vulnerable populations, including inmates, patients, children, and adults with mental disability, when it included within its most serious form of sex trafficking a provision defining coercion to include one who "induces or causes a person in that person's legal custody to engage in prostitution."

Labor Trafficking Laws

Labor trafficking encompasses a broad variety of acts from state to state. In its most basic form, labor trafficking is coercing another person to perform labor or services. The varying forms of coercion specifically associated with labor trafficking, however, illustrate how many methods exist for subjecting another to slave labor, involuntary servitude, and peonage. For example, Florida labor trafficking law prohibits "[r]estraining, isolating, or confining or threatening to restrain, isolate, or confine any person without lawful authority and against her or his will," but to show that the act is against the victim's will, a list of coercive acts is also provided. One coercive act is "[u]sing lending or other credit methods to establish a debt by any person when labor or services are pledged as a security for the debt, if the value of the labor or services as reasonably assessed is not applied toward the liquidation of the debt, the length and nature of the labor or services are not respectively limited and defined." Every state includes a provision defining the act of interfering with a government or immigration-related document belonging to another to be a form of coercion. Hawaii, like several other states, also uses several of the existing common law crimes to establish coercion, including kidnapping, unlawful imprisonment, and sexual assault.

Evidence that local culture and social concerns have impacted the form of labor trafficking laws is most clearly seen in a provision from West Virginia. It provides that labor trafficking "does not include work or services provided by a minor to the minor's parent or legal guardian so long as the legal guardianship or custody of the minor was not obtained for the purpose compelling the minor to participate in commercial sex acts or sexually explicit performance, or perform forced labor or services." This provision begs the question whether birth parents may sell their children for sex or labor without the act rising to the level of human trafficking.

Additional Standard Provisions within State Human Trafficking Laws

State laws generally provide for some form of training for law enforcement and other participants in the criminal justice process. Texas law mandates that a human trafficking task force shall be developed to address human trafficking needs within that state. The task force is also tasked with determining the types of training needed, and to develop that training, for law enforcement, victim services personnel, medical personnel, judges, prosecutors, and their associated staff members. Georgia's and Iowa's training provisions are more in line with other states in that mandated training is limited to law enforcement as determined appropriate by the director of the state law enforcement training academy. Other states, such as Washington, mandate training in providing appropriate care to minors who have been the victims of sex trafficking.

Several states, including Tennessee, Arizona, and Colorado, do not yet mandate that law enforcement receive some form of trafficking specific training. It should be noted, however, that failure to include this type of provision may not correlate to whether the state actually has this type of training or mandates this type of training. Many states do not develop training policies and directions through state legislation. For those states that do mandate law enforcement training through state law, it is likely that training mandates will increase. As criminal justice professionals at the state level become aware of the need for education in recognizing the signs of human trafficking, understanding and applying the newly enacted human trafficking laws, and responding appropriately to the immediate needs of the trafficked victim, more states will develop appropriate training policy and legislation.

Many states have taken action to combat the incentives associated with human trafficking by incorporating human trafficking into those offenses subject to civil asset forfeiture. Civil asset forfeiture is a civil legal process that permits law enforcement to seize goods or property that reasonably appear to be the fruits or instrumentalities of criminal conduct. No charges need ever be filed against the individual from whom the property was seized. Unless that individual files an action against the government to reclaim the goods and/or property, the government that seized the property may use or sell the property as it sees fit. Few individuals from whom goods or property have been seized actually file these lawsuits to reclaim their property because they either do not have the financial resources to do so, do not want the government to have incentive to investigate possible criminal activity any further, or are involved in a criminal case and are unable to deal with the civil asset forfeiture matter. Thus, civil asset forfeiture can create a windfall of goods and monies to be used by law enforcement.

When used appropriately civil asset forfeiture is an effective way of removing all benefits arising from the criminal act from the offender, even before a conviction is obtained. It is also a method of getting the attention of those people who surround the offender, benefitting from the offender's wealth and property. Although these people may escape criminal action based on their claims of lack of knowledge of the ongoing offenses, civil asset forfeiture prevents these people from driving the offender's cars or living in the offender's house while the offender is incarcerated. Civil asset forfeiture is intended to ensure that no individual lives off of the proceeds of trafficked human beings.

Again, there are still many states that have chosen not to use this tool in their efforts to combat human trafficking. The rationale behind this decision varies widely. Some states have adopted negative attitudes toward the use of civil asset forfeiture due to the possibility it will be abused by law enforcement. Other states have not yet determined that civil asset forfeiture will be an effective tool in dealing with the types of human trafficking crimes encountered there.

Assistance to victims of human trafficking can be found in some state human trafficking laws. Typically these laws implement the TVPRA provisions regarding protection and assistance for victims of trafficking found at 22 U.S.C.S. § 7105. Although alien victims of trafficking found within the United States do not qualify for immediate immigration status, individuals certified by federal law enforcement agents to have been the victims of severe trafficking may qualify for a temporary residency status. The goal of the temporary residency is to allow the victim to be available to assist in the investigation and prosecution of their traffickers. The temporary status may be extended during the time necessary to affect a civil lawsuit against the traffickers for compensation for the harms they suffered (18 U.S.C.S. §1595).

Aside from enacting necessary provisions to carry out the goals of the TVPRA, the types of victim assistance made available by states range from none to almost anything imaginable. Some states, such as Mississippi, Vermont, and Nevada, have developed special funds to provide assistance to victims of human trafficking. Other states, including Nebraska, have incorporated duties to be carried out by a delegated task force that includes studying the best approaches to dealing with the myriad of extreme physical and mental health issues, immigration issues, poverty issues, legal issues, and other critical concerns that victims of trafficking present. New Jersey has promulgated a list of services with which a human trafficking victim may receive assistance ranging from parking assistance at the courthouse to assistance filling out forms for federal assistance. New Mexico allows alien victims of trafficking to receive state social services until federal assistance is available. South Carolina law incorporates victims of human trafficking into the existing crime victim's protection laws, which among other things focuses upon protecting the identity and current location of trafficking victims. What all of these varying means of providing assistance to human trafficking victims have in common, though, is an intent to address both the situation that allowed the individual to become trafficked and the harms suffered during the trafficking victimization.

Summary

Human trafficking has become a hot topic in the general media, yet the perception that victims of human trafficking crimes bear a responsibility for their victimization has long hampered the criminal justice system from increasing the priority associated with preventing and ending these types of offenses. The inability to clearly identify the victim or the situation has allowed society to ignore the phenomenon of human trafficking for a very long time, and prevented governments from developing effective legal tools to discourage and end human trafficking. In 2000 Congress passed the Victims of Trafficking and Violence Protection Act of 2000. That law recognized that existing laws were piecemeal and often served to protect the trafficker while further victimizing the trafficking victim. The laws in many states have only recently begun to allow the criminal justice system to effectively address the crimes associated with human trafficking in a manner that both recognizes and protects the victims while actually prosecuting the perpetrators. The effective development and use of both State and Federal laws have assisted victims in recovering from the trauma of victimization and begun to address the issues that allowed these people to have been victimized in the first place.

Key Terms

civil asset forfeiture
coercion
intent
peonage
Peonage, Slavery, and Trafficking in Persons Act
Prosecutorial Remedies and Other Tools to End the Exploitation of Children Today Act
Racketeering Influenced Corrupt Organizations Act (RICO) as part of the Organized Crime Control Act of 1970
Trafficking and Violence Protection Act of 2000
Trafficking Victims Protection Reauthorization Acts of 2003, 2005, 2008, and 2013
Violent Crime Control and Law Enforcement Act, Violence against Women and Combating Domestic Trafficking in Persons

Review Questions

1. Why is the element of coercion a critical element of defining an act as human trafficking?
2. Why is coercion defined differently for adults than for children in most states' laws?
3. How does the legal concept of intent impact the ability to prosecute human trafficking violations?
4. How does civil asset forfeiture and RICO enhance the penalties imposed upon human traffickers?
5. How did the Trafficking and Violence Protection Act of 2000, and its subsequent reauthorization acts, significantly change the ability of federal law enforcement to combat human trafficking?
6. How does the Mann Act protect children who live outside the United States?

References

Customs and Facilitation and Trade Enforcement Reauthorization Act of 2009, S. 1631, 111th Cong. § 308 (2014).

Mann Act, 18 U.S.C. §§ 2421–2424 (2014).

Peonage, Slavery, and Trafficking in Persons Act, found at 18 U.S.C.S. § 1589–1595 (2014).

Polaris Project, http://www.polarisproject.org.

Prosecutorial Remedies and Other Tools to End the Exploitation of Children Today Act, 18 U.S.C. §§ 2251 and 2423 (2014).

Racketeering Influenced Corrupt Organizations Act (RICO) as part of the Organized Crime Control Act of 1970, 18 U.S.C.S §§ 1961 (2014).

Tariff Act of 1930, 19 U.S.C. §§ 1581–1584 (2014).

Trafficking and Violence Protection Act of 2000 (VTVPA), 22 U.S.C.S §§ 7101–7109 (2014).

Trafficking Victims Protection Reauthorization Acts (TVPRA) of 2003, 2005, 2008, and 2013, 22 U.S.C.S §§ 7101–7109 (2014).

Violent Crime Control and Law Enforcement Act, Violence against Women and Combating Domestic Trafficking in Persons, 42 U.S.C.S §§ 14044 (2014).

U.S. v. Kozminski, 487 U.S. 931, 108 S. Ct. 2751, 101 L. Ed. 2d 788, 1988 U.S. LEXIS 3032 (1988).

Conclusion

Man's mistreatment can be traced back to ancient times. The Bible records Cain murdering his brother Abel. The inhumane treatment of human beings has continued throughout the ages and is continuing into the twenty-first century. Even with the development of technology and a world of abundant wealth, acts of violence and mistreatment of humans against one another have not subsided. Today, as in ancient times and throughout the centuries, humans have murdered, beaten, branded, mutilated, and held other humans in bondage and as slaves.

We are all familiar with the Egyptians holding the Jewish people as slaves until Moses was able to obtain their freedom from slavery. Slavery continued even after the Jews were freed. All continents, peoples, regions of the world, countries, and civilized and uncivilized societies along with developing and undeveloped countries have had slavery. Before continuing we need to define *slavery* as holding a human being in bondage who has no freedom and generally has to be the workforce for a family, business, factory, or farm. The victim of slavery is a prisoner to his owner. The slave owner has power over the individual slave victim and can sell him and treat him poorly and in some cases break up slave families.

Slavery during the Middle Ages became a commercial enterprise. As a business for profit, slavery has continued to be a financial success for slave owners till this present day. Slaves have been trafficked for centuries and they are still being trafficked.

One of the cruelest forms of slavery occurred in the United States where slaves were not considered human being but property like a farm, house, or piece of machinery. Many slave owners physically abused their slaves and were so inhumane as to even break up families. Selling mothers or fathers or children to other slave owners was a common practice. Unlike in the United States, slaves in South America were treated more humane where slave families could not be separated and slaves were allowed the opportunity to buy their freedom. Of course slavery is morally wrong and cannot be justified under any circumstances. Slavery must be stamped out wherever it is found. The sad story for our twenty-first century is that slavery still exists. The sad event of our current period is that victims of slavery are looked upon as objects and not as humans. Man's mistreatment to his fellow human is not only a violation of moral values but also a crime against humanity.

One of the common themes found throughout this book is that various forms of bondage are slavery. Whether the bondage is forcing people into the sex trade or forced labor it is slavery. In the early decades of the twenty-first century, slavery in its various forms is referred to as human trafficking. Throughout this book the authors of the chapters use the 2000 Trafficking Victims Protection Act (TVPA) that was passed by the United States Congress as their definition of human trafficking. The TVPA defines *human trafficking* as

> (A) Sex trafficking in which a commercial sex act is induced by force, fraud, or coercion, or in which the person induced to perform such act has not attended 18 years of age; or (B) the recruitment, harboring, transportation, provision, or obtaining of a person for labor or services, through the use of force, or coercion for the purpose of subjection to involuntary servitude, personage, debt bondage or slavery. (As quoted in Wilson and Dalton, 2008, p. 297)

Economics is the main force that drives human trafficking through Mexico to the United States, according to Larry French. Not only is economics a driving force between Mexico and the United States, human trafficking should be considered a driving force from undeveloped countries to the United States. To further emphasize the importance of human trafficking not only do victims of human trafficking come from Mexico and other undeveloped countries, they also come from the United States. As pointed out by French it has always been difficult to separate drug traffickers from human traffickers since major drug cartels operate both types of offenses. This theme exists not only for Mexico cartels but also for other criminal organizations.

A major theme found throughout the book advocates that human trafficking is a global problem. Chris Maloney indicates, similar to other chapter authors, that human trafficking exists in advanced capitalist countries like the United States, developing countries like Cambodia, and in communist countries like China. He further indicates that human trafficking is not equally distributed in all countries and regions of the world. Another point brought out by Maloney and a theme found in other chapters is that victimization for human trafficking usually originates in poor countries and victims are transported to richer countries. This reinforces Larry French's premise that poor Mexicans are transported to the United States for human trafficking.

Another point brought out throughout the book is that the majority of human trafficking victims are women who are forced into the sex business and forced labor. The media has emphasized the sex trade in which trafficking victims are usually women and children. The sex business receives most of the attention by the media and the public has become more familiar with the sexual exploitation of women and children. Just like previously mentioned with the Mexican cartels human trafficking organizations are generally hierarchical organizations. As mentioned by Jodie Beeson, members of a human trafficking organization have a variety of roles they are responsible to work. Various chapter authors mention the hierarchical organizational structure of trafficking offenders.

Although females and children are a greater number of victims, there are adult males and young males who are victims. Some of them are in the sex trade but the majority seems to be in forced labor occupations like construction, farming, or factories. Victims come from various cultures, national, racial, and ethnic groups. Most human trafficking victims usually become victims at a young age. There are a variety of reasons why young people become victims of human trafficking. A major cause of victimization for young victims is that there exists no one to take care of them or to have concern for them. For example, their parents neglect them or they are runaways or drug users.

Little is known about the traffickers who victimize other human beings. There have been a few studies but more research is necessary in this area. Researches recognize the difficulties in studying such a crime as trafficking human beings for profit. The goal of trafficking is to make a profit by selling human victims. According to Beeson, which other authors agree with, traffickers are generally young men who are in the business of selling young women.

A major theme of several of the authors of this book, who have reviewed, studied, observed, and investigated victims of human trafficking, have found that children are frequently victims of human trafficking. Ryan Alexander, who has studied the exploitation of children, found that child sexual exploitation takes many forms and there are many techniques used in targeting children. The approach methods are similar globally and locally. The traffickers take advantage of economic hardships of families or prey on the hardships of children. The exploitation of children can either be sexual exploitation for a financial gain or the offender taking advantage of the child for his prurient interest. The exploitation of children occurs not only in other countries but also takes place in the United States. Jeff Weible, the former director of the Exploited and Missing Child Unit (EMCU), Sedgwick County-Wichita, Kansas, reports that young children are introduced to the world of prostitution with an average age of 12 to 13, as seen in the middle of the country in Wichita, Kansas. Weible along with other contributors considers exploitation of children not only a global or national interest but a hometown interest. Wichita reflects the exploitation of children that may be occurring not only in America's cities but also in its small towns and hamlets. At one time prostitutes were considered criminals; now those with a better understanding realize that young prostitutes are victims, even though they may not realize it. As with other prior crimes such as gang activity and drugs Wichita has become a corridor for transporting victims of human trafficking to such cities south of Wichita, including, Dallas, San Antonio, Oklahoma City, and Tulsa to name a few. The EMCU have recovered victims from Atlanta, New

Orleans, and Chicago. A major point to be emphasized is that no community is immune from the exploitation of young people.

Those working in the field of exploitation of children recognized that no village, town, or city will be immune to this hideous crime. However, the exact number of children who are trafficked seems impossible to determine. As Ryan Alexander reports, one estimate has it that approximately 50,000 (Richard, 2000) children are trafficked into the United States annually while another research estimates that there are approximately 300,000 (Estes and Weiner, 2005) who are of serious risk of being commercially exploited sexually. Alexander and other authors indicate that there exists similarities of children exploited such as poverty, dysfunctional families, and not facing issues that can lead to children being exploited. Contributors to this book seem to be in agreement on the knowledge of identifying the characteristics and methods used by those recruiting children for exploitation. In order to curtail exploitation of children, those responsible for the investigation of child trafficking need to know the strategies, techniques, and methods to prevent the exploitation of children.

Human trafficking has reached the local street gang individual. Recently, local street gangs have become disorganized from the top to the bottom of the gang structure. This lack of leadership has allowed individual gang members to commit crimes on the individual level rather than committing crimes as a gang. The individual gang member has now become involved in human trafficking. The individual gang member exploits females who frequently are juvenile for the use of sex. Gang member victims are similar to victims discussed by other contributors to this book. The victims may be runaways, survivors of abuse, and users of drugs and alcohol.

Adding to the theme of human trafficking functioning as sex trafficking is sexually oriented business as described by D. G. Oblinger. Sex trafficking includes sex workers and other roles of the prostitution ring, escort services, strip clubs, massage parlors, and sneaks and peaks. The exploitation of sex trafficking of women and children is thoroughly explained by the various authors on this topic.

An aspect of human trafficking that seems to be often overlooked has been forced labor. For example, women and children forced into the sex trade are involved in forced labor. Women and children do not have a choice of not being involved in forced labor. They are forced to perform in the sex trade or be abused for failing to cooperate with their traffickers. There are other forms of forced labor in which not only women but also men are forced to work for little or no wages. Women are often forced to be maids or nannies for little or no money. Often they are held as prisoners and not allowed to leave the residence in which they live. They may be beaten or locked into their room or may not even be fed. The various forms of forced labor include slavery, public works projects, agriculture, bonded labor manufacturing, child soldiers, and construction. The United States has all the various forms of forced labor mentioned, except for child soldiers. Many of the victims involved in forced labor are immigrants who have left their native countries to free themselves from poverty.

Human trafficking that violates human rights and takes away the dignity of human beings is also a criminal offense under various United States laws. The crime of human trafficking has to be investigated like any other crime if offenders are to be prosecuted, convicted, and punished. Witnesses and offenders have to be interviewed and interrogated, and their information must be evaluated. Evidence must be legally obtained and follow all the legal procedures as required by the courts. The investigator of human trafficking offenses must be familiar with the different types of evidence such as Miranda warning, exclusionary rule, fruit of poisonous tree doctrine, and direct and indirect evidence. In addition, the human traffic investigator needs to be familiar with the act, means, and purpose of human trafficking. Knowledge of the characteristics of human trafficking is required by the human traffic investigator as well as understanding the problem to prosecute the offender.

Training of human traffic investigators goes along with the process of investigating human trafficking. Human trafficking training for investigators along with knowledge of task force units, policies, and protocols are important. One aspect of training important to trafficking investigators, brought out by Vladimir Sergevnin, is that victims of human trafficking are not necessary offenders, and law enforcement needs to view trafficking victims as victims and not offenders. According to Sergevnin there exists a need for ongoing training and commitment for all levels of agencies. Law enforcement training in human trafficking needs to be provided for crisis intervention. He continues that the Trafficking Victims Protection Act (TVPA) requires the Department of Justice and Department of State to establish training programs for appropriate department personnel to identify victims of trafficking and to provide them with protection. A large number of states have passed antitrafficking laws and about half the states have mandated or encouraged training on human trafficking law enforcement.

Not only are local and state law enforcement agencies involved in investigating human trafficking, so are federal law enforcement agencies. These agencies include the Federal Bureau of Investigation, the Bureau of Immigration and Customs Enforcement (ICE), and with several other agencies not as well known to the public. These include the Department of Justice and Homeland Security, and the Departments of State, Health and Human Services, Education, Transportation, and Interior. Jeffrey Bumgarner provides insight on how these federal departments and agencies play a role in investigating human trafficking. The FBI has established task forces with local police agencies to apprehend human traffickers. ICE is involved in the investigation of human trafficking cases, specifically those involving immigration or those individuals coming from foreign countries. All the departments and agencies mentioned are involved in the investigation of human trafficking. For example, the U.S. Border Patrol concentrates on human trafficking between Mexico and the United States.

In addition to the criminal laws pertaining to the collection and preservation of evidence and laws relating to conducting interviews and interrogations, knowledge of other laws is important. D. G. Oblinger in his chapter indicates that this includes knowledge of Title III of the Omnibus Crime Control and Safe Streets Act of 1968, which allows law enforcement officers to use wiretaps to investigate complex cases. In human trafficking cases wiretapping can document conspiracies and trafficking is vulnerable since traffickers may work over a long distance. The Mann Act can be used for sex trafficking since it can be used for prosecution of prostitution. The Racketeering Influenced Corrupt Organization (RICO), which covers prostitutions, violence, and a number of other offenses, should be understood by the investigator. Many states have laws similar to RICO which local prosecutors can use.

A thorough study of laws relating to human trafficking was researched by Alison McKenney Brown, who sheds light on federal and state laws currently being enforced to control and apprehend human trafficking. The United States Congress has passed federal laws to prevent trafficking, to prosecute traffickers, and to protect victims of trafficking. In addition to the federal government passing federal laws against human trafficking, the federal government is also encouraging state governments to update their human trafficking laws to effectively deal with this hideous crime. The federal and state governments have approached antitrafficking laws from a different perspective. The federal government, according to Brown, deals with issues associated with foreign relations, commerce, immigration, and human rights. On the other hand, states usually address the issue through their criminal laws. The human trafficking laws differ from state to state. It should be expected since each state code is developed independently from one another.

A theme brought up in this book is what can be done to prevent human trafficking and what services exist for victims of human trafficking. Stacie Donaldson outlines what average citizens can do to prevent a hideous offense. Citizens who are concerned about issues can be creative in fighting crimes they consider detrimental to their city. A resident of Wichita, Kansas, reading about human trafficking in other countries was surprised to read in the local paper that human trafficking was occurring in her city. She developed an organization that would raise funds for community organizations that were combating human trafficking in Wichita. The organization, named ICT SOS, had volunteers who meet to develop programs to combat domestic trafficking in their city. Volunteers were encouraged to participate in awareness events, staffing a trafficking prevention booth, and handing out information at events. ICT SOS has an annual 5K race to raise money to give to organizations fighting human trafficking.

Continuing the work of ICT SOS Dorthy Halley has the responsibility for assisting victims in the Kansas Attorney General's Office. Halley describes effective responses and services for human trafficking victims. She describes identification and response, assessment of needs, placement consideration for youth, along with service consideration for youth. Further, she reviews safe harbor laws and their impact on service provisions and ethical considerations.

Human trafficking is a complex issue, and in any one book all the complex issues cannot be covered. The multidiscipline approach of this book attempts to cover several aspects and themes of human trafficking. The themes in summary cover potential victims, offenders, and trafficking of women and children for the sex trade. Various forms of forced labor often go unreported by the media. Forced labor occurs not only in undeveloped countries but also in developed countries like the United States. An important component to controlling and preventing human trafficking is knowledge and an understanding of the investigation of human trafficking. In support of human trafficking investigation is the training of human traffic investigators. The need for the training of human trafficking investigation for law enforcement officers has been recognized by the professionals in the field of investigations.

Finally, residents of a city, village, or community have a responsibility to take action to prevent and eliminate human trafficking. This can be accomplished by participating in events to make the public aware of the severity of this hideous offense. Victims cannot be left out to dry. They need support and assistance to get over the trauma human trafficking has done to them.

References

Estes, R. J., and Weiner, N. A. 2001. *Commercial Sexual Exploitation of Children in NAFA Countries*. Philadelphia, PA: University of Pennsylvania.

Richard, A. O. 2000. *International Trafficking in Women to the USA: Contemporary Manifestation of Slavery and Organized Crime*. DCI report, United States Department of Justice.

Wilson, J. M., and Dalton, E. 2008. "Human Trafficking in the Heartland Awareness and Response." *Journal of Contemporary Criminal Justice* 24(3): 296–313.

Index